MYTH AND THE POLIS

MYTH AND POETICS

A series edited by
GREGORY NAGY

MYTH AND THE POLIS

Edited by

DORA C. POZZI *and*

JOHN M. WICKERSHAM

CORNELL UNIVERSITY PRESS

ITHACA AND LONDON

Cornell University Press gratefully acknowledges grants
from the University of Houston and Ursinus College
which aided in the publication of this book.

First published 1991 by Cornell University Press.

International Standard Book Number 0-8014-2473-9 (cloth)
International Standard Book Number 0-8014-9734-5 (paper)
Library of Congress Catalog Card Number 90-55716
Printed in the United States of America
*Librarians: Library of Congress cataloging information
appears on the last page of the book.*

Contents

Foreword

Gregory Nagy

My goal, as editor of the Myth and Poetics series, is to encourage work that helps to integrate literary criticism with the approaches of anthropology and pays special attention to problems concerning the nexus of ritual and myth.

For such an undertaking, we may look to the comparative testimony of relatively complex societies, like the Ndembu of Zambia, and also of the smallest-scale societies, such as the Yukuna of the Colombian Amazon.[1] Just as important, we must pursue the varied testimonies of the most stratified societies, including what goes under the general heading of "Western civilization." It is precisely here that the meaning of myth is the most misleading—and challenging. In a small-scale society myth tends to be viewed as the encoding of that society's concept of truth; at the same time, from the viewpoint of Western civilization, myth has become the opposite of fact, the antithesis of truth.[2]

Since the ancient Greek concept of politeiā, derivative of polis, serves as the foundation for the very word "civilization" and for our concept of Western civilization, several books in the series treat ancient Greece and the ancient Greek city-state, or polis. A notable example is *Myth and the Polis*. This book explores the ways in which a standard anthropological definition of myth must be modified in the context of

1. V. Turner, *The Forest of Symbols: Aspects of Ndembu Ritual* (Ithaca, N.Y., 1967), and P.-Y. Jacopin, "La parole générative: De la mythologie des Indiens Yukuna" (diss., University of Neuchâtel, 1981).
2. See especially M. Detienne, *L'invention de la mythologie* (Paris, 1981), and my review in *Annales: Economies Sociétés Civilisations* 37 (1982) 778–780.

the Greek polis. The humanism of this modified definition is suggested by Aristotle's dictum that humans are *by nature* organisms of the polis. As *Myth and the Polis* makes clear throughout, the polis tells us as much about myth as the other way around. Centering on myths that illuminate not only the similarities but also the differences between the Greek polis and our own received notions of Western civilization, this book highlights details that will be interesting, of and by themselves, to a wide range of readers.

Myth and the Polis dovetails with three earlier volumes in the Myth and Poetics series: Richard P. Martin's *Language of Heroes* (1989), my own *Greek Mythology and Poetics* (1990), and Stephen Scully's *Homer and the Sacred City* (1991). Scully's book, just like *Myth and the Polis*, addresses the polis directly, in this case by examining the Homeric concept of a "sacred city" and showing that the sacredness of the city depends on the authority of myth in the earlier stages of Greek society. The authoritativeness of *mūthos* or "myth" in early Greek poetics is a central subject in Richard Martin's *Language of Heroes*, and also in my *Greek Mythology and Poetics*. Scully's book shows that the Greek polis, as a concept, is a direct reflection of such authoritativeness. Conversely, as we see from *Myth and the Polis*, the social foundation for the validity of myth is the polis itself—not as a concept but as a reality, the same reality that in the course of ancient Greek history will eventually undermine the very meaning of myth.

Acknowledgments

This book is an outgrowth of the National Endowment for the Humanities Seminar for College Teachers on Ancient Greek Mythology and Criticism, held at Harvard University in the summer of 1985 and attended by the nine authors represented here. We are indebted to the Endowment for that opportunity, and to the seminar director and general editor of this series, Gregory Nagy, for sharing with us his insights and for much critical and friendly comment on our chapters.

The editors acknowledge with gratitude the assistance given by Ursinus College and by the University of Houston toward publication by Cornell University Press. To the University of Houston's College of Humanities and Fine Arts and its dean, James Pickering, thanks are due also for financial and technical support in the early stages of composition of this book. The help of Gary Bisbee, of Harvard University, was invaluable for linking ancient Greek tradition with electronic technology.

Finally, we thank both the University of Chicago Press, for allowing us to reproduce, with adaptations, passages from Richmond Lattimore's translation of the *Iliad*, and the *Classical Journal*, for granting permission to reprint here, as part of Chapter 7, a revised version of an article published therein (Pozzi 1986).

D. C. P. and J. M. W.

MYTH AND THE POLIS

Introduction

John M. Wickersham and Dora C. Pozzi

What was a Greek polis? A territory, of course, with the physical structures of a central town or city, a population (*politai* 'citizens') and a civic constitution (*politeia*). But we lack the core of the concept unless we emphasize the myths, which were a vector for the culture of the polis and an embodiment of its values and sense of identity.

To appreciate the significance of myth, we should perhaps grow what Marcel Detienne has called "a second head." In *Dionysos Slain* (1979) he had entitled the first chapter "The Greeks Are Not like the Others," a way of satirizing those he called "Hellenists," whose basic view of ancient Greece as essentially "rational and enlightened" was threatened by the fact of mythology. "The others" are the peoples studied in anthropology and comparative mythology who supposedly have myth because they lack enlightenment; but *Greek* mythology must mean something else. Detienne returned to the phrase in *L'Invention de la mythologie* (1981), where it appears that the Greeks were indeed alienated from their myths. To the Hellenists' quandary over how the Greeks could have had both enlightenment and myth, he offered the following mock solution: "Granted, the Greeks are like the others, but with one slight difference: they have two heads"—one, that is, for science and philosophy, and the other for "benighted" mythmaking.[1] In this and other ways Detienne correctly, we believe, highlights the marvelous persistence of myth in the ancient communities and its unsuperseded power to verbalize a polis. Older forms of thought do not have to disappear in the face of newer ones.[2]

---

1. Detienne 1986.116–117, on which see Nagy 1982b.
2. The missionary Maurice Leenhardt strove to preserve the preexisting connections of

1

Even post-Enlightenment rationalist historians of Greece have recognized the centrality of myth, at least in part: one of the best modern manuals of Greek myth is still, when allowance is made for its evolutionist foibles, the first volume of George Grote's *History of Greece* (1846). Grote insisted on furnishing this volume because, as he put it, the myths "formed the entire mental stock of the early Greeks."[3] Grote had already in his preface announced the potential of his insight, warning the reader that "there will occur numerous circumstances in the . . . political life of the Greeks which he will not comprehend unless he be initiated into the course of their legendary associations."[4] In the chapters of this book, we propose to explore ancient Greek myth in the spirit of Grote's suggestion, to try the assumption that satisfactory understanding of the polis must include myth and ritual. The hypothesis is that the collective actions of the Greek polis express a culture conveyed in myth, and that the extent to which citizens acted amythically or paramythically was minor or minimal. This polis was exemplary even for an autocrat such as Alexander III of Macedon, who murdered the polis by removing its autonomy—the keystone of political myth—and whose empire is most heavily studied as an expression of Realpolitik. Yet it is far more basic that Alexander also made the *Iliad* his Bible, that in his numerous foundations he was making himself, either directly or through his deputies, the *ktistēs* 'civic founder' of the whole world, and that his life's goal was always the *hērōion* 'hero shrine' at Alexandria.[5]

The polis is a state of mind, and that mind expresses itself in myth. The polis has its physical structure, its buildings and artifacts, and its natural features, but this body has a soul, and it is the myths that animate it. On the western acropolis of Megara there was a rock that rang musically when struck with a pebble (Pausanias 1.42.2). This report is not merely a pleasant oddity for the tourist; when we learn that this was the rock upon which Apollo laid his cithara while lending his hand to the *ktistēs* Alkathoös in the building of this acropolis, we see the depth of the Megarians' conviction that their city was blessed, and suffused with

---

Melanesian myth and society while still shaping people into Christians (Clifford 1982, e.g., pp. 4–5, 7–8, 43, 62).

3. Grote 1846–1862.I.284. See also Bohringer 1980.20, who similarly describes mythical discourse as "the first 'political' language."

4. Grote 1846–1862.I.x.

5. See Green 1985.891 for the dwarfing of the polis in the post-Classical period. Payne in Chap. 8 deals with the success of Alexander's sublimated polis in surviving millennia of diaspora.

harmonia 'harmony, well-constructedness'.[6] One remarkable rock, thanks to its invisible animating *aition*, testifies to the solidity and order of this city.[7] Multiply this example. This city, and every city, was a hugely intricate network of such, and even more overt, signs—temples, hero shrines, boundary stones—of the forces that built it and sustained it.

The precise intricate interdependence between the material city and its vivifying myths determines the identity of each individual polis. We can return to Megara for another example. This is a polis with two citadels, in itself a distinguishing feature, and the individuation carries into complex detail: Karia, the "older" citadel, has as its eponym the hero Kar, who first collected a population for Megara directly after the recession of the primeval flood and the creation of the very land of the Megarid. This hero's tomb, however, is not at the citadel, or even within the walls of Megara, but lies outside, between the city and the sea. There the tomb, with its facing of shell-filled stone, of which many of the city's buildings are made and which only Megara possesses, serves as a link between the sea and the city whose land arose from the sea. Kar was the son of Phoroneus, who, according to the testimony of a myth from neighboring Argos (Pausanias 2.15.5), was the "first man" and who laid the foundations of civilized life in the Argolid by collecting the scattered inhabitants after the ending of the primeval inundation that had covered the entire Isthmus. Kar repeated his father's work in the Megarid. The

6. See G. Nagy 1985.28 for *harmonia* as a complex notion in the poetic diction of the Archaic *polis* that "has a built-in equation of musical beauty with social integration" based on the concrete activity of building. Apollo's rock at Megara appears to embody neatly all these meanings.

7. By *aition* 'cause, ground' we mean the motivating myth behind some institution of a community. There is a powerful circle of validation connecting the two. The institution is an indisputable fact, something "on the ground" which is "set in place" and illuminated by the myth. The institution would not, so runs the belief, be there if not for the events in the myth, and, since the institution is undeniably there, the myth must be true. Each confirms the other. This is especially clear for concrete things such as the musical rock or, most common in the context of the polis, a hero shrine. The latter is obviously someone's tomb, there is no arguing it away, so why should tradition not be correct as to whose it is? Mr. Willett in Dickens' *Barnaby Rudge* would tell how Queen Elizabeth had stayed at his inn and in the morning cuffed a page while mounting her horse; Willett silenced incredulity by pointing to "the very mounting-block!" This example has part of the idea, but in this weaker-than-Greek case the tale is a gratuitous motivation for the mounting block, which was there before the queen came and which was unchanged by her visit. It is far more compelling that such things as a ringing rock or a tomb were perceived in the ancient Greek system of mythmaking as *sēmata* 'signs' that demanded understanding, and myth stepped in to satisfy its own demand. Another example is the outline of Poseidon's trident in the rock of the acropolis of Athens (Pausanias 1.26.5).

exact nature of his fame is encoded in the location and form of his tomb, and he seems to be alluded to in the eerie enigma of Theognis 1229–1230: this hero's tomb is a memorial of drowning survived (Pausanias 1.40.6, 1.44.6).[8] So is Megara as a whole, and that uniquely. No other polis has this arrangement of signs. Megara simply and essentially is the polis that has this cult. Lacking it, Megara would not be Megara nor could another city—lacking at least Megara's peculiar petrography—add it.[9]

Such is "epichoric" myth—the local, often blatantly parochial, myth of an individual polis. Such myth is not, however, what the world most often means by Greek myth. The more familiar notion of myth is that of a unified and coherent corpus current among all the poleis. This too is a perfectly legitimate concept; the Greeks did shape a corpus of unified and canonical pan-Hellenic myth, which is similar in form and spirit to the epichoric myth and agrees with some epichoric myth in its details of narrative, characters, and genealogy but is also to a great extent sui generis. This canon was one of the most striking outcomes of the Archaic age (the eighth through the sixth centuries B.C.). Herodotus named it and explained its importance:

Ἡσίοδον γὰρ καὶ Ὅμηρον ... οὗτοι δέ εἰσι οἱ ποιήσαντες θεογονίην Ἕλλησι καὶ τοῖσι θεοῖσι τὰς ἐπωνυμίας δόντες καὶ τιμάς τε καὶ τέχνας διελόντες καὶ εἴδεα αὐτῶν σημήναντες.

Herodotus 2.53.2

Hesiod and Homer . . . It is these who created a theogony for the Greeks, gave the gods their names, distributed their honors and powers, and indicated their forms.

Herodotus stresses the recentness of the Greek pantheon (as contrasted with the Egyptian):

ὅθεν δὲ ἐγένοντο ἕκαστος τῶν θεῶν, εἴτε αἰεὶ ἦσαν πάντες, ὁκοῖοί τέ τινες τὰ εἴδεα οὐκ ἠπιστέατο μέχρι οὗ πρώην τε καὶ χθὲς ὡς εἰπεῖν λόγῳ.

Herodotus 2.53.1

8. "A corpse of the sea has now called me home. Although dead, it speaks with a living mouth" (ἤδη γάρ με κέκληκε θαλάσσιος οἴκαδε νεκρός, / τεθνηκὼς ζωῷ φθεγγόμενος στόματι). For this explication of the tomb of Kar, see Wickersham 1986.

9. In Chapter 1, we examine a case in which the loss of a physical part of a polis threatened disaster to the whole because of that part's significance in myth.

As to the questions of where each of the gods came from, whether they
were all eternal, who they are and what they are like in form, [the Greeks]
did not know these things until, as we say, yesterday or the day before.

How this canon came into existence is known as "the Homeric question," though of course it is the Hesiodic question as well, and others
besides. The Greeks concealed the process by representing the end products (e.g., *Iliad, Odyssey, Theogony, Works and Days*) as the individual
compositions of individual poets, a view not taken in this book. One
must instead think in terms of a complicated development in the course
of which the traditions of the communities were shaped toward the pro-
duction of a shared canon, a separate container for myth which did not
supersede the epichoric.[10]

Was there a polis to be the referent of pan-Hellenic myth? There
was an abstract ultra-polis in the Hellenic community referred to in such
contexts as the coalition to resist Xerxes:

τὸ Ἑλληνικόν, ἐὸν ὅμαιμόν τε καὶ ὁμόγλωσσον, καὶ θεῶν ἱδρύματά τε κοινὰ
καὶ θυσίαι ἤθεά τε ὁμότροπα.

Herodotus 8.144.2

The Hellenic community, of one blood and one tongue, with common
temples of the gods and common sacrifices and a shared way of life.

This ultra-polis is quite tangible in another great feature of the Archaic
age, namely, the great pan-Hellenic festivals, beginning with the Olym-
pics. Here were gathered representatives of virtually all the poleis into a
single, temporary but recurrent, community, citizens for a few days of a
polis in replica. The name "Olympia" is in itself a programming of the
pan-Hellenic pantheon; this city's epichoric tutelary deity is the tutelary
of all the poleis. Among its hero cults, this fictive community had that of
Pelops, the mythic founder of the polis whose myth furnished an *aition*
for the festival and whose rites both literally (in the earliest state of the
festival) and symbolically initiated the games.[11] The games themselves
are models of epic agonies.[12] They have a reflection in the pan-Achaean
contests held for the funeral rites of Patroklos in *Iliad* XXIII. In such

10. Nagy 1979.7–8; 1982a.43–49; 1985.26–30.
11. Nagy 1990b, chap. 4.
12. Nagy 1990b.118–123.

rites we see the manifestation of the transcendent polis implied by the transcendent myth.[13]

"Greek," that is, pan-Hellenic, myth with its ultra-polis has the appearance of being a magnified, exteriorized projection of something smaller in scale. To be specific, it is modeled upon the myth-cult-community "template" of the individual polis. The pan-Hellenic is thus the epichoric "writ large." The epichoric itself also appears to be modeled upon something smaller. The most striking single indication is that the typical hero cult with its myth expresses funeral rites and thereby implies the family or kinship group (*oikos* 'household' or *genos* 'lineage') as the basic unit furnishing the template. This template appears as if replicated outward, to widen the implied community and evoke a more comprehensive social unit. To be concrete, we mention the example of epinician poetry, which creates an international circle of *philoi* 'members of an integral community'.[14]

The scope of Greek myth looked even farther, stretching its gaze to discover or constitute a community beyond that of the pan-Hellenic ultra-polis. Transcendence of the merely Greek appears in the myths that adopt a far and wide geographic and cultural scope. The myth of Io is expounded by Davison in Chapter 3 as an adventure of Greek self-definition through collision with alienness. Here we want to stress another facet of that myth: it is also an attempt to chart the whole world and thus discover to what extent the exotic and far-flung possesses any kinship with the familiar. The results are largely positive: kinship between Greece and Egypt is asserted, and by the sheer fact of transiting the perimeter Io unites a broad circle of lands. Her journey, because it is guided by Zeus, assures that he and his justice have the widest possible dominion. We also cite the mythic aspects of Herodotus, whose program is to bathe in alienness for the sake of discovering to what extent the world beyond Greece, amid all that is exotic, is governed by the moral laws of the polis. Has the polis discovered a moral law of universal validity? Apparently so, because *hubris* 'excessive growth', the chief bane of the polis, is punished and set straight, corrected by *dikē* 'justice', wherever one finds it—most noticeably in Herodotus' crucial test cases of Croesus and Xerxes.[15] As extreme examples of replication outward,

13. The Delphic sanctuary with its oracles would also merit full discussion as a regulator of myth and cult for all Greeks.

14. See Nagy 1979.241; also Nagy 1986b.89–91.

15. Croesus "was the first I know to begin the injuries [*adika erga*] against the Greeks" (Herodotus 1.5.3); "divine retribution caught him because he deemed himself the most prosperous [*olbiōtatos*] of all mankind" (1.34.1). Xerxes is driven to grand ruin through a

the thought of the early Greek philosophers Heraclitus and Parmenides shows the outward expansion of myth, even though their thought is often interpreted as antimythic or paramythic and therefore a source of the Greeks' "second head."[16] If the Greeks had a second head, it grew out of the top of the first rather than next to it.

In another direction, myth was referred to social units smaller or more restrictive than the family. In Xenophanes we can observe the tendency to develop a reduced and streamlined version of civic myth whose initiates may be fitted within one room and even upon a single couch. The cultural influence of tyrants affords another case: in their *l'état c'est moi* approach, appropriating civic functions to themselves, tyrants did not omit to possess the authoritative vehicles of myth—oracles, poets, and poetry.[17] The case of Hecataeus of Miletus indicates a parallel development for prose traditions. Lastly, Thucydides is an example of the "man without a country" inheriting a historian's form of prose myth but using it to chronicle the suicide of the polis through imperialism and the debasement of its system of values (Thucydides 3.82). Thucydides' program, further, was to develop a power-giving science of action grounded in "human nature" (τὸ ἀνθρώπειον, 1.22.4), not determined by the polis but determining the polis and all other forms of association—or isolation. The work of Thucydides is thus an education for exiles, transients, and the otherwise politically alienated. Thucydides says specifically that he expects his work to yield less *terpsis* 'bliss of communal ceremony' because it is not *muthōdes* 'mythlike'. In an uncivic spirit he calls his work a *ktēma* 'private possession' (1.22.5). Consequently the power of prose myth, which in Herodotus defines the polis and illuminates its triumph, is in Thucydides appropriated by an ersatz—*unshared* power from knowledge of events, deposited to private accounts and thus purloined from the use of the whole polis.[18]

These social units differed in scale, each one striving through its control of myth to be an authoritative vector of culture. The claims of

---

career of barbarian *hubris* (e.g., 7.35.2, where his rebukes to the Hellespont are called βάρ-βαρά τε καὶ ἀτάσθαλα 'barbarian and wanton'. See Nagy 1979.163; also Nagy 1990b, chaps. 8–11.

16. For Heraclitus, see DK 22 B 2: δεῖ ἕπεσθαι τῷ ξυνῷ ... τοῦ λόγου δ' ἐόντος ξυνοῦ ζώουσιν οἱ πολλοὶ ὡς ἰδίαν ἔχοντες φρόνησιν "It is necessary to follow what is common ... although there is a common *logos* most live as though they had private wisdom." In the connotations of *logos* here we include "prose myth" (Nagy 1987a.180–182; Nagy 1988). For Parmenides, see Mourelatos 1970, chap. 1, Nagy 1990a, chap. 8, and Nagy 1988.

17. Ford 1985.87–91.

18. Nagy 1990b.167–169.

one unit might, to be sure, support others. The achievement of Herodotus was to discover a *historia* 'process of inquiry' demonstrating through *apodeixis* 'testimony' that the paradoxical survival of the pan-Hellenic community was a joint product of the cities' obsessional separatism. Honed to hate *hubris* among themselves, they were conditioned to oppose it from outside. We cite the conversation of the Spartan scapegoats with the satrap Hydarnes (Herodotus 7.135: "Spartans, why do you avoid becoming friends of the King? A look at me and my estate shows how well he knows how to reward good men." "Hydarnes, . . . you have good experience of being a slave, . . . but if you had ever tried freedom yourself you would advise us to fight for it, not only with spears but even with hatchets"), together with the succinct proclamation of *to Hellēnikon* (8.144.2). On the other hand, to exemplify "hostile" antagonism among the layers, we can posit that family cult and myth must surrender a great deal, perhaps nearly all, in order for the polis to exist.[19] Myth possessed by a tyrant is similarly subversive of the polis with its myth, and, as we suggested earlier, Alexander's deviant fulfillment of the *Iliad* required neutralizing the autonomy of the poleis. Impingements among the differently scaled social units bring with them corresponding compensations or realignments in the myths involved. If the social units as such come into conflict, their myths are pulled in as well.

The myths as such can also exhibit conflict when they meet. The problem may arise, foreseeably, from simple excess of material—too much myth, too many different versions of the same myth, multiformity where uniformity is needed. The pan-Hellenic community, for example, had the Trojan War—Iliadic themes—as one unifying container for its myths. According to the *Iliad* as we have it, the mustering point for the expedition was Aulis. But as far as epichoric myths are concerned, we may not assume unanimity or consensus on this point, neither before the establishment of the *Iliad* nor after it. There is the specific case of Megara, which had a tradition of its own that the Trojan expedition had been launched from there, not Aulis.[20] Megara not only had this tradition before the fixing of the site at Aulis in the pan-Hellenic version but retained it even afterward. At the same time that pan-Hellenic myth cited Aulis as the place, local Megarian myth claimed Megara, and Megarians had to face a deposition of their polis from this prominence

19. Hamilton in Chap. 5 indicates that Sophocles' *Antigone* deals with a case where tyranny, disguised as polis, has excessively and unjustly constrained the family.

20. G. Nagy 1985.63n.

each time they encountered the Aulis of the pan-Hellenic version. The pan-Hellenic myth is a composite of myriad such inclusions and exclusions.

Our curiosity is strenuously exercised over the ways in which the inclusions and exclusions were made.[21] Did Aulis have a tradition of being the mustering point, and, if so, why did this one prevail? Or was Aulis not in epichoric tradition and could it therefore be chosen without partiality?[22] The appearance of far-flung and hard-to-locate "Nysa" as the birthplace of Dionysos indicates that sometimes it was better to choose nobody's polis and myths than to select invidiously one out of many. The choice of a foreign birthplace for Dionysos thus has a motivation independent of his characteristically exotic ethos; and yet one reinforces the other, parallel to the concept of a "feedback loop" encountered in another context.[23] In this way the transcendent community possessed a transcendent mythology peculiar to itself.

Should we think of the polis and its epichoric myths and cults as historically prior to the ultra-polis and pan-Hellenic myth? No, because insofar as there is a date for the formation of the polis, the current consensus indicates the eighth century B.C.[24] Because, however, this is the same period assignable to the establishment of inter-city institutions, there is no decisive priority to the smaller unit.[25] We must instead be prepared to think in terms of simultaneous development of both. The same is true for the relation of the private local cults to their politicized analogues: the eighth-century "revival" of rural Bronze Age tombs did not cleanly precede the development of the urban sanctuaries.[26] All three levels of myth and ritual—family, polis, and ultra-polis—were capable of developing independently of each other, perhaps because the same common matrix of myth existed for feeding all at once. Ultimately, however, the polis did appropriate cults, singly and wholesale, so that the developed polis, not the *oikos* or *genos*, became the referent of ritual and myth; it was able to do so precisely because it already had its

21. Chapter 1 contains a suggestion for explaining two verses of the *Iliad* as the result of a specific clash between two poleis and their myths.
22. The temple of Artemis at Aulis (Pausanias 9.19.6) fits well with the tradition that the expedition was detained by the wrath of Artemis.
23. Geertz 1983.195, speculating on the reciprocation of physical and cultural evolution.
24. Snodgrass 1980; Murray 1983.63–66; de Polignac 1984.
25. Snodgrass 1980.55–56 cites "Olympia and Delphi, whose athletic festival and oracle, respectively, had already acquired much more than local significance before the end of the eighth century."
26. Snodgrass 1980.39.

own compatible foundations. In the relationship of these two, therefore, we must again see both simultaneity and succession, recognizing that practices of the smaller group were transferred to the larger one, but that both groups were always contemporary. This remained a two-way process, for smaller social units occasionally usurped myth from the larger. We mention again the examples of tyrants and of Thucydides; the latter's apolitical and antimythic stance did not precede the polis but expressed his perception of its inadequacies.

Here concludes this general sketch of the system of ancient Greek myth. We stress myth's pervasiveness and its adaptability; it filled ancient Greek culture and was desired by social units of any scale interested in acquiring authority as vectors of culture. When the social units interacted with each other so did their myths, and both myth and community were liable to be changed; myth and its appurtenant community were thus really in a constant condition of potential crisis. In the following chapters we examine individual aspects of the interdependence and shared vicissitudes of the polis and its myths.

In Chapter 1, Wickersham identifies one of the assumedly numerous crises of myth and polis whereby the poleis of Archaic Greece found, reinforced, lost, enhanced, or otherwise adjusted the dignity of their individual status in myth at both the epichoric and the pan-Hellenic levels. The crisis discussed is the conflict of Athens and Megara over the ownership of Salamis. To assess the factors of this complicated dispute, fragmentarily and subjectively recorded, Wickersham evokes successive formative moments of the mythical traditions of both poleis, as they were involved in the conflict. He argues that Solon buttressed the Athenian claim with the testimony of Iliadic authority at a time when the epic canon was not totally consolidated. Solon recited an oral Athenian variant linking Ajax with Athens; the Megarians in turn resorted to a variant that did the same for themselves. Megarian mythmaking devised a compensation for the loss of Salamis, and the result was a striking genealogy stemming from the hero Skeiron—perhaps a doublet of the centaur Kheiron—which links to Megara not just Ajax and Salamis but Achilles as well. One could say that Megara regained ownership while Athens got possession. The crisis, Wickersham points out, also drew ritual and cult into the battle. The curious brevity of the reference to Ajax in our *Iliad* (in the Catalogue of Ships) is a symptom of the crisis over Salamis and of the blocking influence that epichoric tradition exerted upon the emerging pan-Hellenic canon. Yet balance was eventually struck, in Wickersham's view, thanks to the heroic figure of Ajax, who, hailing from Salamis and linked to Megara in spite of Megara's lost claim, integrated the epichoric and the pan-Hellenic.

Chapters 2 and 3 illustrate how the polis is paradoxically established and consolidated through alienation. In Chapter 2, Freiert delves into the complex of myths and rituals connected with the figure of Orpheus to explain his stance beyond the polis but also at its very center. With his song that enchants wild nature, Orpheus restores order in the human community. Because the body of the primordial poet and his song are renewed through sacrifice, the myth of the dismemberment of Orpheus and the cult of his "talking head" imply the reintegration of the body politic and the continuation of the poet's prophetic mission. Freiert indicates that the widely spread hero cult of Orpheus embodies the mythology in the cults of pan-Hellenic poets. Orpheus is a descendant of Apollo in myth but his rival in cult; myth makes him antagonistic to Dionysos though in cult he is Dionysos' *therapōn* 'attendant squire'. In Freiert's view the quest for Eurydike (Εὐρυδίκη 'Widely Ruling') is parallel to Dionysos' quest for his mother, Semele. Orpheus transgresses not just the boundaries of political space but those of life too—in a journey with shamanistic traits. Life, however, is restored and love prolonged in his song, which sets forth cosmic and civilized order. The tradition of Orpheus shows how myth and ritual can plot the beginnings of both politics and poetics.

An important moment of the foundation of society consists in the marking of its frontiers in opposition and contrast to the spaces beyond it.[27] Using as an illustration the myth of Io's outward wanderings, Davison in Chapter 3 inquires into the role of the *periphery*, the outward limits of the mythic geography, in the self-definition of an emerging political center, in this case Argos. For Davison, mythic narratives of distant travels, stories of remote origins, and descriptions of foreign places are constitutive of a political or cultural self-image. Citing François Hartog's 1980 study of Herodotus, she asserts that spatial difference is myth's mark of social and cultural difference; in myth, distance means alterity. The tales of Io appear as an Argive variant of a Greek and perhaps Indo-European theme of wandering and settling which includes cattle as a *sēma* 'sign' and metamorphosis as well as its reversal. Davison refers to the apparent contradiction in which poleis such as Argos are linked to

27. Theory on the constitution of political space in ancient Greece can be found in numerous works by Marcel Detienne, Louis Gernet, François Hartog, Nicole Loraux, Charles Segal, Jean-Pierre Vernant, Pierre Vidal-Naquet, and others.

non-Greek ancestors or descendants even though the incipient sense of a Hellenic self is predicated upon the ultimate contrast between Greeks and "barbarians." A genealogical tree connecting the Greek world and centered on Io manifests the spatial and temporal bridging of distances implicit in the ultimate function of her myth, namely, the founding of a Hellenocentric view of the identities of Greeks and of non-Greeks, a mapping of the entire world.

Chapters 4 and 5 focus our attention on myths that represent the structure of the family (*genos*) and its conflicting yet foundational role in the polis. In Chapter 4, Segal begins by discussing critically the analyses of the myth of Adonis by James G. Frazer and Marcel Detienne. Against Frazer, Segal argues that the Adonis myth does not belong to the sphere of the supernatural or divine, nor does it symbolize merely the death and rebirth of vegetation; it is a political myth that also posits the necessities and responsibilities of citizenship in which Adonis falls short. Detienne's view of myth in the light of structural oppositions at several levels links Adonis to extremes such as promiscuity and infertility, defining him as "anomalous" in Mary Douglas' terms. But Segal sees in Adonis' failure the result of an inherent lack rather than, as with Detienne, the outcome of his attempt to mediate and overcome antithetical bounds (such as the male and female models). Then Segal supplements Detienne's structuralist grid by applying to the myth of Adonis Carl Jung's theory of the eternal child (*puer aeternus*). Segal shows that the flowerlike, youthful Adonis, who can love only incestuously and who dies an early death, represents a Greek version of the Jungian archetype of a puer personality, attached to the mother archetype and pathetically unfit, be it for marriage and procreation or for a normal life in society. The fast-sprouting Gardens of Adonis, which according to Detienne embody vegetation codes symbolic of Adonis' infertility and of a facile (apolitical) existence, have analogues in Greek mythical "history": Herodotus reports that the domestic lives of Greek and non-Greek tyrants, who share the trait of *hubris* 'excess' (related to botanical exuberance), are aberrations. Adonis is in myth a failed hunter, and this too, in view of the significance of hunting in ephebic initiation myths and rituals pointed out by Pierre Vidal-Naquet, symbolizes his failure to progress to adulthood and to a full role in the polis. The myth of Adonis, concludes Segal, mirrors as a negative model his failure to become part of family structures without which the polis cannot exist and his subsequent inability to become a *politēs* 'citizen'.

Hamilton, exploring in Chapter 5 the myth of Antigone in the famous play of Sophocles, challenges the traditional reading according to which Antigone is pitted against Kreon in an unmitigated conflict of two rights—a conflict that represents the essential incompatibility of private and public codes of value in the Greek Archaic and Classical polis. Against this interpretation, Hamilton observes that Antigone's performance of the forbidden burial rite for Polyneikes makes her, in anthropological terms, an "actor" of kinship morality; that her scale of affection is based on *philotēs* 'nearness-and-dearness'; and that she reestablishes the equilibrium in her *genos* that Kreon's decree upset when he honored Eteokles, one *autadelphos* 'sharer of the womb', while he dishonored the other, Polyneikes. Considering the ideology of Dark Age and eighth-century B.C. death rituals, as well as the curtailment of public family funerals by the fifth-century polis, Hamilton argues that the action of Antigone ('Αντι-γόνη 'deputy of the lineage') is soundly civic and properly compensatory: she redresses an injury to her *genos* inflicted by a tyrant, *not* by the polis. Even in validating kinship she affirms the values of a just polis. For Hamilton the fifth-century myth of Antigone conceives her in the image of *Dikē* 'Justice', the incorruptible virgin dragged off with a murmur of protest from the people in Hesiod's *Works and Days* (220–221, 256). In the Sophoclean play, Antigone, unjustly condemned by Kreon, the *turannos* 'tyrant' who pollutes the polis, receives *kleos* 'glory'.

Further reconsideration of mythmaking in the fifth-century theater is pursued in Chapters 6 and 7. In Chapter 6, Bradshaw studies the *Ajax* of Sophocles, questioning whether indeed—as a prevailing view of this play asserts—the ethos of Ajax, a model of heroic and individualistic (Achillean) nobility, is presented in it as incompatible with fifth-century norms; whether Sophocles in fact proposes that Ajax's anachronistic *aretē* must give way, in the new society of the polis, to Odysseus' sophisticated relativism. Bradshaw's conclusion is very different. Analyzing metaphoric as well as narrative elements in Iliadic passages concerning Ajax, especially in the fight over Patroklos' body, he reevaluates the heroic nature of Ajax in epic. The 'great Telamonian Ajax' (*megas Telamōnios Aias*) who relies on *biē* 'strength' is a paradigm of nobility, for Ajax has *aidōs* 'shame to be thought dishonorable', in contrast to Menelaos and especially to Odysseus, the archetype of *mētis* 'cunning' who lacks *aidōs*. Ajax is the Iliadic figure most constantly associated with the virtue of *aidōs*, yet not for that reason, as Bradshaw's parallel consideration of Pindar's Ajax shows, does he lack *mētis* or *noos* 'perceptive intelligence'. The cult of Ajax as a *daimōn* and his role in the controversy with the Megarians (discussed by Wickersham in Chapter 1) confirm Bradshaw's reading of the code of values attached to pre-tragic Ajax. He argues that Sophocles models the main character of his play upon such genuine Homeric *aretē*, and that this is the virtue that the playwright wants to reaffirm for the benefit of a polis that has woefully forgotten it. The pathetic end of Ajax in this play reflects the injury to civilized values that beset Athens in the middle of the fifth century.

In Chapter 7, Pozzi formulates in a more general way some of the difficult questions that concern the association of myth and ritual in fifth-century Athenian theater. Tragic performances, emerging from earlier performative choral traditions, inherited from religious song and dance the authority of a privileged voice which the polis appropriated and set in the formalized institution of the festival of Dionysos. Tragedy stemmed from sacrifice and initiation; its discourse was mythic and it included the imitation of the *agōnes* 'contests' of civic life; its enactment took place in the religious and political setting of the theater. Greek tragedy, Pozzi submits, reencoded myths in new ideological systems. To illustrate tragedy's reformulation of the mythic tradition she studies the *Ion* of Euripides. Overtly, this play exalts Athens by integrating references to myths and cults related to autochthony and by advancing the figures of Apollo and Athena as allied civilizers. Yet the subtext of the play, she claims, undercuts and supplements the text, for Euripides softens the sharp edges of the image of Apollo by further integrating references to his myths and cult with Dionysiac allusions. Pozzi concludes that *Ion* enacts the advent of Dionysos, a benign god whose symbolic epiphany in the theater, rehearsing new values, challenges and transcends those of the fifth-century polis.

The second half of Chapter 7 points to the roots of Old Comedy, aligning it with very early popular performative traditions. Comic enactment was a carnivalistic celebration (in Bakhtin's sense) culminating in a theatrical manifestation of the Dionysiac temper. Within the formal boundaries of the festival and of the genre, the comedies of Aristophanes offered the polis the critique of a distorting mirror. Examining the *Birds*, Pozzi finds that the mythic motif of Tereus and Prokne encapsulates a pastoral ideal, which Aristophanes deftly employs to bring the fantasy of the plot to a fulfillment that belies its imperialistic nature. The marriage of Peisthetairos and Basileia amounts to a triumphal establishment of the order of Dionysos. Thus did the polis, in the latter years of the fifth century, turn upon itself critically in the theater.

In Chapters 8 and 9 the purview of this book is extended in time and in space. In Chapter 8, Payne reports on the afterlife of Alexander in a Hellenistic account of his life known as the *Alexander Romance*. The historico-mythical Alexander granted continuity to the Greek tradition in Hellenistic Egypt, and the *Romance*, as Payne points out, served the Ptolemies' political interest in syncretism well. Alexander, furnished with a royal Egyptian father who was both human and divine, is given in the *Romance* the title of king of Egypt but also of *kosmokratōr* 'Ruler of the World'. When Egyptian Alexandria was founded, the historical demise of the Greek poleis made such a city an anachronism legitimized by its link to a mythical past. Predictions, prophecies, and miracles attending the foundation, attested in the *Romance*, give Alexander the status of a hero to whom a cult is due. Payne mentions the magnificent tomb of Alexander erected by the Ptolemies and the religious rituals celebrated in his honor. Then, studying the sections of the *Alexander Romance* known as the Letters of Wonders, she relates many motifs to a persistent folk tradition that she illustrates in detail with contemporary evidence and by reference to ancient analogues. Egyptian Alexandria, the ghost of a polis, and other such late centers of myth and hero cult gave Alexander the Great the *kleos* he so passionately desired.

In Chapter 9, Sienkewicz compares the emergence of Greek myth in the ancient poleis with the example of the West African modern epic *Sunjata*. He demonstrates that in this living oral tradition of the Manding people there is a dynamic tension between multiforms and canonicity, a tension apparent too on linguistic, political, and wider cultural levels. Sienkewicz argues that the interaction of performer and audience in *Sunjata* is similar to that which must have existed during the long process of formation of a Homeric canon and cites vestiges of audience participation remaining in the Greek epic texts we possess. He shows how multiform performances of *Sunjata* become communal experiences connecting the singer and the audience, the epic past and the performative present, through the praise of Sunjata, the epic's hero. The modern singer of West African epic, known as a griot or *jeli*, has lost the status of traditional singers, who in their songs partook of the glorious achievements that they sang. Sienkewicz suggests that the pressures of the modern world may force the *Sunjata* tradition into a fixed, pan-Manding version. The comparative study of Greek and West African epics belies the assumption (satirized by Marcel Detienne in an expression that the title of this chapter paraphrases) that Greek culture, the "Greek miracle," was unique.

CHAPTER 1

Myth and Identity in
the Archaic Polis

John M. Wickersham

To emphasize the power of myth and its importance for the *polis*, I consider a specific case of intercity conflict and crisis in which myth was both weapon and stakes. I choose a case from the Archaic period because I suspect that at that time the balance between the epichoric myth and the pan-Hellenic was still being worked out, that not even the pan-Hellenic myth had as yet attained its ultimate fixity. There is also unusually full documentation for this incident, and so we can observe in some detail how adjustments in both layers of myth came about in consequence of the clash.

In the time of Solon, Athens and Megara disputed the possession of Salamis (Plutarch *Solon* 10).[1] Athens actually occupied the island, but Megara succeeded in getting Sparta to arbitrate. The case was heard by

1. Choosing this case from an early period brings problems of historicity. The chief problem is not that the sources are scanty (they are not), nor that the accounts exhibit some confusion or incoherence (they do). It is the danger that the sources may all stem from the tradition about the life of Solon, and that this tradition represents not a genuine historical tradition but merely an accumulation of inferences (some of them fallacious) from Solon's poems: see Lefkowitz 1981.viii, 40–48. The poem in question here was allegedly called *Salamis* and was one hundred lines long (Plutarch *Solon* 8.2). I quote below the surviving eight verses. From these a biographer could indeed infer an incident in which Athens was giving up Salamis but was recalled to the struggle by Solon. I do not, however, find it easy to imagine that the missing other ninety-two lines could have given rise to everything else that is in the sources. I doubt, for example, that living contemporaries were named. The five Spartan arbitrators should therefore come from a source independent of this poem. I would argue likewise concerning the intrusion of Peisistratos into the accounts of the struggle for Salamis. In presenting this affair as history I am basing myself upon the *testimonia* as presented in Gentili and Prato 1979 (with an extension of T 42) and adapting the commentaries in Masaracchia 1958, Legon 1981, and Figueira 1985b. I admittedly diverge from their analyses by presenting the affair as a single episode.

five Spartans: Kritolaidas, Amompharetos, Hupsikhidas, Anaxilas, and Kleomenes. The claims brought forward hinged on ancestral rights, partly as indicated by comparative burial practices, but especially by the myth and genealogy that entered the arena. The Athenians quoted Homer:[2]

Αἴας δ᾽ ἐκ Σαλαμῖνος ἄγεν δυοκαίδεκα νῆας,
στῆσε δ᾽ ἄγων ἵν᾽ Ἀθηναίων ἵσταντο φάλαγγες.

Plutarch Solon 10 (also Strabo 9.1.10 C394)

Ajax led twelve ships from Salamis
and stood them where the phalanxes of Athenians stood.

These lines succeeded in becoming *Iliad* II 557–558. The Megarians had a variant linking Ajax with themselves:

Αἴας δ᾽ ἐκ Σαλαμῖνος ἄγεν νῆας ἔκ τε Πολίχνης
ἔκ τ᾽ Αἰγειρούσσης Νισαίης τε Τριπόδων τε.

Strabo 9.1.10 C394

---

2. Plutarch's account of the use of "Homer" deserves clarification: οἱ μὲν οὖν πολλοὶ τῷ Σόλωνι συναγωνίσασθαι λέγουσι τὴν Ὁμήρου δόξαν· ἐμβαλόντα γὰρ αὐτὸν ἔπος εἰς Νεῶν Κατάλογον ἐπὶ τῆς δίκης ἀναγνῶναι ᾽Αἴας δ᾽ ἐκ Σαλαμῖνος ἄγεν δυοκαίδεκα νῆας, / στῆσε δ᾽ ἄγων ἵν᾽ Ἀθηναίων ἵσταντο φάλαγγες.᾽ αὐτοὶ δ᾽ Ἀθηναῖοι ταῦτα μὲν οἴονται φλυαρίαν εἶναι, τὸν δὲ Σόλωνά φασιν ἀποδεῖξαι τοῖς δικασταῖς, ὅτι Φιλαῖος καὶ Εὐρυσάκης ... παρέδοσαν τὴν νῆσον αὐτοῖς "Most say that the authority of Homer helped Solon in the trial, because he inserted a verse into the Catalogue of Ships and read it during the suit: 'Ajax led two hundred ships from Salamis and stood them where the phalanxes of Athenians stood.' *The Athenians themselves, however, think that this is drivel*; that in fact Solon demonstrated to the judges that Philaios and Eurysakes ... had given the island over to them" (Plutarch *Solon* 10). What I find unclear is exactly what Plutarch's Athenians were calling drivel, and I suggest that they were rejecting the assertion that Solon had "inserted" the second of the two lines, not claiming that "Homer" had not been brought into the case at all. Strabo's citation and discussion (9.1.10 C394) clearly gives this viewpoint. Of greater importance in approaching this case is the matter of what it means to "quote Homer." We need not think that Solon read from a written text of the *Iliad* or from memory of such. If, as is possible but not necessary, by his verb ἀναγνῶναι Plutarch is thinking of "reading aloud" in that sense, then he is most likely being anachronistic. What Solon is really doing is transmitting to the court a traditional Athenian oral variant of a portion of Iliadic poetry; for "read" substitute "performed." The Megarians in turn are doing the same thing, presenting a traditional Megarian version. The pan-Hellenic *Iliad* does not yet exist with complete fixity and authority over epichoric variants. The widespread traditionality of this section, as catalogue poetry, is indicated by the fact that the Hesiodic *Catalogue of Women* also introduces Ajax with the same formula, Αἴας δ᾽ ἐκ Σαλαμῖνος.

Ajax led ships from Salamis and from Polikhne
and from Aigeiroussa and Nisaia and Tripodes.[3]

Ajax, the most pan-Hellenically eminent Salaminian, became one of
the keys to the crisis. Both sides could agree that Ajax was the crux, and
each disputant sought to advance the most telling claim upon him. The
entertaining part starts here, because the Homeric, pan-Hellenic Ajax of
Iliadic tradition did not clearly and decisively show which of the two
cities he belonged to, and thus it was necessary to resort to para-Homeric
traditions. From their local cults and myths the Athenians produced
Eurysakes and Philaios, the two sons of Ajax, who had become Athenian
"citizens." This was an unshakable claim, since the tradition included
the details that Philaios had settled in Brauron and Eurysakes in Melite,
with Philaios being the eponym of the deme Philaidai; the tradition was
anchored by the corresponding tombs and cults (cf. Pausanias 1.35.2–3).
Upon becoming citizens, Eurysates and Philaios had supposedly deeded
Salamis to Athens. Athens could therefore claim to inherit by legitimate
descent from Ajax. As well as citing this stemma, Solon drew further
upon Athenian tradition by reciting oracular responses from Delphi in
which Salamis was called "Iaonia."[4]

This appears to be the extent of the pleas recorded by Plutarch in
Solon; the five Spartan arbitrators decided for Athens. In *Theseus* 10,
however, Plutarch records another clash of myths between Athens and
Megara, highly interesting in itself but most significant in its implications
for Salamis. In Athenian tradition Skeiron, killed by Theseus, appeared
as a brigand, savage and citiless. Those, however, whom Plutarch calls
"the Megarians" insisted that Skeiron was in fact one of their
own civic forebears, a punisher of robbers and a relative and friend of
"good and just" men: Aiakos, they said, is acknowledged by all as
supremely righteous; Kukhreus of Salamis receives "divine honors" in
Athens; Peleus (father of Achilles) and Telamon (father of Ajax) are the
fathers of the prime pan-Hellenic heroes. The Megarian Skeiron was
connected to all of these: he was an in-law (γαμβρός) of Kukhreus, and

3. See Legon 1981.48, n. 25 on the identity of these places. He observes that the omis-
sion of the actual name Megara gives a "pre-Dorian" tone and so connotes high antiquity,
but I do not follow him in suspecting that it was untraditional.

4. For Ionia as a name for Attica on the boundary stones, see Strabo 3.5.5 C171 and
Plutarch *Theseus* 25.

this impressive stemma, adduced by "the Megarians," shows his links to the rest.

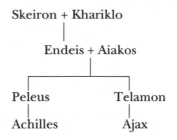

This genealogy, according to Plutarch, was put forward as evidence for the good character of Skeiron. Included also was their account of Theseus' killing of Skeiron, which did not happen during Theseus' initial transit of the Megarid but later, when through skulduggery (παρα-κρουσάμενον) Theseus also undid Diokles, the defender of Eleusis, which in this Megarian myth is claimed as Megarian property. We thus see a rehabilitation of Skeiron's character, with a correspondingly pejorative view of Theseus.

Far more is asserted, because this genealogy radically recasts the status of Megara in relation to the pan-Hellenic heroes. Now a Megarian is the great-grandfather of both Achilles and Ajax, two "best of the Achaeans" (*aristoi Akhaiōn*).[5] Megara regains, indeed surpasses, the luster lost by not prevailing over Aulis in pan-Hellenic tradition as the launching point for the Trojan expedition.

The appearance of Skeiron and Megara in this eminent genealogy shows an admirable accommodation of the needs of local myth to the pan-Hellenic. The stemma as a whole accords with the pan-Hellenic stemma, and Skeiron himself is the only peculiarity. As the father of Endeis and the key to the whole family, he has supplanted Kheiron, who is elsewhere famous as the centaur tutor of Achilles and who is named as the father of Endeis by scholia on Homer (*Iliad* XVI 14), on Pindar (*Nemean* 5.7), and on Apollonius (1.554). Pindar himself, in hymning the sons of Endeis and Aiakos in *Nemean* 5, did not name the father of Endeis and thus avoided this controversy.

The change of Skeiron for Kheiron may at first appear trivial, but a second look may show more seriousness. In the first place, given the

5. For this traditional ranking, compare the two *skolia* cited below.

fluid nature of myth, we should not assume without proof that Kheiron is the correct name, or that Skeiron does not have equal validity in tradition. In fact, our own concept of a correct version must first come under scrutiny before we regard the Megarian version as less legitimate than the other. Furthermore, it could just as easily be the case that Skeiron had even greater legitimacy than Kheiron, and that the latter name was the supplanter. Second, the difference between the two names amounts to an initial sigma alternating with an initial aspiration. These two sounds have an equivalence in Greek, and there are many examples of general fluidity in mythical names.[6] It is not, after all, the case that we see one name changed to the other in a forced or gratuitous alteration. The two names are in a real sense doublets of each other—the same name in two different presentations, both of them linguistically and mythically valid.

The Megarian preference is understandable for the following reasons. It seems plain that, if the Megarian Skeiron was the ancestor of Ajax, and Ajax was the key to the Solonian crisis over Salamis, then the Megarian genealogy is a response to that crisis. To puzzle out the nature of this response provides an enlightening example of the subtle interdependence between myth and polis. If we take the evidence at its face value, then it appears that Megara did not produce the tradition about Skeiron during the actual sixth-century arbitration, because it is not part of the proceedings as found in *Solon*. It is found in the separate passage of *Theseus*, and this *testimonium* does not make a connection with the affair of Salamis. This must be precisely because it was not brought into the proceedings. It was not a part of the proceedings, but it reflects their aftereffect upon Megarian myth. Plutarch's source (referred to above as "the Megarians") for the Megarian version of Skeiron was the group of writers he calls "the historians from Megara" (οἱ Μεγαρόθεν συγγραφεῖς), belonging to the fifth and fourth centuries B.C.[7] I infer that the Solonian crisis revealed a deficiency in Megarian myth, a deficiency so serious that it led to the loss of something of great value to Megara. Megara responded to the shock by modifying its mythic traditions to compensate for the loss. I do not mean that the "historians from Megara" modified the tradition from their own resources; rather, in accord with the dominant ethos of historians in antiquity, their role was to record tradition as they found it already shaped by its community.[8]

6. See Kretschmer 1894, although this specific alternation does not appear.
7. See Okin 1985.19–20; Figueira 1985a.115–124; Ste. Croix 1972.387.
8. Veyne 1983 chap. 1, esp. p. 24.

There was quite adequate time between Solon and the historians for the myth to reform, especially in view of the minuteness and naturalness of the crucial transformation (Kheiron ⇌ Skeiron). The rest of the genealogy was already in place, with general validity. The development may have happened very quickly indeed, and Plutarch may appear jejune when he says (adapting Simonides) that the Megarians with their "variant" lore on Skeiron were "at war with antiquity" (τῷ πολλῷ χρόνῳ πολεμοῦντες, *Theseus* 10.2).

What the historian as such could do, however, was shown by the Megarian Hereas, who confuted one of the subsidiary Athenian arguments. Solon had claimed that the graves on the island matched the Athenian westward-facing custom, rather than the eastward Megarian practice. Hereas (*FGH* 486 F 4 = Plutarch *Solon* 10) fought this point by insisting that Megarian burials did indeed face west. In a sense Hereas' contribution is too late, since the case was centuries finished; but in his own time it was still critically important as a shield for the mythical tradition as the tradition reacted to the loss of the arbitration. Solon's argument about the graves implied that Salamis had never been Megarian. Although Megara had to accept the historical loss of Salamis, there were still great stakes to be won in preserving the mythical possession of the island.

The loss of Salamis had been a severe blow to the Megarians, whose identity needed the possession of that island. Megara was prevented from being Megara. Although the Spartan decision was not to be reversed in the real world, Megara did not let the affair end thus. The polis and its amanuenses such as Hereas stayed on the case, determined not to remain caught, as had happened, with its myths unready. Thomas Figueira observes that the Megarians' claim to Salamis "was grounded in the formative period of their communal existence," and its loss made them "turn to the distant past to redress contemporary grievances."[9] Hence, the "new" myth of Skeiron gave Salamis back to Megara and—a brilliant coup—linked Megara to Ajax and Achilles. There was nothing to be done about the transfer of Salamis to Athens by the sons of Ajax, but repairs were made in another time, and Megarian title to Salamis was established as valid for the age *before* the sons of Ajax, in the time of Ajax himself and earlier. Now, although Athens was the current owner, it was not the original owner. Athens had the current descent,

9. Figueira 1985a.120.

Megara the crowning ascent. When the heroes were prime, Salamis was Megarian.

The crisis over Salamis, as a matter of realpolitik, was ended by the Spartan decision.[10] But this crisis of the historical polis produced a crisis of myth. As a crisis in the myths of Megara it persisted until Salamis had been reestablished as a civic truth. A myth and its polis possess each other. A loss of territory leaves a gap, and myth has the ability to substitute, to fill the breach. Myth may be exchanged for territory; a physical part of the polis can be converted into myth.

In this way Megara lost an island today but recaptured it yesterday, and also discovered its claim to be the polis of several distinguished heroes and heroines revered by the opponent Athens or the Greeks generally. This example illustrates well the principle derived from Grote, that a political act is also an exercise of myth: a war was settled through an examination of cult and myth.[11] We observe that Megara, having failed in its suit, did not renege, and it would be hasty to infer that this was merely a matter of yielding to force. Wagering on the arbitration and honoring its outcome, Megara must be viewed as also acquiescing in the superiority of the decisive Athenian claim, which I take to be the transfer by the sons of Ajax. Megara did not refute this and could not, because this claim, solidly grounded in Athenian cult and myth, could not be shaken as part of truth about Athens. I cite Paul Veyne's point that, where tradition is concerned, the natives are in the best position to know the truth about themselves and that "this truth about their city belongs to them with the same force of ownership as the city."[12] It is a corollary that one polis cannot manage the myths of another; the Megarians therefore had to accede to this Athenian civic truth, and so had to be guided by the consequent judgment.[13] Comprehension of this event requires that we acknowledge the myth-mindedness of all parties.

Complete homage to Grote necessitates a look at what use he made of his own strictures and how he himself handled the Salamis affair,

10. Plutarch *Solon* 12.5 indicates that Megara struck back and forcibly recaptured Salamis not long after, when Athens was distracted by the Cylonian curse. In ignoring this report, I follow, for example, Legon 1981.136. If, however, one accepts the report, in accordance with a discussion such as that of Figueira 1985b.291, then I suggest that retaliation by Megara, admittedly implying repudiation of the arbitration, could indicate that Megarian tradition had already reformed itself enough to reestablish the ancestral claim to Salamis.

11. See Wickersham and Pozzi in Introduction.

12. Veyne 1983.107.

13. A polis can, however, manage its *own* myths, and Megara did so, as described above.

when he came to it in his exposition of "Historical Greece": "Such a title [sc., from the sons of Ajax] was held sufficient, and Salamis was adjudged by the five Spartans to Attica, with which it ever afterwards remained incorporated until the days of Macedonian supremacy. Two centuries and a half later, when the orator Aeschines argued the Athenian right to Amphipolis against Philip of Macedon, the legendary elements of the title were indeed put forward, but more in the way of preface or intro- duction to the substantial political grounds. But in the year 600 B.C., the authority of the legend was more deep seated and operative, and ade- quate by itself to secure a favourable verdict."[14] Grote, true to his princi- ple, was plainly impressed by the fact that argument from myth was decisive. Such argument, to adopt his phrase, was what constituted "sub- stantial political grounds," because it constituted the heart of the polis, its sense of identity and self-esteem.[15]

According to the narrative in Plutarch (Solon 8–10), myth was part of the strategy of the war even before featuring so critically in the arbitra- tion. With Megara still in possession of Salamis, Solon had advice from Delphi to initiate action by propitiating the heroes of Salamis, and so a night expedition crossed over; its mission was to sacrifice to Periphemos and Kukhreus. The action that followed gave the Athenians military control of the island, and Solon crowned it with a new temple to Enu- alios. The campaign was thus bracketed by acts of cult, with intense local importance in the case of the two heroes: approval to possess a place must be sought from its heroes, and one can seek that approval only by offering cult on the spot, because of course that is where the myth says the heroes are buried. Success in arriving to offer the cult is simultane- ously the first step in successful possession. The whole campaign appears as one seamless action, with a sincerity lent by a sacral inaugura- tion and conclusion.

We also see the centrality of myth to a polis' self-concept, and how all its myths are interwoven. The historical loss of Salamis changed Megara's and everyone's view of what it meant to be Megara. Megara became not only a city that did not now have Salamis, but one that perhaps never really did. A way had to be found to reconnect, or else the loss would be compounded; all the rest of the myths predicated

14. Grote 1846–1862. II.299; also Wickersham and Pozzi in Introduction.
15. Grote himself perhaps underestimated the force of myth at the later period; see Mar- kle 1976, especially p. 98, who agrees with both Grote and Bohringer in saying that myth was still, in the fourth century B.C., a language "familiar to all Greeks" and that there was "no alternative" to it "in inter-state or hegemonic political theory."

upon Megarian kinship with Ajax and possession of Salamis were shaken. For example, I cite the Megarian cult of Athena Aiantis.[16] Pausanias (1.42.4) says that his guides (*exēgētai*) had no information to give him on this. He therefore acted as his own exegete, reckoning by the following genealogy.

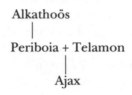

Combining the name with the genealogy, Pausanias inferred a demystifying but politically critical *aition*: "that Ajax, who succeeded to the throne of Alkathoös, made the statue of Athena." Like the stemma previously cited, this puts Ajax—and with him Salamis—into the civic genealogy of Megara. The other made him the great-grandson of Skeiron; this one makes him the son-in-law of Alkathoös, who was the most prominent hero of Megarian myth, a Megarian equivalent to Herakles, and, most important, the "true founder of a true polis, Megara."[17] Alkathoös is the keystone of Megarian civic myth; his throne passed to Ajax. Did Ajax's sons inherit Ajax's title to Megara as well as to Salamis? Did they give away more than Salamis? When Salamis was awarded to Athens, connection to Ajax became actually dangerous to Megara. The loss of the material island was one thing, but the disturbance of the web of myth threatened the whole polis.

The interdependence of myth and polis also appears from the chain reaction of crisis. The general political crisis of war between the two cities led to a crisis of arbitration in which myth was most prominent; the judgment here issued in a transfer of territory, altering the political configurations (of both parties), and this change put a strain upon the

16. The Latinizing translation "Ajacian Athena" of the Loeb is opaque. Actually the sanctuary's name is suggestive of cultic enigma: "Athena offspring of Ajax," or "Athena divine counterpart to Ajax" (Palmer 1980.248; Nagy 1979.289–295). This reinforces the suggestion of Bradshaw in Chap. 6 that with Ajax and Athena we have another example of hero and deity being antagonistic in myth but symbiotic in cult. This is also relevant to the discussion of Orpheus by Freiert in Chap. 2.

17. Bohringer 1980.9, followed by de Polignac 1984.134–135. This emphasis on Alkathoös is to distinguish him from the first founder of Megara, Kar the son of Phoroneus; to Bohringer and de Polignac, Kar's creation was not yet a full-fledged polis, marked off both from the wild and from other poleis.

myth of the loser, a strain that was relieved by the realignments of the myth described above.

We should also look at the crisis from the viewpoint of the winner Athens. Before the Athenian occupation led by Solon, Athens had become despondent over the course of the war and there was even a public prohibition against pressing the struggle. Solon injected new spirit with his poetry on Salamis, of which the following verses survive:

αὐτὸς κῆρυξ ἦλθον ἀφ' ἱμερτῆς Σαλαμῖνος,
 κόσμον ἐπέων ᾠδὴν ἀντ' ἀγορῆς θέμενος.
εἴην δὴ τότ' ἐγὼ Φολεγάνδριος ἢ Σικινίτης
 ἀντί γ' Ἀθηναίου, πατρίδ' ἀμειψάμενος·
αἶψα γὰρ ἂν φάτις ἥδε μετ' ἀνθρώποισι γένοιτο·
 "Ἀττικὸς οὗτος ἀνὴρ τῶν Σαλαμιναφετῶν"...
ἴομεν εἰς Σαλαμῖνα, μαχησόμενοι περὶ νήσου
 ἱμερτῆς χαλεπόν τ' αἶσχος ἀπωσόμενοι.

Solon F 2 Gentili-Prato

I came in person as a herald from longed-for Salamis,
 dedicating a song, a garland of poetry, instead of speaking a proposal.
Would that I might change homelands and be a
 Pholegandrian or Sikinite instead of an Athenian;
for the reputation among mankind would soon be this:
 "This man is an Athenian, one of the Salamis-betrayers"...
Let us go to Salamis, to fight for the longed-for island
 and repel harsh disgrace.

If Megara's sense of itself as a polis was strained by the loss of Salamis after the Spartan judgment, so had the Athenians gotten into a similar crisis of civic spirit before the successes of Solon in the field and in court. To them Salamis was *himertē* (ll. 1, 8); they desired the island with the urgent and distracting sort of desire marked as *himeros*. So strong was this Athenian yearning and need for Salamis that, just as Megara was faced with damage to its identity, so Solon makes the lack of Salamis equivalent to a destruction of Athenian identity: to be Athenian without Salamis is worse than to be Pholegandrian or, what is next to it, Sikinite (3). To be Athenian (*Attikos*) now is to also have the reputation (*phatis*) of having relinquished Salamis (*tōn Salaminaphetōn*, 5–6), a mark of disgrace (*aiskhos*, 8).

Without Salamis, Athens is a polis not worth belonging to. Why take it so hard? Is there not something remarkable about this? Such harping upon this island as essential to the concept of "Athenian" should lead us to infer that the strong bond between Athens and Salamis was forged of myth.[18] We know that the connection given by the sons of Ajax was already there, because it was cited in the arbitration against Megara and was probably the decisive element in the case. I wish to include it among the motives as well. The cult, the status of eponym for Eurysakes and Philaios—these facts were evidence for the *aition* in the myth that they exchanged Salamis for Athenian citizenship, and it was therefore true. To abandon or overlook the claim that obviously issues from the myth would be to destroy the constitution "Attica-includes-Salamis" that was established by the heroes. It would also mean denying the reality of the sons of Ajax in cult and eponymy—an institution as undeniable to the Athenians as to the Megarians. Myth or cult can be added, though it should be done carefully, and the Megarians were careful about it in discovering the posterity of Skeiron. But to remove such an institution is extremely difficult—practically impossible—as Kleisthenes of Sikyon found out in his attempt to eliminate the cult of Adrastos (Herodotus 5.67). The Athenians were therefore in the uncomfortable position of having a myth that entitled them to Salamis while Salamis was in the hands of foreigners, who were themselves also driven by a tradition of ownership. This battle of Salamis was a battle of myths well before it went to the arbitrators.

Whose tradition was the stronger? What did it mean to have a stronger tradition? It meant that Athens' torpor could be ended by Solon's appeal to the axiom that Athens included Salamis, while Megara fought no more in war after Solon's successful seizure; it meant also that the Athenian tradition proved stronger in the minds of the five Spartans. We should infer that it prevailed with the Megarians as well, as I have already said; here let me emphasize the fact that the Megarian reaction in myth did not take the form of a denial or a "countermyth" that would somehow negate the myth behind the Athenian claim. Instead it was Megarian tradition that adapted.

Does the Athenian position show any reflection of Ajax himself? In Chapter 6, Bradshaw argues that Ajax in the *Iliad* is the Homeric figure "most consistently associated with *aidōs* 'shame'. . .; who takes control of defensive retreats . . .; who proves most resolute when the Achaean

18. Legon 1981.129–131 argues that economic or strategic considerations are inadequate to explain the fervor of the struggle over Salamis, concluding that it was "primarily an emotional, patriotic issue for both sides."

cause seems most endangered." *Aidōs* keeps Ajax a steadfast defender of his *hetairoi* 'companions', and he calls upon them to remember *aidōs* when they flag and are deserting the cause:

αἰδώς, Ἀργεῖοι· νῦν ἄρκιον ἢ ἀπολέσθαι
ἤε σαωθῆναι καὶ ἀπώσασθαι κακὰ νηῶν.

Iliad XV 502–503

Shame, Argives; now it is certain that we will either be killed
or be saved and repel destruction from the ships.

It was into such a crisis, when the city had wavered in its struggle for the isle of Ajax, that Solon stepped and like Ajax recalled them to the fight by appealing to their sense of shame, "to repel the disgrace" (*aiskhos apōsomenoi*, Solon F 2.8). Solon thus alluded to the Homeric Ajax, so centrally involved anyway in the mythic dimensions of the crisis.

The loss of Salamis reacted upon Megarian myth, and the winning of Salamis affected Athenian myth. Athenian traditions about the sons of Ajax, thrown into the ring and put at risk, were won back with renewed validation. The gaining of Salamis facilitated the flourishing of Ajax himself in Athenian myth. Possible indications are the following two *skolia* 'traditional Athenian banquet songs', which Martin Ostwald has connected with this period of Athenian activity in Salamis:[19]

παῖ Τελαμῶνος Αἶαν αἰχμητά, λέγουσί σε
    ἐς Τροίαν ἄριστον ἐλθεῖν Δαναῶν μετ' Ἀχιλλέα.

τὸν Τελαμῶνα πρῶτον, Αἴαντα δὲ δεύτερον
    ἐς Τροίαν λέγουσιν ἐλθεῖν Δαναῶν μετ' Ἀχιλλέα.

PMG nos. 893 & 896

Son of Telamon, they say that you were
    best after Achilles of the Danaans who went to Troy.

They say that Telamon was first and Ajax second
    after Achilles of the Danaans who went to Troy.

19. Ostwald 1969.129, who, besides Salamis, mentions also Athenian interest in the Troad, another site of great relevance to both Ajax and his father Telamon; both fought there, and the father in collaboration with Herakles captured it (Homer *Iliad* V 638–651; Apollodorus 2.6.4); the son died and was buried there (see Pausanias 1.35.4–5 on the relics).

The creation of the Kleisthenic tribe Aiantis is a symptom of Athenian elation over Ajax made possible by the victory in the struggle over Salamis. The Ajax of Sophocles acquires new authority as representative of Athenian values through the demonstration of both the true excellences of Ajax and his accumulating connections to Athens (see Bradshaw, Chapter 6). Ajax could not have been so clearly united with Athens if Salamis had remained Megarian.

We have been looking at the importance of myth at the level of the single *polis* and at the clashing or meshing of complementary myths between two *poleis*. How did this crisis relate to the ultra-*polis* and its overarching myth? I want to discuss first the appearance of Ajax in Homer. Considering his strong presence throughout the narrative of the *Iliad* and his well-documented rank among the Achaeans, it is strange that Ajax has such a small section (II 557–558) in the Catalogue of Ships. The two lines as performed by the Athenians during the arbitration over Salamis are all that Ajax now gets, and the brevity of the notice makes it stand out from the rest of the Catalogue. It is not merely the brevity that I stress, but the nature of what is omitted. A typical Catalogue entry lists place names in the hero's land of origin, as for example the one for the lesser Ajax:

Λοκρῶν δ' ἡγεμόνευεν Ὀϊλῆος ταχὺς Αἴας,
μείων, οὔ τι τόσος γε ὅσος Τελαμώνιος Αἴας,
ἀλλὰ πολὺ μείων· ὀλίγος μὲν ἔην, λινοθώρηξ,
ἐγχείῃ δ' ἐκέκαστο Πανέλληνας καὶ Ἀχαιούς·
οἳ Κῦνόν τ' ἐνέμοντ' Ὀπόεντά τε Καλλίαρόν τε
Βῆσσάν τε Σκάρφην τε καὶ Αὐγειὰς ἐρατεινὰς
Τάρφην τε Θρόνιόν τε Βοαγρίου ἀμφὶ ῥέεθρα·
τῷ δ' ἅμα τεσσαράκοντα μέλαιναι νῆες ἕποντο
Λοκρῶν, οἳ ναίουσι πέρην ἱερῆς Εὐβοίης.

Iliad II 527–535

The Locrians' leader was Oileus' son, swift Ajax,
lesser, by no means so great as Telamonian Ajax
but far lesser. He was short and had a linen corselet,
but he outmatched all Hellenes and Achaeans with the spear.
Those who dwelt in Kunos and Opous and Kalliaros
and Bessa and Skarphe and lovely Augeiai
and Tarphe and Thronion and around the waters of the Boagrios
—there escorted him forty black ships
of the Locrians, who live across from holy Euboea.

I also cite for comparison a full catalogue entry for the greater Ajax, from the Hesiodic *Catalogue of Women*:

Αἴας δ' ἐκ Σαλαμῖνος ἀμώμητος πολεμιστὴς
μνᾶτο· δίδου δ' ἄρα ἕδνα ἐοικότα, θαύματα ἔργα·
οἳ γὰρ ἔχον Τροιζῆνα καὶ ἀγχίαλον Ἐπίδαυρον
νῆσόν τ' Αἴγιναν Μάσητά τε, κοῦροι Ἀχαιῶν,
καὶ Μέγαρα σκιόεντα καὶ ὀφρυόεντα Κόρινθον,
Ἑρμιόνην Ἀσίνην τε παρὲξ ἅλα ναιεταώσας,
τῶν ἔφατ' εἰλίποδάς τε βόας καὶ ἴφια μῆλα
συνελάσας δώσειν· ἐκέκαστο γὰρ ἔγχει μακρῷ.

Hesiod F 204.44–51 MW (adapted)

Ajax from Salamis, the faultless warrior,
came as a suitor [sc., to Helen], and he gave suitable gifts—
    marvelous deeds:
for he said that he would drive together the shambling oxen and
    the strong sheep from
those Achaean youths who inhabited Troizen and seaside Epidauros
and the island Aigina and Mases
and shady Megara and beetling Corinth,
Hermione and Asine that lie near the sea,
and would give them; for he was supreme with the long spear.

A catalogue entry should itself be a miniature catalogue, and indeed the Megarian variant was, although brief, the right sort of thing:

Αἴας δ' ἐκ Σαλαμῖνος ἄγεν νῆας ἔκ τε Πολίχνης
ἔκ τ' Αἰγειρούσσης Νισαίης τε Τριπόδων τε.

Strabo 9.1.10 C394

Ajax led ships from Salamis and from Polikhne
and from Aigeiroussa and Nisaia and Tripodes.

These comparisons show the availability of a far richer, more informative, and, especially, more localized entry for Ajax. Instead, the canonical *Iliad* has merely two lines, and those two are completely uninformative in regard to the dispute: they show that Ajax was from Salamis, and that is really all. I do not in the least agree that saying, as it goes on, that Ajax put his camp near the Athenian camp has any relevant legal consequences; it merely tells where Ajax camped, and the motivation for mentioning this appears to be simply that the Athenian entry has just preceded (Il 546–556).

I say "appears" because I would like to suggest that the dispute between Athens and Megara over Salamis had a formative effect on this section of the *Iliad*. I am suggesting that at the time of this dispute the *Iliad*, at least this section of it, was not yet canonically fixed, that there was not yet a set, officially pan-Hellenic version. When the Athenians and Megarians were having their contest of couplets, I do not imagine that there was a third, "correct" version to compare them with. Lines 557 and 558 of Book II of the *Iliad* did not yet exist; it still remained to be seen what Ajax's entry would be like and so it is not the case that Megara's variant was discounted because it disagreed with the correct version while that of the Athenians agreed. There were in court *only* the two epichoric variants; from them a judgment was not possible and therefore other evidence was needed. The outcome of this pan-Hellenic arbitration was to award Salamis to Athens, and the pan-Hellenic catalogue entry for Ajax afterward had to be harmonious with the award. Therefore the Megarian version, because it did indeed strongly imply that Ajax was Megarian, had to be rejected. The Athenian variant was acceptable because it hinted as inoffensively as possible that Ajax or Salamis might have some connection to Athens not realized at the dramatic time of the *Iliad*. The couplet was placed immediately after the Athenian entry in the same spirit. Extension of the entry was blocked by the fact that Ajax was not in the Athenian king list and therefore could not fill ships from Attic places; the only gazetteer extension available for his entry (attested in the Hesiodic *Catalogue*) would be one that took him around the Saronic gulf and away from Athens.[20]

I can be less speculative in drawing conclusions about the more familiar diplomatic facets of the crisis. Athens and Megara were able to settle their dispute through arbitration because the pan-Hellenic myth included the figure of Ajax, prominent and prestigious, and made it clear for arbitrators that Ajax was the hero of general belief with title to Salamis. Arbitration was possible on the basis of connection to Ajax, and he became the key to the judgment. The ultra-polis with its canonical myth has a function of providing touchstones such as Ajax to adjust or regulate affairs between the poleis. As transcendent myth, it puts over the epichoric a span from which an arbitrator can have a perspective.[21] It

20. The fifth-century Athenian capture of Aigina (459 B.C.; Thucydides 1.108.4) would make sense as a way to get hold of another place for an entry for Ajax in the Catalogue of Ships.

21. On the concept of the exalted perspective that issues in arbitration and as such is central to Herodotus' program of *historiē*, see Nagy 1987a, 1988, 1990b, chaps. 8–11.

permits the application of a rule roughly like this: let us put matters back where they were in the time of the heroes; let us agree upon a certain *status quo ante*. But this operation was complicated, for it only partly covered the case. It furnished Ajax but left the rest to the clash of epichoric myth, in case the generic status quo had accepted a mythic alteration—in this case an updating that answered the question of which disputant *now*, as a result of the actions of Eurysakes and Philaios, represented the heritage of Ajax. The limitations of the generic myth preserve the local, while the local myth pays its due to the generic by agreeing on a mutual mythic touchstone. The two layers are kept discrete but are joined in balance. When the system worked, this was how. On the beach at Troy, Ajax was at the midpoint of a journey from a past in Megara to a future in Athens.

CHAPTER 2

Orpheus:
A Fugue on the Polis

William K. Freiert

In this chapter I discuss the figure of Orpheus, whose story is one of absence and journeys to other worlds. In ancient Greek myth Orpheus is a boundary crosser who passes the ultimate frontier, that of death. His music is a language that antedates and then parallels the conventional language of the polis. I argue that, through the myth of Orpheus, Greek culture reaches back to its oldest traditions to reflect a mythico-ritual complex that transcends the institution of the polis and, curiously enough, in so doing consolidates it. One might look upon the myth of Orpheus as a fugue on the polis, a contrapuntal flight from the tonic key of the polis to a dominant key that helps create a richer organic synthesis.

The Cosmogonic Singer

A universal trait of Orpheus in myth is his music.[1] With it he can enchant plants, animals, rivers, and even rocks. Subduing the forces of nature with song represents an inversion of the Hesiodic cosmogony, wherein the direst threat of disorder and destruction, manifested in an incongruous combination of animate and inanimate elements of nature

---

1. The myths that concern Orpheus have been narrated in detail only in late sources, the most important of which are Ovid *Metamorphoses* 10.1–11.84 and Virgil *Georgics* 4.453–527. Yet Orpheus appears in many texts as a mythic figure of great antiquity and prestige. His name served to legitimate poetry, ritual, and doctrine of diverse nature. See Linforth 1941, Guthrie 1952, Burkert 1972 and 1985, and West 1983. Segal 1989 explores the paradoxical meanings of the myth of Orpheus and his poetry in the Western literary tradition.

and embodied in the monster Tuphoeus, could only be vanquished by Zeus's supreme intelligence allied with supreme violence (Hesiod *Theogony* 820–868). Yet theogonic and cosmogonic texts related to Orpheus are in a sense "Hesiodic": like Hesiod's *Theogony*, these texts develop patterns belonging to older and vaster traditions.[2] The cosmogonies sung by Orpheus, by rehearsing the origin of the universe, promote order. When Orpheus sails with Jason and the Argonauts, for example, the very first song he sings for the heroes, to calm the strife arisen among them, is a cosmogony.[3] This song has a cosmic significance for the cosmic journey of the Argonauts.[4] In addition, it demonstrates one of the commonest features of cosmogonies: they are intimately related to the restoration of order in situations of strife.

Knowledge of the cosmos implies knowledge of the polis, for the word *kosmos* 'order' is multivalent: it embraces both the notion of "universe" and that of the constitution of the polis. Herodotus (1.65), for example, cites *kosmos* as the official Spartan word for the constitution of Sparta. Ideally, the city is a cosmos, and all of its constituent elements work together for the good of the whole.[5] But no matter how tightly ordered a polis may be, the spirit of *eris* 'discord' is never long dormant.[6] Plutarch (*Lycurgus* 4.1) tells of a Cretan lawgiver named Thaletes whom Lycurgus persuaded to go to Sparta. Thaletes masked his injunctions as lyric poetry, which was so full of *to kosmion* 'decorum, order' that it drove away the strife and mutual hatred of the citizens. As the singer of cosmogonies, whose function is to abate *eris*, Orpheus transcends the dynamic of strife that drives the polis. Orpheus' relevance to the polis stems from his knowledge of cosmogony. In a well-ordered polis, one that enjoys the Solonian *eunomia*, each organ of the body politic contributes to its total health. In Pythagorean doctrine such order is identified with the harmony of music.[7]

2. For a study of the far less solidly traditional "rhapsodic" theogonies, see Detienne and Vernant 1978.133–174; for the Derveni theogony, see West 1983 and Rusten 1985.

3. Apollonius Rhodius *Argonautica* 1.494–515.

4. Detienne and Vernant 1978.182 show that Orpheus' hymn about the birth of the world helps the Argonauts open up and establish the paths of the sea by setting a τέκμαρ 'point of reference' in the sky. In his song earth, sea, and sky had been confused together until, as the result of strife, they separated from each other: ἠδ' ὡς ἔμπεδον αἰὲν ἐν αἰθέρι τέκμαρ ἔχουσιν / ἄστρα σεληναίης τε καὶ ἠελίοιο κέλευθοι (499–500) "and thus forever the paths of the moon and the sun have a sign fixed in the sky."

5. Plato *Republic* 4.430d-432a; see Vernant 1982.128–129.

6. Hesiod *Works and Days* 11–16.

7. Burkert 1972.

Dismemberment and Reintegration

Mary Douglas has developed the idea that the symbolism of the body, especially the human body, carries profound significance for relating myth and ritual to political and social systems.[8] The physical body is a symbolic medium for working out problems of social organization through myth and ritual. Victor Turner has carried these ideas further. Linking the symbolism of the body with the color triad of white, black, and red, common among small-scale societies of Africa, he posits that human physiology serves as a model for social, cosmic, and religious ideas and processes. Basic group relationships are conceptualized by analogy with the structure of the body, which is a microcosm of the universe: "Culture, the superorganic, has an intimate connection with the organic."[9] In small-scale societies a primary metaphor for music is the body. "A legend from the Sudan tells of a musician who acquired a lute from a blacksmith. But the lute 'did not sing.' The smith said, 'This is a piece of wood. It cannot sing if it has no heart. You must take it into battle with you on your back. The wood must resound at the blow of the sword; the wood must soak up dripping blood; blood of your blood, breath of your breath. Your pain must become its pain, your fame its fame.' "[10] Jesper Svenbro points to an analogue of the body in early Greek poetry. In an analysis of Pindar's *Olympian* 1 he shows the connections made between the body of a sacrificial animal and the text of the poem. According to an ancient biographic tradition Pindar, as he arrived in Delphi and was asked what he was bringing to be immolated to the god, answered, "a paean."[11] And in *Paean* 6.127–129, addressing Aegina (island and nymph), for the Aeginetans had furnished the chorus for the Delphian festival, Pindar says:[12]

οὔ σε παιηόνων
ἄδορπον εὐνάξομεν, ἀλλ' ἀοιδᾶν
ῥόθια δεκομένα κατερεῖς . . .

Paian 6.127–129

8. Douglas 1966.128.
9. Turner 1967.88–91, 107.
10. Schneider 1957.48.
11. Such traditions, though of dubious historical value (see Lefkowitz 1981), are valuable witnesses of myth and cult.
12. See also Pindar F 111 Bowra and F 109.1–2 Bowra. On sacrifice and poetry, see Svenbro 1984.217, 229 nn. 28–33.

We shall not lull you to sleep without a supper of paeans, but you will vow
to have received the waves of our songs . . .

There is more than literary metaphor in this identification of song and
sacrificial victim: an actual commerce, an exchange between man and
god is implied. A bull was a prize for a dithyrambic victory, as well as a
sacrifice for Dionysos. In a perfect circle of compensation, the choral
song is given instead of and in exchange for the sacrificial victim.[13]
     What makes the carving of a poem especially pertinent here is the
fact that Orpheus, the poet himself, was in myth the subject of a ritual
sacrifice. I refer here to the tradition that he was torn to death by Thracian women in an act of Dionysiac *sparagmos* 'dismemberment'. Several
reasons are adduced for this violent death of Orpheus. Eratosthenes
Catasterismi 24.140 Robert (= *OF* T 113) tells that Orpheus incurred the
anger of Dionysos because he worshipped Helios-Apollo.[14] According to
Virgil and Ovid, Orpheus angered the maenads because, in his sorrow,
he disdained women; the reason given in Conon 45 (= *OF* T 115) is that
he refused to initiate them in his mysteries. Tradition, then, presents
Orpheus rejecting a dominant religion, or spurning sex that leads to
procreation (or even killing himself, Pausanias 9.30.6), that is, refusing
to participate in the social systems that serve as the foundation of the
polis. With his death the threat he represents for the structures he
defies is eliminated. The rending of his body carries another symbolism:
it preserves the cohesive unity of the community that he would—were he
alive and whole—threaten to break, to "dismember."[15]

13. Ancient metricians and philologists, in *analyzing* ("cutting up") poems, availed themselves of terms related metaphorically to the ritual carving up of a dedicated animal. See
Svenbro 1984.222.
14. For a discussion of literary and visual evidence on the death of Orpheus, see Guthrie
1952.32–33, 54–55, 61–62.
15. In one of the versions of the myth of Romulus (Plutarch *Romulus* 27), the senators
who revolted against his royal rule dismembered him in the temple of Hephaistos and later
each carried a piece of his body away to inter it secretly. Burkert 1962a.365–368 (cited by
Lincoln 1986.43–45) explains the cosmogonic symbolism of the story: Romulus' body
became the earth—and also its significance for the genesis of the society. As the body of
Romulus was shattered, so was Rome, which existed as the sum of families or *gentes*. But
each meeting of the senate reconstituted the primordial totality. Lincoln mentions ritual
counterparts of such a separation and reintegration of the sociopolitical whole.

Alterity in Myth and Cult

Myth makes Orpheus remote and inimical to the polis in one way after another. Like Dionysos, Orpheus is an example of "the other." As Gregory Nagy argues, it is "a common traditional theme that the culture-hero of a given polis is really a foreigner or at least one who introduces his cultural boon from a foreign source."[16] The mythopoeic center seems to have been, for Dionysos and even more so for Orpheus, not a particular polis but a "Greek" one.[17] Both Dionysos and Orpheus are alien to what must have been a developing pan-Hellenic consciousness. The myths of Dionysos are an example of the use of the stranger as a repository for the mysterious and prohibited features of a remote culture. Unsavory characteristics that the Greeks tend to ascribe to foreigners are attributed to him, and various myths depict his initial rejection by the authority of a polis. Yet Dionysos' birth in Thebes, as well as the appearance of his name on Linear B tablets, indicates that he is no stranger but in fact a native, and that the rejected alien characteristics ascribed to him are in fact Greek characteristics.[18]

On the one hand, myths of foreign ("barbarian") lands serve as a means for the culture to project its own unacceptable traits onto non-Greeks. Medea, the barbarian daughter of Aietes, is an example of this phenomenon. The mythical country that Aietes rules, Aia (aia 'earth, land'), is a remote land. The story of Aphrodite's origin in the East might also illustrate this "tendency to attribute foreign origins to early elements of Greek culture which, with the passage of time, appeared somehow exotic."[19] On the other hand, the remoteness of Dionysos' origins enhances the sense of a god's, a hero's, or a shaman's extraordinary power and magic resourcefulness and indicates the privilege of having been chosen for a divine epiphany, a civilizing mission, or a revelation, as the case may be. Even as Dionysos, Orpheus, whose birth in Thrace gives him a wild and semibarbarian origin, can be shown to be thoroughly Greek. But in his relationship to the polis, he offers an unorthodox perspective.

All of the myths of Orpheus demonstrate that he is a figure of alterity. To begin with, his home is Thrace, that most un-Greek part of Greece. By most accounts, he comes from Thrace (and, as we have seen,

16. See Nagy 1990a.273–274 and Davison in Chap. 3.
17. See Wickersham and Pozzi in Introduction.
18. See Boedeker 1974 and Wickersham and Pozzi in Introduction.
19. Boedeker 1974.4.

dies there.)[20] Most revealing is his rejection of *logos* 'speech, argument, reason', the discursive system of the polis. Orpheus' mode of discourse is not the "*log*ical" language that served as a medium of debate and opposition in the *agōnes* 'contests' of the polis but the arcane manner of communication represented by song. Bruno Nettl writes about the affinities between speech and music, concentrating on the three features they hold in common: pitch, stress, and duration.[21] While Socrates eschews the countryside to talk in the *agora*, Orpheus charms the rocks and the oaks. Orpheus transcends the forensic and civic life of the polis; he stands beyond the polis rather than in the center.

As a cult founder, Orpheus has an ambivalent relationship with the polis. He was widely acclaimed as a founder of mysteries throughout the ancient Greek world, and Apollonius in the *Argonautica* has him incite religious activity. At 2.927–929, for example, the Argonauts sacrifice to Apollo and Orpheus dedicates his lyre, thus providing a foundation story for the city of Lyra.[22] Pausanias notes that rites in honor of Hecate (2.30.2), the Savior Maid (Κόρη Σώτειρα, 3.13.2), and Demeter Chthonia (3.14.5) were attributed to Orpheus. Yet there is a fundamental difference between this use of Orpheus' name and the eighth-century practice whereby a city-state would establish a public cult for its patron deity in order to achieve political unity.[23] Political, civic cult is the opposite of the kind of cult that is believed to have originated with Orpheus, for civic cult is public and depends on a central city sanctuary, where all may participate and view the ritual. The rituals attributed to Orpheus, on the other hand, tend to be those of mystery religions, and the groups of ascetics who claimed him as their founder kept their mysteries hidden from the public scrutiny of the open polis.[24] That communal appropriation and "publication" of religious ritual which takes place in the polis is alien to the spirit of Orpheus.

It is Orpheus' nature as an outsider that enables him to transcend the organization of social space in the polis.[25] What was new about the polis was that power, authority, and sovereignty were located, not at the top, but *es to meson* 'at the center', in the middle of the human group.[26]

---

20. See *OF* T 30–37, and, for evidence on fifth-century B.C. vases, Linforth 1941.13.
21. Nettl 1956.134–137.
22. See also Apollonius *Argonautica* 1.516–518, 1.1134–1138, 2.684–693.
23. See Snodgrass 1980.33, 38–40.
24. See Guthrie 1952.201–205; Burkert 1972; 1985.301–303; Graf 1986.86.
25. Vernant 1983.95–109.
26. See Cerri 1969 for the meaning of *es to meson*.

The centered social space was an arena for debate and confrontation, as Vernant notes.[27] But Orpheus stands for the removal of argument and strife in the secular sphere; he stands opposed to the public sharing of religious cult; he stands, ultimately, in his myth, for the avoidance of human society. Thus, once again, Orpheus seems to stay on the fringe rather than in the center.

Both in myth and cult Orpheus appears as alien to the social space, inimical to the primordial structures of the social group (*genos*, without which there can be no polis) and opposed diametrically to the values of the polis.[28] From the viewpoint of its individual members (*politai*), *sōphrosunē*, the political virtue of self-control, which includes such qualities as discipline, balance, moderation, and temperance, is the counterpart of *eunomia* 'good government' or *kosmos* 'law and order, the social order'. Although Orpheus' cosmogonic music calms strife, there is still the contradiction that the life of Orpheus in myth reveals anything but *sōphrosunē*. Immoderate in his passion for Eurydike, immoderate in his grief, immoderate in his misogyny, immoderate even in the manner of his death, Orpheus is the antithesis of the good citizen whose virtue includes *sōphrosunē*. The myth of Orpheus appears as an alternative to the dominant myth-ritual complex of the polis. The mythological figure of Orpheus appears as nonheroic, alien to the warrior-hunter ethic, and alien to the poetry of praise (*kleos*) and blame that legitimizes heroic behavior in the archaic Greek society.

Orpheus as a Hero

There is evidence from cult that, in spite of the myths, Orpheus was revered as a hero.[29] Pausanias notes an image of Orpheus, attributed to the Pelasgians, in the sanctuary of Eleusinian Demeter at Therae in Laconia (3.20.5) and a statue of him together with statues of Dionysos and Zeus at Olympia (5.26.3). At 9.30.4, he describes another statue of Orpheus in the sanctuary of the Muses on Helicon, surrounded by an audience of stone and bronze animals. The ancient sources give two burial places for Orpheus. The *Palatine Anthology* 7.9 mentions his tomb in the northern foothills of Olympos. Eratosthenes *Catasterismi* 24 (*OF*

27. Vernant 1982.125–126.
28. See Aristotle *Politics* 1253a.
29. *Pace* Pfister 1909.I.323, who, making an unconvincing analogy from Christian cult, claims that the cult at Lesbos was not a relic cult because the head was never displayed.

T 113), drawing upon Aeschylus' *Bassarides* (*TGF* Aeschylus F 22; *TrGF* 3.138–139), describes his burial at Leibethra in Macedonia, and Pausanias (9.30.9–12) relates at length the story of the destruction of Leibethra in fulfillment of an oracle, because the tomb was carelessly knocked over and the bones of Orpheus exposed. The bones were then moved to the neighboring town of Dion, where a pillar was set up surmounted by a stone hydria to hold the bones. Diogenes Laertius (*Proem* 5) provides the epitaph from the Dion tomb, which is the source of the story of Orpheus' death by thunderbolt.

In addition to the apparent rivalry over the bones of Orpheus in Thrace, a similar contention over his head existed in Ionia. The decapitated head of Orpheus floated out to sea and landed at Lesbos, where it continued to prophesy. Lucian (*Adversus indoctum et libros multos ementem* 11) tells that the temple of Dionysos at Lesbos stands over the spot where the head of Orpheus was buried in an underground cave at Antissa and that Orpheus' lyre hung for a long time in the temple of Apollo. Philostratus in his *Life of Apollonios of Tyana* 4.14 (= *OF* T 134) says that Apollonios visited Orpheus' shrine at Lesbos, which Apollo had shut down because of the competition. But Smyrna, too, laid claim to the head of Orpheus, so there was competition over the talking head in Ionia just as there was over the bones in Thrace.[30] Conon 45 (= *OF* T 39 and T 115) tells the entire story of Orpheus and adds that he was buried under a big *sēma* 'grave mound' in a sacred precinct which was at first a *hērōion* 'hero shrine' but later became a *hieron* 'temple'. So both pairs of rivals, Leibethra / Dion and Lesbos / Smyrna have the preserved relics of Orpheus. It is not uncommon for hero cults to be the object of political rivalry, and in the contention over Orpheus' relics we have good evidence that he received a genuine hero cult. That the cult places continued to be respected in Hellenistic times may be inferred from Plutarch's story (*Alexander* 14) that it was interpreted as a bad omen that the cypress image of Orpheus at Leibethra sweated when Alexander was about to set out for Asia. Alexander himself was heartened when one of his advisers interpreted the omen to mean that poets would sweat with the great labor of singing all of Alexander's coming exploits.[31]

30. Lesbos and Smyrna also share a comon interest in Dionysos and the ship of Arion (Burkert 1983.200). Parke 1977.109 mentions a Dionysiac procession at Smyrna similar to that of the Athenian Anthesteria.

31. The continued use of his *persona* for purposes of legitimization can be seen in the Lesbian story found in Nicomachus of Gerasa (*Encheiridion Harmonikes* II *init.* = *MSG* 266) that Terpander, who brought Aeolic music to the mainland in the seventh century from Antissa, had inherited Orpheus' lyre.

Recalling Angelo Brelich's findings on the life of Hesiod, Gregory Nagy has argued that the mythology that motivated a poet-hero's cult was similar to the mythology surrounding a warrior-hero.[32] God and hero were institutionalized, he says, as the respectively dominant and recessive members of an eternal symbiotic relationship. In the case of Orpheus it is not a matter of one god alone.[33] Orpheus, as we have seen, is intimately associated both with Apollo and with Dionysos: with one, as his son or pupil as well as his priest or missionary; with the other, as antagonist and victim.[34] An apparent contradiction emerges here, for Orpheus is thought to have shamanistic characteristics and, as Mircéa Eliade observed, we know of no connections of Dionysos with other shamanistic figures. The ecstasy of shamans is different in structure from the Bacchic enthusiasm, and, in fact, Greek shamanistic features are rather related to Apollo.[35]

One possible solution to this tension lies in the convention that equates the hero (be it warrior or poet) with a *therapōn* 'attendant squire'.[36] The etymology of *therapōn* in the sense of 'ritual substitute' indicates its latent subtext. Nadia Van Brock showed that the Greek word *therapōn* was borrowed, probably in the second millennium B.C., from Hittite *tarpassa / tarpan(alli)*. The Hittite words connoted an alter ego upon whom impurities could be projected—in other words, a ritual substitute. The god is typically both beneficent and maleficent toward the hero.[37] Applying the notion of *therapōn* to Orpheus is not so simple, for in his case we have not one god but two, and it appears that each god assumes a different relationship with the hero-poet.

On the surface, Dionysos is certainly antagonistic to Orpheus, being in some versions the cause of his death. Eratosthenes records such a tradition:

τὸν μὲν Διόνυσον οὐκ ἐτίμα, τὸν δὲ Ἥλιον μέγιστον τῶν θεῶν ἐνόμισεν, ὃν καὶ Ἀπόλλωνα προσηγόρευσεν· ἐπεγειρόμενός τε τὴν νύκτα κατὰ τὴν ἑωθινὴν ἐπὶ τὸ ὄρος τὸ καλούμενον Πάγγαιον ἀνιὼν προσέμενε τὰς ἀνατολάς, ἵνα ἴδῃ τὸν Ἥλιον πρῶτον· ὅθεν ὁ Διόνυσος ὀργισθεὶς αὐτῷ

32. Conon 45 (= *OF* T 39, T 115) makes him a king. It is interesting to compare his life with that of his teacher, Linos (Farnell 1921.25–30).

33. Brelich 1958.321–322; Nagy 1979.307.

34. I refer here again to Burkert 1972 and 1985, Guthrie 1952, Linforth 1941, and West 1983.

35. See Eliade 1964.388.

36. Nagy 1979, chaps. 17–18. See also Puhvel 1987.241–255.

37. Van Brock 1959.119; Nagy 1979.33, 292.

ἔπεμψε τὰς Βασσαρίδας, ὥς φησιν Αἰσχύλος ὁ τῶν τραγῳδιῶν ποιητής· αἳ
διέσπασαν αὐτὸν χωρὶς ἕκαστον· αἱ δὲ Μοῦσαι συναγαγοῦσαι ἔθαψαν ἐπὶ
τοῖς καλουμένοις Λειβήθροις. τὴν δὲ λύραν οὐκ ἔχουσαι ὅτῳ δώσειν τὸν Δία
ἠξίωσαν καταστερίσαι, ὅπως ἐκείνου τε καὶ αὐτῶν μνημόσυνον τεθῇ ἐν τοῖς
ἄστροις· τοῦ δὲ ἐπινεύσαντος οὕτως ἐτέθη· ἐπισημασίαν δ᾽ ἔχει τῷ ἐκείνου
συμπτώματι δυομένη καθ᾽ ὥραν.

Eratosthenes *Catasterismi* 24.140 Roberts (= *OF* T 113)

[Orpheus] did not honor Dionysos but deemed Helios, whom he also
called Apollo, the greatest of the gods. After staying awake the entire
night, toward dawn he used to go to Mount Pangaios and await the sunrise
so that he might see Helios as he appeared. This angered Dionysos, who
sent to him the Bassarids, as the tragic poet Aeschylus says. The Bassarids
tore him up and rent his members one by one. But the Muses, gathering
the pieces, buried them in the place called Leibethra. Not having one to
give the lyre to, they resolved to set it in the sky for Zeus, as a memorial of
him and of themselves among the stars. Zeus consented and it was thus
made into a star. It gives a sign of Orpheus' fall, because it sets in the hor-
izon at the same time as the sun.

Apollo also has a symbiotic relationship with Orpheus, as his patron
and teacher. *OF* T 22 illustrates Apollo's paternity of Orpheus. Pindar
mentions Orpheus, who came to join Jason with another nine heroes, as
follows:

ἐξ Ἀπόλλωνος δὲ φορμιγκτὰς ἀοιδᾶν πατὴρ
ἔμολεν, εὐαίνητος Ὀρφεύς.

Pindar *Pythian* 4.176–177

And the son of Apollo, master of the lyre and father of songs, the much-
praised Orpheus, also went.

As Ella Schwartz argues, the myths show that the opposite qualities
represented by Apollo and Dionysos are always present in Orpheus as his
intrinsic aspects, and neither needs to be considered a later or foreign
addition to his story.[38]

Closer analysis, however, reveals that both Apollo and Dionysos are
at the same time beneficent and maleficent toward Orpheus. In fact
there is a tidy inversion in the respective relationships, for Apollo is
beneficent toward Orpheus in the realm of myth, while we find evidence

38. Schwartz 1984.186.

for opposition to the cult of Orpheus from Apollo in the ancient testimony that Apollo suppressed the oracular head of Orpheus at Lesbos out of rivalry: "Cease from the things that are mine, for I have borne enough with thy singing" (Philostratus *Life of Apollonios* 4.14 [= *OF* F 134]).

While Dionysos' opposition to Orpheus lies in the realm of myth, he is in fact supportive of Orpheus with respect to cult, in view of Pausanias' story (9.30.9) that an oracle of Dionysos warned the Leibethrans of the dire consequences of not caring for Orpheus' tomb. So we have a bipolar pattern:

	Orpheus in myth	Orpheus in cult
Apollo	symbiosis	antagonism
Dionysos	antagonism	symbiosis

Beyond the symmetry of this pattern, we should note the dynamic relationships it involves. If we keep in mind the sense of *therapōn* as ritual substitute, it becomes clear that the rending of Orpheus makes Orpheus a ritual substitute for Dionysos, for the victim of the Dionysiac mysteries is both the enemy of the god (like Pentheus) and the god himself.[39] Not only is Orpheus a ritual substitute for Dionysos, but he can also be seen as a multiform of the god from the point of view of the structure of the myth. Although Orpheus forfeits his life as *therapōn* of Dionysos, not of Apollo, we should remember the Delphic identification of Apollo and Dionysos. There is evidence for an early alliance between Dionysiac and Apollonian cult.[40]

Further association of Orpheus with Dionysos is implied in the description by Pausanias (10.19.3) of a ritual at Methymna involving veneration of a phallus head made of olive wood which had washed ashore. Bodiless heads were cult objects among Indo-Europeans.[41] The evidence suggests that the head was seen as the seat of the *psukhē* and also as the source of life.[42] The birth of Athena from the head of Zeus, rather than

---

39. On the theogonic myth of Dionysos rent by Titans, see West 1983.74.

40. Privitera 1970.146–147.

41. J. F. Nagy 1990 relates the story of Orpheus' talking head to "the tripartite schematization of the uses of the human voice and its analogues" pointed out by G. Dumézil with reference to Apollo. The pattern actually becomes quadripartite since, according to Dumézil 1982.11–108, song or music "actually holds the social fabric together."

42. See Onians 1954.109–111 and Bremmer 1983.16–17.

being a mere metaphor of *mētis* 'intelligence', may point to primitive notions that equate the cerebrospinal substance with semen.[43] If the head is the creative force, then the union of head and phallus in one olive wood relic is perfectly appropriate. Like the Dionysiac phallic head at Lesbian Methymna, the talking head of Orpheus is a source of life through his sacrificial death as *therapōn* of Dionysos. This association of Orpheus with the seed of life takes us to the next section.

Orpheus as a Shaman

Because he appears as a magician and a healer and because he transcends the opposition of life and death, it is widely thought that Orpheus represents a Greek version of shamanism.[44] Shamanism was first recognized as proper to north and central Asia, then as a far more widespread religious phenomenon. A shaman is a magician whose spirit can, in a trance, abandon temporarily the body and travel in the beyond. The shaman, a healer and a sage, understands and controls nature and converses with gods and spirits (without being "possessed" by them) on behalf of a community.[45] A characteristic of Orpheus that clearly fits the shaman pattern is his control of nature—animals, rocks, and trees—through the power of his music. Among the trees he charms, oaks are especially mentioned. The close association of rocks and oaks in Indo-European thought,[46] as well as the story (Pausanias 9.30.5) of Orpheus' death by thunderbolt (like the oaks of Zeus), hints at the great antiquity of the figure of Orpheus. Perhaps the great musician who calms strife by singing cosmogonies and who goes to the underworld is the remnant in Archaic Greece of its own prehistoric shamanism.[47] As the *keleustēs* 'boatswain' for the journey of the Argo, Orpheus has traits of the archetypal guide to the other world, to the land of mystery at the end of civilization, to the ultimate destination of heroic quests. As Eliade says, passing from one cosmic region to another is a preeminently shamanic

43. Onians 1954.109–111.
44. See Graf 1986.
45. See Dodds 1951.147, Eliade 1964, West 1983.4–7, 140–150, and the bibliography West cites.
46. A Greek proverb is attested in *Odyssey* xix 163 (οὐ γὰρ ἀπὸ δρυὸς ἔσσι ... οὐδ' ἀπὸ πέτρης 'you were born neither from an oak ... nor from a rock'), Plato *Apology* 34d, and elsewhere. It is applied in these passages to contrast nature with shared human life in a community.
47. On the antiquity of Orpheus' shamanism, see Burkert 1972.163–164.

technique. Orpheus' singing of cosmogonies is parallel to his journeying to the other world.[48]

A typical shamanistic function is the retrieval of a stolen soul; the story of Orpheus' descent to Hades is the tale of an attempt to rescue one who is dead, Eurydike. This is the best-known part of the story of Orpheus in literature and the part that often has been taken to be the whole point of the Orpheus myth. But the love story, as romanticized by Virgil (*Georgics* 4.453–527) and in the ironic version of Ovid (*Metamorphoses* 10.1–11.84), is intimately connected with the primordial functions of Orpheus as cosmogonic singer. Diodorus Siculus (4.25) compares Orpheus' rescue of Eurydike with Dionysos' raising of his mother Semele from Hades. Seeing Orpheus as a multiform of Dionysos sheds light on the function of Eurydike as a surrogate. Her name is really an epithet, 'widely ruling'; it would apply to any queen or princess. In fact, the name of Orpheus' wife does not appear as Eurydike until the first century B.C., in Bion's *Lament for Adonis*. Prior to that, Hermesianax in the third century had called her Agriope 'savage watcher'. Both names could be applied as epithets to Persephone herself. And when Offenbach in his comic opera on Orpheus cast Aristaeus the lecherous beekeeper as Hades in disguise, he captured the ambivalence of the Greek myth.

Eurydike dying after the attempted rape by Aristaeus is Persephone raped by Hades. From one perspective, then, the myth of Orpheus and Eurydike means that the wide-ruling, or savage-watching, Mistress of the Underworld is carried off by death. Her rescuer is Orpheus, her earthly consort and the *therapōn* and mythic antagonist but ritual surrogate of Dionysos. Like Dionysos, the figure of Orpheus is traditional and central in Greek culture. Yet, at the same time, his shamanistic nature makes him totally external to the culture of the polis. Singer of life's beginnings and traveler to the dead, Orpheus transcends the cosmos of the polis.

Death and growth, logically antithetical processes, are represented together in mythic and religious thought in a manner often referred to with Nicholas of Cusa's famous expression *coincidentia oppositorum*, borrowed by Eliade. Victor Turner describes this polarity as the principle of economy (or parsimony) of symbolic reference. The coincidence of opposite processes and notions in a single representation characterizes, says Turner, the "peculiar unity of the liminal: that which is neither this

---

48. See Eliade 1964.259.

nor that, and yet is both."[49] A clear illustration of *coincidentia oppositorum* is found in the Hermes and Hestia duality that was common in Greek iconography. Like Orpheus, Hermes is the great boundary crosser, who comes and goes freely from Olympos to the underworld and whose image guards the boundary of every piece of property. It seems ironic, therefore, that this most fleeting of gods should appear paired with Hestia on the base of the statue of Zeus at Olympia, for Hestia is the ultimate symbol of stability at the center. But as Vernant points out, her very stability joins her to Hermes.[50] Hestia, the hearth, is rooted in the earth, even identified with Mother Earth, and supports the column or mast (*histos*) that reaches straight up to heaven. Thus neither Hermes nor Hestia can be viewed in isolation; one implies the other. Hermes / Hestia represents "the polarity which exists between the static and the mobile, the open, the interior and the exterior."[51]

The Tradition of Orpheus

It is time now to recapitulate and, if possible, synthesize the various paradoxical aspects of Orpheus. In his relation to the polis, Orpheus illustrates the principle of *coincidentia oppositorum*. Crossing the boundary, he stays at the center. He represents unity and cosmos as well as the forces of dissolution and destruction. His dismemberment is the key to his position in respect to the polis: simultaneously central and alien.[52]

After detachment from its body, the head of Orpheus floated away, continuing to sing the name of his beloved Eurydike. As *therapōn* of Dionysos, Orpheus forfeits his life in a sacrifice of purification, but his sacrifice is not that of the poet-hero whose name makes him the one who "emits the voice" (Hesiod) or the one who "fits the song together" (Homer).[53] The etymology of Orpheus' name suggests, like that of his

49. Turner 1967.99.
50. Vernant 1983.127–175.
51. Vernant 1983.142.
52. On the basis of a detailed comparison with similar tales in the Indo-European tradition, J. F. Nagy (1990.234) sees in the afterlife of Orpheus' head "the signification of the oral tradition in its function as a mechanism for establishing a continuity of verbal discourse—that is, for preserving and renewing the spoken word." In the lore of other Indo-European peoples the surviving severed head often occurs on the occasion of an act of written communication; for Nagy the head is an icon that represents the preeminence of voice or song over written records; in other words, it represents the strength and the endurance of the oral tradition.
53. Nagy 1979.296.

wife, an epithet. The suffix -*eus* is attested in Linear B, where it forms adjectives with the basic function of indicating an agent or instrument: 'One who has to do with'.[54] The root of Orpheus' name (*orph-*) has been variously derived; Chantraine traces it to Indo-European *orbh-* 'deprived'. To be Orpheus is to be deprived, to be "orphaned." Because of his loss of Eurydike, Orpheus is the archetypal griever. Separated from his love, separated even from his body, the head of Orpheus is emblematic of the otherness of the myth of Orpheus with respect to the polis. Like so many other significant names in Greek mythology, Orpheus' name defines his essence.

Orpheus' alterity, then, comes ultimately from his separation, which is the cause of his great grief. Walter Burkert traces the Greek words *goaō* 'to mourn' and *goēs* 'an enchanter' back to an original sense of shaman.[55] Orpheus the shamanistic conjurer of animals is fundamentally the mourner, whose nature it is to be orphaned, deprived of his wife, separated from love, and eventually separated from his own mantic head, which even in death goes on singing his love (Eurydike). Orpheus is the singer, not of *kleos*, but of *penthos* 'grief'.[56] As the one deprived of his love, Orpheus is the central figure in the primordial love-death antinomy. It is this that is the basic fact about him. The parallel between Orpheus' cultic head on Lesbos and the Dionysian phallic head of Lesbos suggests Orpheus' sexuality. If the head is the source of life, then the decapitation that Orpheus suffered is a symbolic castration. Indeed, the ultimate reason for his decapitation was the loss of the object of his love, that is, his psychological castration. After Eurydike, he was unable to love women again. This makes all the more poignant Virgil's story that the truncated head of Orpheus continued to sing the name of Eurydike (*Georgics* 4.525–527). It was Orpheus' psychological castration that led him to transgress the ultimate boundary in the first place. Like Gilgamesh and other boundary crossers, he leaves the polis yet is always at its core.

In death, Orpheus sang of Eurydike. Perhaps Eurydike is Orpheus' own poetry; in Jean Cocteau's film *Orphée* (1949), for example, Orpheus journeys to the underworld because he has lost his ability to write. But the self-referential nature of the figure of Orpheus is inherent in the Greeks' use of the myth. Orpheus may be seen as a reflection of the

54. Palmer 1980.249.
55. Burkert 1972.164.
56. See Nagy 1979, chap. 6, on lamentation and the hero.

intrinsic nature of music itself, refracted through the lens of shamanism—for Orpheus' loss of Eurydike is his central concern and essence.

Susan Shelmerdine has shown how the *Homeric Hymn to Hermes* celebrates both its own origins and those of the power of music, which comes from a death-conquering sacrifice. After sacrificing the tortoise and inventing the lyre from its shell, Hermes sings about his own origin in the love of Zeus and Maia (52–61). And it is the lyre that brings about the reconciliation of Hermes and Apollo, when Hermes gives the instrument to Apollo and sings a cosmogony (418–512).[57] Orpheus' otherness is not unlike that of the musician in small-scale societies whose instruments have magic power because they are made from parts of sacrificed animals or human beings (bones or skin). The mythology of musical instruments is rich and bespeaks the intimate relationship of music to sacrificial ritual. According to Burkert, "any new creation, even the birth of music, requires ritual killing. Underlying the practical use of bone-flutes, turtle-shell lyres, and the tympanon covered with cowhide is the idea that the overwhelming power of music comes from a transformation and overcoming of death."[58] Elsewhere Burkert reminds us of the death of Hesiod, who like Orpheus was slain and thrown into the sea.[59] A dolphin rescued Hesiod's body, which became the object of a cult in the sanctuary of Zeus Nemeios. It is interesting to compare one variant of the lore regarding Hesiod's death, that it was caused by a woman, the girl he had raped and who subsequently bore his successor, Stesichorus.[60] Death, sex, and the poet lead us back to the Methymna ritual of the olive wood phallus head. Like the Dionysiac phallic head at Lesbian Methymna, the Lesbian talking head of Orpheus is a source of life through his sacrificial death.

Among the Melanesians, songs are thought to have a hidden supernatural energy. For Cocteau too, Orpheus is the song itself, the force of art, that inherently human activity whose function it is to transcend the limits that individuation imposes on us. Likewise for the Greeks, the art of Orpheus is inseparable from the art of music.[61] The myth of Orpheus functioned in the culture of the polis as a means of transcending the limits set by the Olympian myth-ritual complex that defined the polis.

57. Shelmerdine 1985.
58. Burkert 1983.39.
59. Burkert 1983.202–203.
60. Lefkowitz 1981.4–5.
61. Linforth 1941.165.

To Cornford it seemed an obvious fact that "the content of every divine, semi-divine, or heroic figure is, either wholly or in part, a projection from the mind of the group which carries on the cult."[62] Similarly, the early Greek poets appear as cult figures with identities determined by the genre of their poetry.[63] What is peculiar about Orpheus is that the tradition that creates him is not his own writing, which even the ancients regarded as spurious, but the stories told about him. From a diachronic point of view, the myth of Orpheus is song's self-reflection. In Orpheus, song sings what it is. When his truncated head floated away singing the name of his love Eurydike, it sang the essential meaning of Orpheus. His name means the one orphaned, separated from the source of his life. His truncated head is an emblem of his self-separation. As Orpheus calls Eurydike forever, Greece calls Orpheus forever, Orpheus who is cut off from her, the shaman who crossed the border. Crossing the border to Thrace is crossing the border to the underworld, both as *keleustēs* for the Argo and as bereaved husband. In Orpheus, the polis reaches back into the Greeks' earliest cultural traditions in order to reflect on alterity, on the separation from self, that projection and mirroring of self that is essential for all self-definition and identity.

62. Quoted in Guthrie 1952.57n.
63. Nagy 1979.296; 1982a.49–52; 1990b, chap. 2.

CHAPTER 3

Myth and
the Periphery

Jean M. Davison

In numerous ancient Greek myths, wandering figures traverse the "savage" spaces—inhabited by the "others"—in journeys that culminate in the foundation of a civilized center. Such myths demarcate the world, defining what is beyond the mythmaking center and also thereby assuring that the center is indeed the center. The contours of this periphery are usually blurred and do not cohere completely from the standpoint of scientific geography. Regions and peoples on these outer edges of the world are polarly opposed to the center qualitatively as well as spatially.[1] Diachronically the periphery offers a double valence. It may define the center, providing the mythmaking community with a remote and prestigious (divine or heroic) origin, or else the center may define the far-away peoples as its descendants.[2] Furthermore, civilizing feats are accomplished by local heroes from a polis as a center (an example is Theseus, civilizing "peripherally" as an Athenian Herakles). Such myths buttress the claims of a polis to territorial dominion and power.[3]

To some extent, myths of wandering reflect an interest in geography that was fostered by exploration, piracy, trade, and colonization, intense activities from the eighth to the sixth centuries B.C.[4] Herodotus (4.152)

1. Curiously, the "other" serves both as an opposite and as an analogue of the self. See Hartog 1980.226 and J. Nagy 1985.10.
2. See Hartog 1980.45 and Bickerman 1952.65–81, esp. pp. 68, 77–78. The myths thus can be interpreted or expanded to justify contradictions that they themselves establish: "at the very time when Greeks were beginning to sense a closer kinship among themselves, and to distinguish between Greeks and barbarians, the work of the poets and compilers invited a belief in the relationship of Greek cities and families with one or other barbarian people" (Braun 1982.31).
3. See Wickersham Chap. 1 for conflicting traditions of different poleis.
4. Ramin 1979.7–10.

describes the accidental voyage of Kolaios of Samos, who was blown off course to Spain while on a trading voyage to Egypt ca. 630 B.C. Planned colonization took Greeks to every corner of the Mediterranean world and spawned as well a host of foundation myths. These wanderings, and the trading stations and settlements established from the western Mediterranean to the coast of Phoenicia, from the Black Sea to the coast of Africa, brought the Greeks into contact with a variety of peoples, civilized and savage, and a plethora of landscape and experience.[5] Naturally, "real" geography and actual historical exploration furnished materials for the mapping of mythical journeys and adventures. Myth appropriates and elaborates geography. This creates a setting for the narrative that signifies much more than mere background. François Hartog, in his book on Herodotus, furnishes a fundamental interpretation of this phenomenon through the concept of alterity. Myth uses exotic places and peoples as representations of what it is like to be "not us" as a way of clarifying by contrast and comparison who and what "we" are.[6]

Literary evidence of a mythical geography appears early, in the Homeric poems and in the fragments of the *Catalogue of Women* attributed to Hesiod.[7] In the prose tradition, there are the fragments of Hecataeus' *Periēgēsis* 'Journey around the World'.[8] These references present or imply an extensive mythic geography, of which the following is merely a brief evocation. Olympos, Hades, and the Isles of the Blessed, distant peoples dear to the gods such as the Hyperboreans and Ethiopians, and abodes of the gods and of dead or translated heroes are all common. Historical places, especially of course poleis, are exalted in myth as scenes of the trials and adventures of live heroes or as centers of

5. Boardman 1980 and Ramin 1979.9–10.
6. Hartog 1980, esp. pp. 224–269. Similarly, for an interpretation of the *Odyssey* as a survey of encounters with nonagricultural societies, see Vidal-Naquet 1986b. For a parallel approach to the role of the outsider in Irish myth, see J. Nagy 1985. For tales of wandering as a political metaphor for exile, see Bernand 1985.15: "le héros tragique est essentiellement défini comme un vagabond, un Grec errant, le plus grand malheur de l'homme étant le déracinement."
7. For the *Catalogue* fragments as witnesses of geographic lore including the far-flung, see F 150–157 MW and West 1985.84–85. F 150 features exotic peoples—the Κατουδαῖοι 'Subterraneans', the Pygmies, the Μέλανες 'Negroes', the Aithiopes, the Libyans, and the Scythians. F 151 (= *FGH* Ephorus 70 F 42) indicates that at least a portion of the *Catalogue* was so rich in this sort of material that it was referred to as *Gēs Periodos* 'Tour of the World'. The portion in question may have been specifically that dealing with the descendants of Inakhos, with Io near the head of the stemma, as the figure who initiates its great geographic spreading (see West 1985.84, 177–178).
8. *FGH* 1 F 36–359.

civilization founded by them; such are Athens, Thebes, Argos; Herakles, Perseus, Jason, Odysseus. The far reaches of the earth include the theriomorphic and biform creatures with whom the heroes contend, or—no less interesting from myth's viewpoint—those beings of alterity that populate places of alterity: centaurs, griffins, Gorgons, Cyclopes, sirens, Arimaspians. Myth makes use of well-known permanent folk, such as Egyptians, and of peoples who may be barbarous and shifting, such as Cimmerians, Amazons, and Scythians.[9]

It is characteristic of this mythic geography to furnish a realm for wanderings. The gods travel often on divine business. Zeus and Poseidon (on separate occasions) visit and feast with the Ethiopians, as Apollo does with the Hyperboreans.[10] Demeter is given an extensive itinerary in her search for Persephone.[11] Various deities make regular journeys to their appropriate cult places. Heroic travels are equally purposeful, involving as they normally do some important trial or quest. Perseus undergoes a series of trials, and Herakles experiences a combination of labors, quests, and incidental adventures—carried out en route to or from another goal. Jason sets out on a quest that results in a trial and an ensuing series of travels. Odysseus' homeward journey is beset with dangers, and Kadmos wanders far from home in search of Europa.

Piracy too appears as a feature of many mythic voyages.[12] The Achaeans at Troy may claim to be seeking Helen, but Nestor recalls incidents of plunder on the way, and both Menelaos and Odysseus behave like pirates on their return voyages (*Odyssey* iii 105–106; iv 80–85; ix 39–42). The *Homeric Hymn to Dionysos* praises the victory of the god over Etruscan pirates.[13] The Phoenicians have mythic status as sailors of fortune. Homer limits their transgressions to kidnapping and the slave trade (*Odyssey* xiv 288–289; xv 415–484). In Herodotus 1.1, the Persian λόγιοι 'tellers of prose tradition' claimed that the Phoenicians had abducted Io, the daughter of Inakhos, from Argos to Egypt. Greek myth made elaborate and imaginative use of Io's journey.

9. For the special fascination arising from the Scythians, see Hartog 1980.
10. See Ramin 1979.74–75, 69.
11. See Picard 1927.
12. Historically the Greeks themselves actively practiced piracy during their earlier days (Thucydides 1.5–7; Herodotus 1.166). The distinction between piracy and commerce is often blurred, and both Phoenicians (Thucydides 1.8) and Etruscans (Pallottino 1975.82–84) are recognized as traders as well as pirates.
13. *Homeric Hymn* 7; Strabo 6.2.2 C267 refers to the fear men had of Etruscan (Tyrrhenian) piracy as they approached Sicily, until the Greeks founded colonies. See also 5.2.2 C220 and 5.3.5 C232.

The Myth of Io

Io's wanderings are in a special category. She is not divine, though being a priestess of Hera she is connected to the goddess and may even be her surrogate; nor is she a human male heroic deliverer (as are Herakles and Theseus). Though her travels appear similar to those of Medea, she differs radically from Medea, a sorceress and barbarian herself who journeys with a Greek hero but has her own center outside the confines of the familiar world. Whereas Medea's travels are purposeful, Io's peregrinations are at once frantic and aimless.

Io's sufferings do serve a purpose, however; she is a girl who will become the mother of a founder, Epaphos. This makes her myth comparable to those of Auge, Kallisto, Danae, Tyro, Antiope, and others whose tales belong to the category described by Walter Burkert as the "girl's tragedy."[14] The additional element of animal metamorphosis also has many parallels. Io can be compared with Kallisto, also loved by Zeus and changed into a bear, and because of her transformation into a cow the parallel with Europa is equally clear. Most impressively, both Europa and Io through their adventures become the centers of international families, mothers of nations.[15]

The story of Io is one of the most complicated and interesting of Greek myths, covering as it does the widest expanses of chronology and geography.[16] The core of the tale is fixed in Argos, where Io, the daughter of King Inakhos, is a priestess of Hera. Zeus falls in love with her and, in the earliest variant, changes Io into a cow to deceive the watchful Hera.[17] Hera sets the shepherd Argos to guard Io; Argos is

14. Burkert 1979.7: "a fixed sequence of departure, seclusion, rape, tribulation, and rescue as a prelude to the emergence of the hero."

15. See West 1985.84

16. See Hesiod F 124–126 MW (from the *Catalogue of Women*) and 294, 296 (from the *Aigimios*, attributed to Clinias of Carystus by the testimonium added in Merkelbach and West 1983.232). The source—a strange one—of the Scythian itinerary is probably Aristeas of Proconnesus and his story of the Arimaspians, tentatively dated ca. 658 B.C. (*FGH* 35 and Herodotus 4.13–14; see Bolton 1962.) An informative discussion of Io's representation in ancient literature and vase painting is given by Bernand 1955 and Yalouris 1986. For a broad spectrum of discussion and interpretation, see Linforth 1910; Severyns 1926; R. D. Murray 1958; Hicks 1962; Wehrli 1967; Albini 1975; Duchemin 1979; Gourevitch and Gourevitch 1979.

17. Io is daughter of Inakhos in Aeschylus, but in the *Catalogue of Women* (Hesiod F 124 MW) she is daughter of Peiren, with Inakhos higher in the stemma. In later variants, it is Hera who effects the transformation, and Zeus changes himself into a bull "eager for his mate" (Aeschylus *Suppliants* 299–301).

killed by Hermes on order of Zeus. Hera retaliates by sending a gadfly (or the ghostly image of Argos) to torment Io (Aeschylus *Suppliants* 307–309; *Prometheus Bound* 567– 574, 681–682). Maddened with pain or terror, Io sets off on a series of wanderings which take her to the far north, to the East, and finally to Egypt. Here she is restored to her human shape by the breath and gentle touch of Zeus and bears him a son, Epaphos ('He of the touch'), who will be the first ruler of Egypt.

The next episode occurs five generations later with the flight of the Danaids from Egypt to Argos (Aeschylus *Prometheus Bound* 853–856). Aigyptos and Danaos, descendants of Epaphos, become involved in a brotherly dispute which in one variant concerns the marriage of Aigyptos' fifty sons with Danaos' fifty daughters (Aeschylus *Prometheus Bound* 855; *Suppliants* 392–395). Danaos and his daughters (the Danaids) seek refuge in Argos, on the basis of their original descent from Io. Aigyptos' sons appear in hot pursuit and force marriage upon the unwilling girls. All but one of the girls respect their oath to their father to kill their husbands on their wedding night. Danaos later becomes king of Argos, and through his one remaining daughter, Hypermestra, and her descendants he will be a founder of the Greek race (the Danaoi in Homer).[18]

To detail Io's journey from Argos to Egypt, this time with emphasis on the separate sources, we have but brief fragments of the Hesiodic version (F 124–126, 294, 296 MW). The fullest detail is offered in two plays by Aeschylus, *Prometheus Bound* and *Suppliants*. Io's itinerary is described in both plays, but with considerably more detail in the *Prometheus Bound* (848–851).[19] In *Suppliants* (547–564) the journey as described by the Danaids is simple and direct. Io moves first through various sections of Asia Minor: Phrygia, Mysia, Lydia, and across the mountains of the Cilicians and the Pamphylians. Then comes an unclear stretch over rivers and fertile lands and "the wheat-rich land of Aphrodite" (variously interpreted to mean Cyprus or Syria) to "the snow-fed meadow," the Nile.

The itinerary of Io in the *Prometheus Bound* is considerably more complicated, for Prometheus first prophesies Io's future wanderings (707–735, 790–814) and then describes to her the route she has taken to reach his place of torment (828–841). In geographic order, Io goes first to Dodona and to the Ionian Sea (which receives its name from her);

18. The line of descent from Io back to Argos and then through Danaos is the main line, but also, as the center of a circle, it is only the center; for the rest, see the stemmata of West 1985.177–178.

19. Much of this geography and genealogy is mentioned in various passages of Herodotus book 2. For comment on these passages, see Lloyd 1975, 1976, and 1988.

then she moves northeastward to the Scythian nomads and thus to Prometheus. When she leaves Prometheus, she is to go along the shore of the Black Sea, bypassing the unfriendly metalworkers, the Khalybes, and crossing the Caucasus. She moves south to the Amazons and crosses the Cimmerian Isthmus (this region will be named, after her, Bosporos 'Cow's Crossing'), leaving Europe and entering Asia. Now she is in an eastern wonderland, from which she crosses the sea to the Gorgoneion plains of Kisthene; she passes the daughters of Phorkys (the Graiai) and the Gorgons, the hounds of Zeus (griffins), and the one-eyed horse-riding Arimaspians near the river Plouton. Finally she reaches the "land of the dark race," the river Aithiops; passing along this to the cataract where the Nile flows from the Bybline mountains, she will arrive at the land of Nilotis, where it is ordained that she and her descendants are to found a colony, Kanobos.[20]

Implications of Myths of Wandering

It is as a cow that Io wanders around and beyond the known world, finally to settle in a place, Egypt, and mark it as an origin. Following a cow is an old theme, of which Io's tale may be seen as a specially elaborated Argive / Greek variant. Io's metamorphosis and its reversal, while encapsulating other complex meanings, also reinforce in her story the basic theme of peregrination and settlement. To define the conclusion of the search, the myth has her recover in Egypt her human figure and receive the magic touch and the seed of Zeus (Aeschylus *Prometheus Bound* 848–851). Io's descendants will found Kanobos (*Prometheus Bound* 814–815, 846–847).

The motif of cattle as a mark for settlement in Greek myth continues beyond Io. Europa, another descendant, is an involuntary instigator of two major wanderings and foundations involving cattle: Zeus changes himself into a bull to lure her from Tyre to the land which will bear her name, and Kadmos, in his search for her, travels from Phoenicia to Greece and follows a cow to the future site of Thebes.[21] A still later descendant, Herakles, is an active participant in adventures of wandering and foundation myths which involve cattle.[22] When he is on his way

20. See Bianchetti 1988 for the most recent discussion of Aeschylean geography.
21. See Bühler 1968 and Edwards 1979.
22. Lacroix 1974.38, 50.

home from Spain after seizing the cattle of Geryon, he traverses the full length of Sicily with the herd.[23] Here he conquers the settlement of Eryx, which he marks for his descendants.[24] In a further episode on his roundabout way home with these cattle, he founds the race of Scythians (according to the Greeks of Pontus; see Herodotus 4.8–10). Not linked to Io, but a fine parallel to the case of Kadmos, is that of Ilos, who follows a dappled prize cow to the site where he founds Ilion (Apollodorus 3.12.3). On a more exalted level, the Egyptians believed that a celestial cow conducted the dead pharaoh to a heavenly throne.[25] A tenuous link to Io exists in the fact that the Greeks recognized a similarity to her in the horned representations of Isis / Hathor (Herodotus 2.41) and that one of the many epithets of Hathor was the "Queen of Heaven."

The traditional basic motif of the cow is combined in the myth of Io with a developed rhetoric of travel and wandering marked by strong contrasts. The course moves from "near" to "far," from "now" to "then" and from "identity" to "alterity"; these are the dimensions of thought wrapped up in the myth's narrative contrast of wandering with ceasing to wander. With reference to the first two oppositions, in space and time, Greek myths of wanderings related to foundations are usually journeys of penetration, moving inland beyond the accessible coasts of the Mediterranean. Io's itinerary takes her from Greece to Scythia, Asia Minor, the East, and the Nile valley. Her descendant Herakles also visits Scythia and Asia Minor, touches at North Africa and Egypt, and adds a western dimension by trips to Spain, Italy, and Sicily. The Argonauts sail a direct route from Iolkos to Kolkhis through the Black Sea, with stops at Lemnos and along the coast of Asia Minor; but their homeward voyage takes a northward swing along normally nonconnecting rivers—the Danube, the Po, and the Rhone—whence they take the southern route through the Tyrrhenian Sea, North Africa, past Crete and so back to Iolkos (Apollonius Rhodius 4.303–1781).

The story of Io is a particularly illuminating example of the representation of extremes of geography and other oppositions. That geographic pairings and oppositions are significant is especially noticeable in Aeschylus' treatment of the myth. The Scythians of the far north find an analogue in the Ethiopians of the far south. Geographic features and boundaries are also antithetically paired: the (nonexistent) river

23. Hesiod *Theogony* 287–293, 979–983; see Lacroix 1974.53, n. 6.
24. Herodotus 5.43; Lacroix 1974.38 lists Motya and Solous but not Eryx.
25. Bergman 1968.127 (*Pyramid Texts* 1153–1154).

Hybristes northeast of Scythia is opposed to the section of the upper Nile which Aeschylus calls the river Aithiops. In the same way, the Caucasus forms the boundary between Scythia and Asia, while the (nonexistent) Bybline mountains mark the boundary between Ethiopia and Egypt.

Despite all the mythic otherworldness inherent in these adventures, the bulk of the journeys take place in areas surely known to be inhabited. Asia Minor at various periods held and was held by the Hittites, by the later and better known Phrygians and Lydians, and by a host of less powerful or urbanized tribes whose names were known to the Greeks at least from the time of the fixation of the Homeric epic. Asia was successively or contemporaneously populated or controlled by Phoenicians, Hebrews, Neo-Hittites, Aramaeans, Urartians, Assyrians, Neo-Babylonians, and ultimately Medes and Persians. Egypt was inescapably her idiosyncratic and independent self, regardless of shifts in dynasties. The coasts of Spain and North Africa were encrusted with Phoenico-Punic emporia, and North Africa itself was largely supervised by Carthage and Libya. Italy from the eighth century on was populated by Etruscans, Italic tribes, and nascent Rome, while Sicily was under Punic control at the western end and populated by Sikels and Sikans elsewhere.[26] All of these cultures were known to the Greeks to have been in place earlier. Therefore mythic adventures in these areas were placed in a mythic time, a period before the rise of known civilizations. In fact the basic function of some myths seems to have been that of explaining the actual origins of these civilizations. Where this could not be appropriately done, the adventures would take place in an undifferentiated, generalized area, localized merely by a compass direction or broad geographic term such as "south" or "Asia."

Tales of wanderings tend to superimpose upon the temporal remoteness and the pairings and oppositions in space a polarity in *ēthos* 'character'. The far frontiers, in particular, serve as a metaphor for extremes of social organization and human types. The Scythians are described as nomads, and the mention of the river Hybristes (*hubristēs* 'one who commits *hubris*') lying beyond them, apparently to the east (see *Prometheus Bound* 717–719), suggests that they are as unbridled in nature as they are unsettled in their way of life. The Khalybes, according to Prometheus' instructions, are unfriendly and must be avoided

26. See Trump 1980.229–293.

(714–716). They are ironworkers, but unlike those of the Greek world they have no part in the normal economic structure of a *polis*. They do not even seem to fulfill the useful function of Homer's itinerant crafts-men (*Odyssey* xvi 383). The man-hating Amazons will be kind to Io, Prometheus says (*Prometheus Bound* 723–728). Like the Khalybes, they too represent a social anomaly, a group that has rejected the conventions of the polis and the Greek family.[27]

When Io reaches the generalized area of the East, she is in a region of no civilization at all. The only human touch is provided by the one-eyed horse-riding Arimaspians, who are clearly nomads like the Scythians. Otherwise, she must make her terrified way past the Graiai (hags living in a cave), the Gorgons, who have a more comprehensive hatred of mankind than even the Amazons, and the griffins, composites of eagle and lion. A pendant for Io's travels through the strange and marvelous East is provided by those of her distant descendant, Herakles, in the dangerous West.[28]

The mythical environment provided in Aeschylus is reinforced by descriptions of geography and customs in Pindar *Isthmian* 6.22–23 and Herodotus 3.114. For Pindar it is the Hyperboreans rather than the Scythians who represent the northernmost people, but both agree that the Ethiopians are the southernmost. Extremes of space involve extremes not only of climate but of ways of life. Egypt represents the oldest population, according to Herodotus 2.15 (contradicting the comment on the Phrygians in 2.2), while the Scythians are the youngest (4.5 and 4.7), being only a thousand years old. Pontus on the Black Sea has the most ignorant inhabitants (4.5), and Egypt the wisest.[29]

The pairing of Egypt and Scythia by contrasts (of climate, age, and learning) is matched by a pairing of similarities as well. Each is represented as being averse to adopting the customs of others (Scythia 4.76, Egypt 2.95) and each is given as an example of a region that is difficult to reach and from which one does not return (Scythia 4.46, Libya 3.26 and 4.179).

27. See the discussion of Tyrrell 1984.xiii–xix.
28. See Ramin 1979.105–119 and Lacroix 1974.36–38 and 50, n. 5. That Io's itinerary included a swing to the West is indicated by Prometheus when he says (*Prometheus Bound* 839–841) that she has come by way of the Ionian sea.
29. Egypt's wisdom is implicit in Herodotus' statements concerning Egyptian cultural priority and influence upon early Greece (2.4.1–2; 2.54–55; 2.160.1). See Bernal 1987.98–101.

The Periphery and the Identity of the Polis

Travels like those of Io and Herakles, which reach the other regions of the inhabited world and beyond, put a mark upon the Greeks' sense of their own identity. The outer limits of geographic description serve as a directional device by which the Greeks recognize their centrality in the Mediterranean world. These tales thus function at one and the same time as a separating and identifying factor. Experience of what is not Greek serves as an affirmation and reinforcement of what is. The myths of wandering indicate that such a representation aroused in the Greeks not only an extravagant idea of the alterity of other peoples but also a Hellenocentric—in a full range of senses—view of the world. This is a case in which the phenomenon of ethnocentrism is clarifiable.

The Greek tradition of localizing their deities offers a strong geographic argument for the development of a sense of centeredness, especially when these deities themselves are also thought to have played a part in the divine ancestry of peripheral civilizations. The gods are centered at Olympos, while one of the major entrances to Hades is at Eleusis, where the cult of Demeter, dating perhaps since Mycenean times, eventually became pan-Hellenic.[30] The stone at Delphi known as *omphalos* 'navel' explicitly marks for the Greeks the center of the *oikoumenē* 'inhabited world'. Contrast the Scythian analogue to an *omphalos*, represented by a *human sēma*: the tombs of their kings—for a stranger to find them is also to raise a gage of war (Herodotus 4.127). Greece was thus centered on the horizontal axis of the Mediterranean in relation to the mythic *periēgēsis* 'journey around the world' and on the vertical axis of the "above" and the "below" represented by Olympos and Hades.[31]

There is attested from the time of Homer a clear equation of travel with wisdom. Odysseus has wandered far and has seen the cities and known the minds of many men.[32] King Croesus of Lydia tells Solon of

30. See Burkert 1985.285–290.

31. For the general concept of a symmetrical universe with the horizontal plane of the earth divided into equal segments by the Mediterranean / Black Sea (east-west axis) and the Danube / Nile (north-south axis), see the discussion on the theories of Anaximander in Kirk, Raven, and Schofield 1983.133–137 and in Kahn 1985.76–85. For the concept of the vertical plane (along a single axis), see *Iliad* VIII 13–16 on Tartaros, "as far below Hades as heaven is from earth," and Hesiod *Theogony* 720–725, solid glimpses of a strongly traditional scheme: Tartaros-Hades-Earth-Olympus-Heaven. For a thorough consideration of the mythical and speculative aspects of ancient cosmogony, see Ballabriga 1986.

32. μάλα πολλὰ πλάγχθη / . . . πολλῶν δ' ἀνθρώπων ἴδεν ἄστεα καὶ νόον ἔγνω (*Odyssey* i 1–3).

Athens that he has heard much about him, "on account of your wisdom and your travels," and that "seeking wisdom you have traversed many a land for the sake of sightseeing" (Herodotus 1.30.2). Two distinct extremes appear in these tales. The regions traversed by the wanderer are either dangerous and terrifying or desirable and unattainable (in any permanent sense). The dangerous and terrifying may be assumed as a given possibility in any heroic adventure, but the pervasive element of the alluring creates an unexpected and provocative contrast. Aside from the Isles of the Blessed, the land of the Lotus-eaters, and Kalypso's island, which require no noticeable effort to gain a livelihood and are thus clearly "out of this world," the major references to gladsome regions represent them as ideally productive lands.

The abodes of the Hyperboreans and the Ethiopians are pictured not only as geographic extremes but also as examples of unattainable blessedness. The Ethiopians reach human perfection as the tallest and handsomest of men (Herodotus 3.17–24). The Hyperboreans lead a happy and peaceful existence and inhabit a fertile country which, despite its northern climate, produces two harvests a year (Aeschylus *Libation Bearers* 372–379; Pindar *Pythian* 10.46–59). Although both peoples are thought of as having an existence in space, they can be visited only by gods; consider again Zeus and Poseidon entertained by the Ethiopians and Apollo's annual sojourn with the Hyperboreans (*Iliad* I 423–424; *Odyssey* i 22–24; Pindar *Pythian* 10.53–55). Homer describes the uninhabited island opposite the Cyclops' cave in pictorial detail and makes a uniquely Greek observation, that it would be perfect for colonization (*Odyssey* ix 121–135). On Io's trip, when she leaves Asia Minor and turns south, she enters "the wheat-rich land of Aphrodite" (Aeschylus, *Suppliants* 555), which is not otherwise identified. Similar terms are used to describe the Delta region of Egypt: "all-nourishing" (*Suppliants* 558); productive with the least amount of effort (Herodotus 2.14.2); having "very beautiful fields" (*Odyssey* xiv 263).

From the Greek point of view, a wheat-rich land is a metaphor for an Isle of the Blessed for those living in a post-heroic age, and some of their colonizing enterprises of the seventh and sixth centuries were motivated by just such a search.[33] In historical times we hear Sardinia being described by Herodotus as a desirable and fruitful land for refugees from

33. Boardman 1980.153 (Cyrene), 178–180 (Sybaris, Croton, Metapontum), 186 (Selinus), 229 (Po valley), 229–232 (Macedonian and Thracian coast), 241–242 (Megarian settlements along eastern Propontis); also 242, 244 (Black Sea).

Persian control of Asia Minor (1.170) and on another occasion as a fruit-ful enterprise for the extension of the Persian empire (6.2, 5.106). The "blessed isles" had already been located by Hesiod in the vicinity of Italy, and the desirability of the West for colonization is implied by the settle-ments that develop within the mythic context of Herakles' travels. Both Homer (*Odyssey* iv 563–569) and Hesiod (*Works and Days* 167–173) say that certain heroes will be translated, still living, to a paradise located at the ends of the earth, near Ocean. For Homer the paradise is Elysium, for Hesiod the Isles of the Blessed. This haven for favored heroes is fixed generally in the West by Homer's comment (*Odyssey* iv 567–568) that Ocean will send breezes of the west wind to cool them. Hesiod locates it more precisely, near Italy where Agrios, Latinos, and Telegonos are said to have ruled over the Tyrsenians (= Etruscans) "far away in a nook of the blessed islands" (*Theogony* 1011–1016).[34] Still, all these ideal landscapes represent as much an antithesis to life as experienced in the polis as do Io's experiences amid nomads, Amazons, and monsters. Paradise and barbarism are equally antithetical to civilization.

To the Greeks the broadest and most versatile distinction between civilization and barbarism was marked by permanent settlements versus nomadism.[35] Among permanent inhabitants a further nuance was developed and often called upon for political effect: a distinction between autochthonous inhabitants and immigrants.[36] The Athenian claim to autochthony was never challenged by the rest of the Greek world, and Athens often boasted of it in depreciation of the immigrant origins of the other Greeks (the Herakleidai of Sparta, in particular).[37] Herodotus describes the Athenians as one of the recognizable remnants of the original Pelasgians (1.57–58).

Embedded within the myth of Io is a claim to autochthony on the part of Argos, as is clear from the fact that Io is represented as the daughter of the local river god, Inakhos. A charming irony also appears in the fact that, when the Danaids arrive, Pelasgos is king of the territory which will become the historical Argos; thus, on this showing, the

34. For Herakles as a founder of cities in the West (and elsewhere), see, e.g., Lacroix 1974.37–39.

35. For an impressive survey of such distinctions, see Hartog 1980.208–209.

36. According to Nilsson 1951.14, Athenians and Arcadians were unique in their claims to be autochthonous. On Athenian autochthony see Loraux 1979 and 1981.

37. Loraux 1979.3–7. There is also a local distinction between true-born Athenians and unfranchised metics (p. 10), understandable as a standing model of the polarity native / immigrant as an always-present reminder of Athenian specialness vis-à-vis other Greeks.

Argives, like the Athenians, were also originally Pelasgians. Actually, Pelasgos' rule is described in Aeschylus *Suppliants* 254–259 as extending to include all of mainland Greece, thus representing a pan-Hellenic unity that was never achieved historically.

A Pan-Hellenic Vision of the World

The major significance of the myth of Io for the Greeks of the sixth and fifth centuries B.C. was that it authenticated and legitimized the traditional genealogies on which their history was based—to the extent that they could find a link to Io. Io provides the crucial connection between Greece and Egypt—crucial because, if the Egyptians were correctly perceived as having existed "from the beginning of man," they must be the ancestors of the Greeks despite the clearly non-Greek character of their whole culture.[38] Besides forging this essential link, the Io story serves as a "charter" myth for the major Greek tribes (the Danaoi, the Argives, and, later via Herakles, the Herakleidai), as well as for such later historical peoples as the Phoenicians, the Medes, and the Persians. The later episodes of the story centering around Herakles also provide an indispensable framework of chronology by generations. Thus, to the extent that itinerary and genealogy formed the basis of the Greek view of their own prehistory, the myth of Io was central to this comprehension.[39]

Aeschylus places the story of Io in a broader context, not merely pan-Hellenic but universal. Through the itinerary of the *Prometheus Bound*, he offers his audience a Greek genesis, with Io appearing as the original progenitrix of the later Mediterranean cultures, so that they may have names and be told from each other.

Egypt is never mentioned by name in the *Prometheus Bound* but is indicated only by such terms as the river Nile or the river Aithiops. Syria

38. Herodotus 2.15; see Hartog 1980.193, n. 5 and Bernal 1987.

39. Lloyd 1975.180–182. Various cultures of the ancient Near East showed a similar interest in itinerary and genealogy, often with the added support of native documentation (e.g., the Abydos Table listing the Egyptian pharaohs and the Assyrian king lists, both emphasizing royal succession). The Hebrews expressed their sense of history through their word for *generations* (*toldoth*); *Genesis* 10–11 gives the family trees of Noah's three sons down to Abraham in the tenth generation, whence the actual "history" of Israel takes its beginning. Here the emphasis is on lines of descent, including as well geographic areas of expansion by the various families and the peoples to whom they give rise, and thus this genealogy legitimates territorial claims. Egyptian and Assyrian mythic genealogies, place names, and itineraries overlap, just as in the Greek traditions, with real geography and actual travels. See Hallo 1964 on a text listing caravanserais at the time of Hammurabi.

is mentioned only as a regional boundary. Even by the time of the Danaids, five generations after Io, Pelasgos is ruling an aboriginal Greece, called Apia; Danaë, Perseus, and Herakles are still to come.[40] Thus mankind already exists but not the distinctive cultures, races, and political entities. The place names of major areas are not indicated because they cannot come into existence until after Io. There is there-fore no Egypt, only the Nile; no Syria-Palestine except as a place of mon-sters. Scythia can be specifically labeled for two reasons: first, it has no share in Io's genealogy; second, just as it was inhabited by barbarians in prehistoric times, so it continued to be in historical times—it stayed the same place, "then" and "now."

Aeschylus' use of the tale, therefore, serves as a kind of no-fault genesis of civilization based on the absence of a preemptive culture. Io does not come from a Greece such as that historically defined by the polis but from one of the many inhabited pre-Greek or, equally to the point, pre-polis regions of the Mediterranean. In the *Prometheus Bound* there is no emphasis on Io's origin, only on her future and the future of the Mediterranean world. Whatever Aeschylus' intention, however, his treatment of the story allows an interpretation that would satisfy Helleno-centric notions of the mid-fifth century: Egypt must be recognized as the *geographic* location of the beginnings of civilization, but the original seed comes ultimately from a source that is recursively Greek, from the land that will contain a fully conceived and polis-ready "Greece."

Just as Io serves as the indispensable ancestress of the historical peoples of the Mediterranean world, so does her descendant Herakles serve as their benefactor and civilizer. The journeys of Herakles form a true peregrination of the known world, and everywhere he establishes settlements and fights against the savagery of man and beast. Herakles thus assures the future of the human race that Io has endowed with a genealogical identity.[41]

The actual centrality of Greece in the geographic space of the Medi-terranean was reinforced by the various myths of wanderings, which helped to create among the Greeks a sense for balance between extremes of climate, customs, and the various stages of civilization. Given this accumulation of tradition, it was not hard for the Greeks to see the development of the polis as a clear antithesis to barbarism. This

40. Rare references to Hellas and the Hellenes appear in Aeschylus but only in contexts emphasizing a contrast between barbarian and pan-Hellenic customs (*Suppliants* 220, 234, 237, 243, 914).

41. Lacroix 1974.41.

outward view directed at the rest of the Mediterranean world is balanced by an inward view based on genealogical cohesion. Despite tribal disparity and growing geographic dispersion through colonization, all the Greek world was connected by a genealogical tree centered on Io.[42]

The peculiarity and exotic nature of other areas, combined with an internal cohesion provided by extended genealogies, made the Greeks conscious of their own singularity.[43] The initial sense of a sort of reciprocal difference from other peoples in language, customs, and political development gradually evolves into a stronger feeling of basic incompatibilities. This development of a sense of pan-Hellenic community is a natural concomitant of the Greek view of the world as consisting of two major divisions, Hellenes and Barbarians.[44] The mythic wanderings that were, from one aspect, responses to concretely geographic exploration and discovery were also an expression not only of the Greeks' sense of their own identity but also of the identity of other peoples as created through Greek experience of them.[45] The myth of Io encapsulates the diversity of the experiences and representations, conceptualizing the Greek world of poleis as the special product of a pre-polis background shared by many nations that have since passed through a richly diverging evolution.

42. See the genealogical tables of West 1985.177–178. It must be conceded that this is, from one viewpoint, merely an Argive view of the world with Argos holding the center.

43. Schaefer 1955.281 expresses the same idea: "Religion and myth become carriers of an incipient historical consciousness."

44. Schaefer 1955.282. This "us / not-us" concept has of course parallels: e.g., Old High German *diutisk- 'of the people' > New High German deutsch 'German' vs. Old High German walhisk- > New High German welsch 'foreign' (with Old High German Walh 'Roman', Old English Wealh 'Celt'—it depends on whom one is surrounded by). Although Herodotus appreciates the differences in non-Hellenic cultures without denigrating them, a hint of depreciation is present in the Aeschylean exchanges between Pelasgos and the "barbarian" descendants of Io (see the commentary of Friis Johansen and Whittle 1980 on Suppliants 746–747).

45. See Bickerman 1952.

CHAPTER 4

Adonis:
A Greek Eternal Child

Robert A. Segal

The myth of Adonis describes, in many versions, the miraculous birth of a preternaturally beautiful human out of a tree, the fighting over him by goddesses, and his annual death and rebirth.[1] This myth seems as far removed from the world of the polis as it could be. The events it narrates are supernatural, and they take place in either the woods or the underworld rather than in any society. Yet I argue that, despite appearances, the myth in fact concerns neither the physical nor the supernatural world but the social one. The characters are really humans, not gods, and live in society, not outside it. The myth, I assert, is a political myth: it dramatizes the prerequisites for membership in the polis. But it does so negatively, by presenting the life of one least equipped for the

---

1. Adonis is the Greek counterpart—more clearly in cult than in myth—of a Near Eastern dying god. His name is related to the Semitic invocation *adon* 'Lord'; he appears in other cultures as Dumuzi, Tammuz, or Attis and is the son / lover of a goddess: Inanna, Ishtar/Astarte, and Cybele, respectively. Early in Greek tradition Adonis is mentioned (Hesiod F 139 MW) and mourned, perhaps as Aphrodite's lover (Sappho F 140 LP). He is born from the incestuous union of Myrrha (*murrha* 'myrrh') and her father, Cinyras. Aphrodite and Persephone fall in love with the young Adonis, and in one variant of the myth Persephone, to whom Aphrodite entrusts him, refuses to give him back (Apollodorus 3.14.4). Zeus's arbitration assigns Adonis to Aphrodite for one third of the year and to Persephone for another third and lets him spend as he will one third, which he chooses to devote as well to Aphrodite. This variant of the myth depicts the annual absence and presence of Adonis. Yet even in it, as in others (Ovid *Metamorphoses* 10.708–739), he is killed while hunting. The motif of a young hunter's accidental death is not uncommon in Greek myth. The tradition of Adonis in cult is very complex, yet some traits recur. Summer festivals in his honor were celebrated by women, and they included the use of incense, ritual lament, and the dedication to him of pots sown with fast-growing plants, known as Gardens of Adonis. For sources and parallels of the myth and the cult of Adonis, see Boedeker 1974.64–66; Burkert 1985.176–177; 1979.105–111.

responsibility entailed by citizenship. One learns what to do by seeing a model of what not to do. Adonis is ill suited for life in the polis because he is ill suited for its cornerstone, the family. His life involves the severest violations of family life: incest, murder, license, possessiveness, celibacy, and childlessness.[2]

I examine in this chapter the myth of Adonis in the light of three theories of myth. Two, those of James Frazer and Marcel Detienne, have been applied to the Adonis theme by their authors. The third, Carl Jung's, has not. His theory is the key to my claim that the myth has a political message.

Frazer's Adonis

The most popular interpretation of the myth, James Frazer's, assumes that the myth of Adonis is about gods rather than about humans and gods and, even more, is about nature itself, which the gods merely personify. If Adonis symbolizes only an impersonal entity like a tree, his life can scarcely constitute a model, positive or negative, for others. His behavior is mechanical rather than deliberate. The myth cannot teach a lesson, negative or positive, unless Adonis has behaved improperly or properly, which he can have done only if he has chosen his behavior, in which case he must have a mind and so be a personality, divine or human. Furthermore, Frazer views myth as the primitive counterpart to modern science. In that case it can only explain, not evaluate, events. Even if, then, Frazer deemed human beings the true subject of myths, myths would still yield no norms. They would merely describe, not assess, human behavior. One would still have to venture outside myths to secure political or other norms. For Frazer, the myth of Adonis is, then, apolitical.

Frazer places Adonis in all three of the prescientific stages he distinguishes—those of magic, religion, and magic and religion combined. Though to differing degrees, in all three stages Adonis, for Frazer, is a mere personification of vegetation rather than a personality. Vegetation does not symbolize Adonis; Adonis symbolizes vegetation. Frazer locates the potted gardens of Adonis, a feature of the cult, in his first, magical stage. Since, according to him, in this stage humans

2. The story of Myrrha and Adonis in Ovid (*Metamorphoses* 10.300–509, 708–739) is a part of the song of Orpheus, with its theme of distorted sexuality. See Freiert in Chap. 2.

believe that impersonal forces rather than personalities cause events, Adonis here cannot be a personality. Greeks would be planting seeds in earth-filled pots not to persuade a divine personality to grant growth but, by the magical Law of Imitation, to force the impersonal earth itself to grow: "For ignorant people suppose that by mimicking the effect which they desire to produce they actually help to produce it."[3] Mimicking the growth of crops would ensure their actual growth.

In Frazer's second, religious stage, Adonis is an outright personality. He is the god of vegetation. Indeed, Frazer distinguishes religion from magic on precisely the grounds that here divine personalities rather than impersonal forces cause events. As the god of vegetation, Adonis could, most simply, be asked for crops—and could be influenced by ritualistic or ethical obedience. Frazer himself says that rites of mourning were performed for Adonis—not, as in the next stage, to undo his death but to seek his forgiveness for it.[4] For Adonis has died not, as in the next stage, because he has descended to the underworld but because in cutting, stamping, and grinding the corn—the specific part of vegetation he symbolizes—humans have killed him. Rather than "the natural decay of vegetation in general under the summer heat or the winter cold," the death of Adonis is "the violent destruction of the corn by man."[5] Yet Adonis is somehow still sufficiently alive to be capable of punishing humans, something which the rituals of forgiveness are intended to avert. Since, however, Adonis dies because vegetation itself does, the god is here really only a metaphor for the element that he supposedly controls. As vegetation goes, so goes the god.

In Frazer's third stage, which combines the first with the second, Adonis' death means his descent to the underworld for his stay with Persephone. Where in stage two as vegetation goes, so goes Adonis, now as Adonis goes, so seemingly goes vegetation. Frazer assumes that whether or not Adonis wills his descent, he is too weak to ascend by himself. By acting out his rebirth, humans facilitate it. On the one hand the enactment employs the magical Law of Imitation. On the other hand it does not, as in the first stage, compel but only bolsters Adonis, who, despite his present state of death, is somehow still hearty enough to revive himself, just not fully. He needs a catalyst, which the enactment provides. In this stage gods still control the physical world, but their

3. Frazer 1922.396.
4. Frazer pp. 393–394.
5. Ibid.

effect on it is automatic rather than deliberate. To enact the rebirth of Adonis is automatically to spur not only his rebirth but also that of vegetation itself.[6]

Against Frazer, I note that even if Adonis chooses to descend to the underworld—how much choice he has is not clear—he is not choosing infertility, which is simply the automatic consequence of his sojourn below. Likewise, even if he chooses to return, he is not thereby choosing fertility, which similarly simply follows automatically from his resurfacing. Again, Frazer is minimizing the role of decision and so of personality. Indeed, Adonis proves to be not the cause of the fate of vegetation but only a metaphor for that fate, so that in fact in stage three as well as stage two as vegetation goes, so goes Adonis. The myth that Adonis spent a portion of the year in the underworld "is explained most simply and naturally by supposing that he represented vegetation, especially the corn," which lies buried half the year and reemerges the other half.[7]

In a much larger sense Frazer, in all three of his stages, reduces Adonis to the mere personification of vegetation. For even where Frazer does deem Adonis an independent personality, the only aspect of his life which he considers is that which parallels the natural course of vegetation: death and rebirth. Yet Adonis' birth is anything but natural. For both Apollodorus and Ovid, his birth results from his mother's incestuous yearning for her father.[8] Adonis' split schedule may become routine, but it is not therefore natural. For Apollodorus, it stems from love and jealousy on the part of Aphrodite and Persephone. Nor is Adonis' eventual death natural. He is killed, and in various versions even murdered—by either a spurned lover, Artemis, or a bested rival, Ares. To be sure, Frazer need not take the myth literally and therefore supernaturally, as indeed I myself do not. But he must *translate* the supernatural terms into natural ones, not simply ignore them.

Frazer ignores above all something not supernatural but human: Adonis' final death. And so he must. For Adonis' life to symbolize the course of vegetation, Adonis must continually die and be reborn. But in fact he does not. He eventually dies "permanently." Not only Ovid's version, which does not involve a trek to the underworld and therefore a cycle of death and rebirth, but even Apollodorus', which does, ends in Adonis' permanent demise. By whatever means Adonis has overcome

6. Frazer p. 377.
7. Frazer p. 392.
8. Apollodorus 1.116, 3.182, 183–185; Ovid *Metamorphoses* 10.708–739.

death annually, he cannot do so now. He is gone forever, which is why, in Ovid's version, Aphrodite is so disconsolate. How, then, can his mortal life symbolize eternal rebirth? How, then, can he be a god, who may die but does not stay dead, rather than a human being, who does?

Because Frazer reduces Adonis to vegetation, Adonis cannot serve as a model for others, who can hardly be implored to act like or unlike sheer vegetation. Frazer considers the gods as impersonal forces, viewing them in relation to the men who celebrate their rituals, but he disregards the narrative of the myth that portrays their mutual relationships and mirrors human interrelation in society. For Frazer, the myth of Adonis has no political import. Impersonal entities cannot be held accountable since they are not thinking, willing, motivated agents—in other words, personalities. The fundamental problem in his interpretation is that he ignores the values that the myth encodes.

Detienne's Adonis

Marcel Detienne faults Frazer's interpretation of the myth of Adonis on two grounds: for associating Adonis with rebirth rather than with death and for making the function of the myth technological rather than social. Where for Frazer Adonis is an impersonal force rather than a god, for Detienne he is a human rather than a god. Where for Frazer Adonis symbolizes vegetation, for Detienne one form of vegetation symbolizes, or parallels, Adonis. Where for Frazer Adonis, like vegetation, annually dies and revives, for Detienne Adonis, like the vegetation associated with him, grows up quickly and then just as quickly dies, once and for all. As a structuralist, Detienne differs with Frazer over not just the meaning and function but also the "operation" of the myth. Though Detienne later rejects the structuralist approach to myth of Claude Lévi-Strauss, his interpretation of the Adonis myth is Lévi-Straussian.[9] The meaning of myth therefore lies not, as for Frazer, at the narrative level but at the structural one. It lies not in the plot itself—the birth, adolescence, death, and rebirth of Adonis—but in the dialectical relationship among the elements of the plot—characters, places, times, and events.

For Detienne, following Lévi-Strauss, this dialectical relationship exists on a host of levels—dietary, botanical, astronomical, seasonal, religious, social, and by species. At each level a middle ground lies between

9. See Detienne 1986, esp. pp. 114–116.

extremes. The levels parallel, not symbolize, one another. The relationship among the elements at, say, the dietary level is isomorphic with that at the botanical. Still, the dietary level—with cereals and cooked meat lying between spices at one extreme and lettuce and raw meat at the other—most tightly links the others. If the *meaning* of the myth is the presentation of an almost endless series of levels, the *function* of the myth is social. It advocates marriage as the middle ground between promiscuity on the one hand and sterility or celibacy on the other.

Detienne first associates spices with the gods, cereals and cooked meat with humans, and lettuce and raw meat with animals. Spices get burned during sacrifices to the gods. The smell ascends to the gods, who inhale it as the equivalent of food. Because the meat is cooked rather than burned, it goes to humans, who also cultivate cereals. Just as burned meat goes to the gods in the form of fumes, so raw meat goes to animals, with which Detienne also somehow links lettuce. Spices are further associated with the gods because of their relationship to the sun and so, as the place atop earth, to Olympos. Spices not only are burned by the sun but also grow where and when the sun is nearest: in the hottest places and on the hottest days of summer. By contrast, lettuce is cold and is therefore connected with the coldest places and times: the world below earth—the seas and the underworld—and winter. To eat meat raw is to eat it "cold."

Cereals and cooked meat lie between spices on the one hand and lettuce and raw meat on the other. Just as, for humans, meat must be cooked rather than either burned or eaten raw, so cereals, to grow, need some sun but not too much: "In the middle range, situated at a fair distance from the fire of the sun, are the edible plants . . . the cereals and the fruits."[10] Cereals are therefore grown neither above ground nor below it but in it. Whereas spices are gathered during the summer and lettuce somehow during the winter, crops are harvested in the fall in between.

Spices are tied to the gods for other reasons. Less cultivated than gathered, they require no work and so fit the lives of the gods. Conversely, animals, eating only what they find, do not work for their supper either. But the gods eat what they want. Animals eat only what they find. The gods, then, do not have to work to eat better than humans. Animals, by not working, eat worse than humans. Humans again fall in between. They must work to eat, but when they work, they have enough,

10. Detienne 1977.14.

if barely enough, to eat. In Hesiod's Golden Age, humans were like the gods precisely because they had plenty without working. In the future they will be like animals, refusing to work and so presumably going hungry.

Spices are associated not only with gods but also with promiscuity. Rather than making promiscuity a divine prerogative, Detienne deems Zeus and Hera the perfect couple—despite Zeus's escapades—and makes Demeter the epitome of motherly and so familial concern: "Where the Demeter–Persephone couple lays emphasis upon the fruit of marriage and the relations between the mother and her legitimate child, the Zeus–Hera couple stresses the ritual consecration that sanctions the unity of husband and wife."[11] Not gods but spices, with their fragrant, hence seductive, aroma, are connected to promiscuity: "In the form of ointments, perfumes and other cosmetic products they [spices] also have an erotic function."[12] Not coincidentally, spices pervaded the Adonia festival, which was notorious for its promiscuity.[13] Conversely, Detienne links not animals but lettuce and raw meat to sterility and celibacy, for the foul smell of at least rotten, if not raw, meat—Detienne somehow equates the two—repels rather than attracts and thereby fends off sex. Not coincidentally, the women of Lemnos were spurned by men because of their stench.[14]

Between promiscuity on the one hand and sterility or celibacy on the other stands marriage, with which, notes Detienne, the Thesmophoria festival was connected. Though barred to men, the festival really celebrated marriage.[15] If its celebrants were all female, they were also all married. Falling between the fragrance of the Adonia and the stench of Lemnos, the mildly foul smell of the festival served to dissuade men during only the festival.[16]

Detienne connects all of these levels with the life of Adonis and with the ritualistic gardens dedicated to him. At every level, argues Detienne, Adonis falls in either extreme rather than in the middle. In fact, Adonis

11. Detienne p. 89.
12. Detienne p. 60. Myrrh (Myrrha or Zmyrna, the mother of Adonis) is attested as a potent incense and object of conjuring in erotic charms. See Luck 1985.96–97: "Everyone calls you Zmyrna [i.e., myrrh], but I call you Eater and Burner of the Heart . . . I am sending you to X, daughter of Y, to serve me against her and bring her to me. She may think only of me, Zmyrna, desire only me, love only me and fulfill my every wish."
13. Detienne pp. 64–66.
14. Detienne p. 94.
15. Detienne p. 80.
16. Detienne pp. 80–81.

jumps from one extreme to the other, bypassing the middle. Adonis'
fate represents that of any human who dares to act like a god: he is
reduced to the equivalent of an animal. Daring to be promiscuous, he
proves impotent.[17]

For Detienne, as a structuralist, the extremes on each level do not
symbolize the life of Adonis; rather, they *parallel* it. At each level the
extremes are to the middle as Adonis is to normal humans. The
extremes are analogous to the life of Adonis. Whereas for Frazer the
myth uses symbols of humans to describe impersonal forces of nature,
for Detienne it uses impersonal forces of nature as analogues to humans
to evaluate human behavior.

The gardens of Adonis, planted during the Adonia festival, involve
little work. The plants shoot up immediately. Tending them parallels
the toilless lives of the gods. In fact, the gardens are like the spices of
the gods. They are merely gathered, not cultivated, and grow in the hot
test places and times. They are carried to the roofs of houses at the
height of summer. Whereas regular crops take eight months to grow,
the gardens take only eight days. Whereas regular crops demand the
strength of men, the gardens are tended by women. Unlike the spices,
however, the gardens die as quickly as they sprout, and unlike regular
crops they die without yielding food.[18] Having begun above the earth,
they end up below it—cast into the sea. In short, the gardens are a futile
"get rich quick" scheme to get food without work. Gods need not work,
but humans must. When they seek "fast food" instead of regular fare,
they get no food at all.[19]

Adonis himself is related to spices through his mother, Myrrha, who
becomes a myrrh tree. Adonis' gestation takes place in the tree, and his
birth requires his breaking out of it. In Ovid's version wood nymphs
even bathe the infant in the myrrh formed from his mother's tears.
More important, Adonis is tied to spices through promiscuity. Unable to
control her desire, Adonis' mother commits incest with her father.
Unable to control their desire, Aphrodite and Persephone fight for custody of the infant Adonis. Adonis himself, for Detienne, is less an inno-

17. The union of a mortal lover with a mother goddess, in Greek and Near Eastern
myth, involves dire dangers. The son/lover may be killed (like Orion, the lover of Eos),
may be granted immortality without youth and thus become pathetically weak and old (like
Tithonus, also lover of Eos), or may become impotent, as Anchises fears he will if he yields
to Aphrodite's seduction (*Homeric Hymn to Aphrodite* 189–190). See Boedeker 1974.67–84.

18. Detienne 1977.10.

19. Detienne pp. 103–104.

cent victim of divine seduction than a seducer of divinities: "No sooner is he born from the myrrh tree whose form his mother has taken than Adonis arouses, first in Aphrodite and then in Persephone, the possessive and exclusive desire that a mistress feels for her lover."[20]

Adonis is a precocious seducer. Like the gardens, he grows up quickly. But like the gardens as well, he dies quickly. While young, he is killed by a boar. Just as the gardens die too early to yield any food, so Adonis dies too young to marry and have children. Having begun promiscuous, he ends up sterile. Conversely, his mother, who began sterile or at least abstinent—she had spurned all males—becomes promiscuous at the least. Jumping from one extreme to the other, mother and son alike reject and, more, threaten the middle ground of marriage.[21]

Adonis' sterility takes the form of not only childlessness but also effeminacy. His death from the boar shows his unfitness for the masculine hunt. Instead of the hunter, he becomes the hunted: "The perfect antithesis of a warrior hero such as Herakles," Adonis "is nothing more than a victim as weak as he is pitiable."[22] Adonis' effeminacy signifies insufficient distance between male and female. His mother's initial rejection of all males signifies the opposite. The ideal lies, again, in between: males and females should be related but distinct.

Just as Detienne links Adonis' promiscuity with spices, so he links Adonis' sterility and death with lettuce, in which, in several versions of the myth, Adonis tries vainly to hide from the boar. Just as myrrh "has the power to arouse the desires of an old man," so lettuce "can extinguish the ardour of young lovers." Lettuce "brings impotence, which is equivalent to death."[23]

Detienne argues that Adonis is, in Mary Douglas' terms, anomalous.[24] He literally does not know his place. He does not know that he is neither god nor animal but human, or that what is distinctively human is marriage. In dying before marrying, Adonis fails to fulfill his human nature. Detienne himself does not consider the role of marriage in the polis. For him, the myth advocates marriage as an end in itself. I argue later in this chapter that the myth advocates marriage as a bulwark of the polis.

20. Detienne pp. 63–64.
21. Detienne pp. 81–82.
22. Detienne p. 67.
23. Detienne p. 68.
24. See Douglas 1966, esp. chaps. 2–3.

Jung's Adonis

Detienne's interpretation of the myth of Adonis is a double improvement on Frazer's. First, his interpretation of Adonis as not an impersonal force but a personality, divine or human, enables him to stress Adonis' motives. Adonis becomes not just something that automatically lives and dies but someone who wills the course of his life. One can therefore hold him accountable for his behavior and can praise or condemn it as a model for others. Second, Detienne's interpretation of Adonis as not a god but a human enables him to stress Adonis' mortality.

Detienne's analysis of the myth is nevertheless skewed, for he deems Adonis an active culprit rather than a passive victim. According to Detienne, the myth berates Adonis for daring to transcend his human bounds, but Adonis in fact acts out of blindness, not boldness. Far from striving to venture too far, he has no idea of how far he has gone or can go. Far from yearning to be more than human, he is oblivious to what being human means. As a personality, he remains responsible for his actions, which can therefore still be condemned, but his motivation is the opposite of what Detienne depicts. In noting Adonis' effeminacy, Detienne half recognizes his true nature, but he then interprets effeminacy as an attempt to transcend the ordinary human bounds of male and female rather than, as it surely is, the expression of his failure to recognize them in the first place. Adonis fails to marry not because he dares to go beyond the confines of marriage but because he has no conception of marriage.

The theory of myth which, I believe, best illuminates the character of Adonis is Carl Jung's. Jung himself mentions Adonis only in passing, but he does mention him as an instance of the archetype of the eternal child, or *puer aeternus*.[25] The archetype as well Jung discusses only in passing, though he does devote many pages to an allied archetype, the Great Mother.[26] Marie-Louise von Franz, one of his keenest disciples, has

25. On Adonis, see Jung 1958.442, 1970c.372; 1967.219, 223n., 258–259, 343n. Jung discusses archetypes in nearly all his writings; see esp. Jung 1968a.3–72, 75–80, 151–162; 1969.129–158; 1966.64–113; Jung, von Franz et al. 1968.56–71; see also Jacobi 1967a.39–51; 1968.31–73. On the archetype of the puer aeternus, see Jung 1967.257–259, 340; 1968a.106; 1973.I.82; see also Neumann 1970.88–101 (Neumann himself uses the term "son-lover" for puer); Jacobi 1967b.27–28, 147–148; 1968.21–22; Singer 1973.286–288; Whitmont 1969.182–183; Harding 1965.145–148; Mattoon 1981.98–99; Samuels 1985.204–205.

26. On the archetype of the Great Mother, see Jung 1968a.75–110; 1967.207–444; Neumann 1972.1–336; 1970.39–101, 152–169.

written a book on the puer archetype, but she deals largely with the cases of the Little Prince and the character Fo in Bruno Goetz's novel *Kingdom without Space*, not with Adonis.[27]

Elaborating on Jung's brief remarks, together with von Franz's work, I interpret Adonis as a puer. Following Jung on myth generally, I argue that the myth functions not merely to present the archetype but also to assess it.[28] The myth serves as a warning to those who identify themselves with the puer archetype. To live as a puer, the way Adonis does, is to live as a psychological infant and, ultimately, as a fetus. The life of a puer in myth invariably ends in premature death, which psychologically means the death of the ego and a return to the womblike unconscious.

As an archetype, the puer constitutes a side of one's personality, which, as a side, must be accepted. A puer personality is one who simply goes too far: he makes the puer the whole of his personality. Unable to resist its spell, he surrenders himself to it, thereby abandoning his ego and reverting to sheer unconsciousness.

The reason a puer personality cannot resist the puer archetype is that he remains under the spell of the archetype of the Great Mother, who initially is identical with the unconscious as a whole. Unable to free himself from her, he never forges a strong, independent ego, without which he cannot in turn resist any smothering female he meets. His surrender to the puer archetype means his surrender to the mother, to whom he yearns only to return. A puer "only lives on and through the mother and can strike no roots, so that he finds himself in a state of permanent incest." Jung even calls him a mere "dream of the mother," who eventually draws him back into herself.[29]

The development of the ego depends considerably on society. The institutions of marriage and work serve to anchor one to the external world, with which the ego deals, and thereby to keep the ego from falling back into the unconscious. The ego is strong exactly insofar as one is in touch with the external world. At the same time, participation in a society, including the polis, requires the development of a sturdy ego. In contrast to slavery, citizenship requires decision making, which only connectedness to the external world, and so only a strong ego, provide. Adonis is a puer personality because he has no society to nurture him. Never free of smothering mother figures, he is never free to live in

27. Von Franz 1981.
28. Discussion of myth is found in nearly all of Jung's writings; see esp. Jung 1968a.151–203.
29. Jung 1967.258.

society and thereby to develop psychologically. Exactly because he is retarded psychologically, he is retarded politically. Participation in the polis is beyond him.

Biologically, a puer can range in age from late adolescence to middle or even old age. Psychologically, however, he is an infant. Whereas for Freud a person in the grip of an Oedipus complex is psychologically fixated at three to five years of age, for Jung a puer is fixated at birth. Whereas an Oedipus complex presupposes an independent ego "egotistically" seeking to possess the mother for itself, a puer involves a tenuous ego seeking to surrender itself to the mother.[30] A puer seeks not domination but absorption—and thereby reversion to the state prior even to birth.

For Freud, attachment to the mother at any stage means attachment to one's actual mother or mother substitute. It means attachment to the person herself. For Jung, attachment to the mother means attachment to the mother archetype, of which one's actual mother or mother substitute is only a symbol. Whereas for Freud a boy should free himself of his yearning, infantile or Oedipal, for his own mother, for Jung a boy should free himself of his inclination to identify himself with the mother archetype. For Freud, failure to free oneself means eternal attachment to one's own mother. For Jung, it means the restriction of one's personality to the mother archetype within. Whereas for Freud the struggle for freedom is between one person and another—son and mother—for Jung it is between one part of a person and another—ego and unconscious, which, again, the mother archetype first symbolizes. For Jung, "the mother corresponds to the collective unconscious, and the son to [ego] consciousness."[31]

Because an archetype expresses itself only through symbols, never directly, the aspects of the mother archetype which a child knows are only those filtered through his actual mother or mother substitute. A mother who refuses to let her child go limits him to only the smothering, negative side of the mother archetype. A mother who, however reluctantly, finally lets her child go opens him to the nurturing, positive side of the mother archetype. Initially, any child is reluctant to leave. A smothering mother, by revealing only the smothering side of the mother archetype, tempts him to stay. A nurturing mother, by revealing the nur-

30. On the Oedipus complex, see, most succinctly, Freud 1969.44–51. On Freud's theory in general, see likewise Freud 1969.1–64.
31. Jung 1967.259.

turing side of the archetype as well, prods him to resist the temptation. In all its aspects, the mother archetype, as an archetype, is for Jung innate. One's experience of mother figures determines only which aspects of the archetype are elicited. A child who never experiences a nourishing mother figure never develops that dimension of the archetype latent in him.

Approached properly, the puer archetype provides an ego that has managed to sever itself from the unconscious reentry into it. Taken rightly, the puer dimension of a person evinces itself in moments of playfulness, imagination, and spontaneity—moments that complement the rationality and sobriety of the ego. Taken to excess, the puer personality amounts to nothing but these moments. Taken rightly, the puer is childlike. Taken to excess, it is childish.

Although the puer personality arises in infancy, it manifests itself most dramatically at adolescence. A puer personality is even called an eternal adolescent. A puer is impulsive, dreamy, irresponsible, and self-centered. He dreams of accomplishing great deeds but never does them. He makes great plans, but they never materialize. He may work hard, but only sporadically and only when he is interested. A puer avoids commitments and refuses to be tied down. He craves excitement and seeks risks. Scornful of the mundane, everyday world, he waxes spiritual and otherworldly. Sexually, he is promiscuous. He dreams of a perfect mate but, never finding her, scorns anyone else. He refuses to become attached. He may be a Don Juan. He may turn to homosexuality.[32] The difference between a puer personality and a normal adolescent is that a puer remains an adolescent for life.[33] In fact, it is normally at adolescence that the son finally breaks away from the mother. Rites of passage serve precisely to force a break.[34] Still, the puer personality is infantile. It arises in infancy, not adolescence, and at adolescence merely expresses its infantilism in adolescent form.

There is no inconsistency between the promiscuity of adolescence and the reluctance to leave the mother at birth. The puer is promiscuous because he cannot choose a mate, and he cannot choose a mate

32. See von Franz 1981.1, 4–5, 9, 125–126, 138, 160, 201–202; Jung 1968a.85; Singer 1973.287.

33. Von Franz 1981.1.

34. See Pozzi on Euripides' *Ion* in Chap. 7. Ion leaves his enclosure (the temple of Apollo, an adolescent god himself) and undergoes a rite of passage when he learns to see his real mother (Kreousa) as nurturing rather than threatening. In Jungian terms, he becomes a hero.

because he remains attached to the mother. Without the institution of marriage to spur him to mate, he remains a puer forever. To say that a puer is attached to the mother is to say that he knows the world only through the projection of her onto it. He thereby really knows her rather than the world. He is promiscuous not because he dares to defy the convention of marriage but because he is unaware of it. Every female he encounters is either a manifestation of the Great Mother, in which case she is to be outright embraced, or an unworthy inferior to her, in which case she is to be dismissed.

A puer may be either conscious or unconscious of his character. To be sure, even a conscious puer experiences alluring females as epiphanies of the Great Mother, but at least he recognizes that other males experience women differently—as possible mates. He simply takes for granted that mystical union alone is right for him. He is both aware and proud of his unconventionality. Examples of conscious pueri are Casanova and Aleister Crowley.[35]

An unconscious puer, by contrast, assumes that everyone else is like him. He assumes that all other males seek unity with women, for no other relationship exists. He considers himself wholly conventional. A literary example of an unconscious puer is Goethe's character Werther, who dismisses the values of both aristocratic and bourgeois society as artificial and therefore unnatural and who blames society for coming between him and an otherwise responsive Lotte, with whom, moreover, he seeks not intercourse but maternal absorption. A more spectacular, contemporary example is Elvis Presley, a quintessential mamma's boy who lived his last twenty years as a recluse in a womblike, infantile world in which all of his wishes were immediately satisfied yet who deemed himself entirely normal, in fact "all-American."[36]

A puer can thus be either an actual person or a symbol. Indeed, some famous historical pueri eventually become symbols themselves. While a historical puer is biologically an adult, a symbolic one may never grow up. These symbolic pueri exemplify exactly the eternally young life that actual puer personalities strive to emulate. Other symbolic pueri are Peter Pan and the Little Prince, and of course Adonis. Just as a puer may be conscious or unconscious, so he may outwardly be adjusted or maladjusted. Outwardly, he may be settled in a marriage and a job, but he finds no satisfaction in them. Or he may be unsettled even outwardly—like the cases of Don Juan and the eternal student.

35. See Casanova 1966–1971; Crowley 1970; Regardie 1982.
36. Goldman 1981.

The opposite of the puer archetype is that of the hero.[37] The hero is the opposite precisely because he succeeds where a puer fails. Strictly, there are two stages of heroism. In the first half of life an ego is heroic in managing to liberate itself from the unconscious and establish itself in society. A hero manages to secure a fulfilling mate and job. A puer fails to do either. In the second half of life a now independent ego is heroic in managing to break with society and return to the unconscious without thereby falling back into it. Whereas a hero in the first half of life establishes himself in the conventions of society, a hero in the second half defies those conventions. But a hero is consciously defiant. A puer is only unconsciously so. Whereas a hero risks everything to which he has committed himself, a puer has committed himself to nothing and so risks nothing. Because a puer never establishes an independent ego, he never faces the possible loss of it. Whereas a real hero is like Daidalos, a puer is like Ikaros. Because a puer is a failed hero in the first half of life, he is necessarily one in the second half as well. Indeed, there is no second half for him.

Adonis is a quintessential puer because he never marries, never works, and dies young. He simply never grows up. His puer personality spans the period from infancy to adolescence. He must first break out of a tree in order to be born. His mother, transformed into the tree, is reluctant to let him out. Like any other mother, she may be overjoyed at his conception, but unlike normal mothers she wants to hoard him. In Ovid's version (*Metamorphoses* 10.504) Adonis himself has to find an exit.

Adonis' mother has herself proved unable to break out of her father, the only male who ever arouses her. Even if her incestuous desire results from a curse, the curse is punishment for her indifference to other men, for which a *prior* attachment to her father is likely the latent cause. In any event her desire is not really for intercourse with her actual father but for absorption in the father archetype. For she, too, has never severed herself from the unconscious and therefore has never grown up. Not coincidentally, she is incapable of raising Adonis, whom others, whatever their motives, must raise instead. She is a *puella*.[38]

---

37. On the hero archetype, see Jung 1968a.151–181; 1967.171–444; 1970a.117–123; 1968c.333–339; Jung, von Franz et al. 1968.103–125; Neumann 1970.131–256; 1972.203–208; von Franz 1970.41–46; Harding 1947.237–296; Jacobi 1967a.182–187; 1967b.60–79. On the hero as the opposite of the puer, see Whitmont 1969.182–183.

38. On the puella archetype, see von Franz 1981.81–84, 150–151, 152–154; Whitmont 1969.178–180; Singer 1973.287–288.

No sooner does Adonis emerge from the tree than, in Apollodorus' version, Aphrodite thrusts him back—not, to be sure, into the tree but into a chest. She thereby undoes the birth that had proved so arduous. She tells no one, for she wants Adonis all to herself. When Persephone, to whom Aphrodite has entrusted the chest without revealing its contents, opens it, she likewise falls in love with Adonis and refuses to return him. Each goddess, just like his mother, wants to possess him exclusively. Though Zeus's decision leaves Adonis free for a third of the year, Adonis readily cedes his third to Aphrodite. Never, then, is he outside the custody of these manifestations of the mother archetype.

Rather than the seducer, as for Detienne, Adonis is really the seduced. He may scurry from goddess to goddess, but only because he is attached to them. He does not come and go on his own. He cannot imagine an independent life. Adonis is unable to resist the blandishments of the goddesses not because his will is weak but because his ego is. Indeed, for Jung the ego controls the will. Adonis is unable to resist the goddesses not because they arouse him sexually but because he does not even recognize them. He sees them not as beautiful women but as his mother, with whom he wants not intercourse but absorption. Between him and the goddesses there exists the primordial state of mystical oneness that the philosopher Lucien Lévy-Bruhl, whom Jung often cites, calls *participation mystique*. Psychologically, Adonis is at exactly that stage of humanity to which Lévy-Bruhl and, following him, Jung apply the term "primitive."[39]

Adonis is the most extreme kind of puer—an unconscious as well as outward one. Since he never marries, never has children, never works, and dies young, he is conspicuously an outward puer. Since he has no idea of the difference between his life and anyone else's, he is clearly an unconscious puer as well. He lives in a fog.

Seemingly, a Jungian interpretation of the myth of Adonis faces the same contradiction as a Frazerian one: that Adonis annually breaks free of the mother yet eventually dies permanently. Like Frazer, one might dismiss Adonis' final death as an aberration and stress his perennial liberation from the mother. In that case Adonis would be a hero rather than a puer. Indeed, Jung himself identifies Adonis with Frazer's annually reborn corn-god: "The corn-god of antiquity was Adonis, whose death and resurrection were celebrated annually. He was the son-lover

39. See Lévy-Bruhl 1966.22–87; Jung 1970b.50–73; 1968a.153–154; Jung, von Franz et al. 1968.6–8.

of the mother, for the corn is the son and fructifier of the earth's womb."[40]

A Jungian interpretation, however, need not ignore Adonis' final demise, which is reconcilable with his recurrent revival. The annual cycle of death and rebirth symbolizes not Adonis' annual liberation from the mother but the opposite: his annual return to the mother, even if that return ends in release. Whereas a normal child needs to be born only once to liberate himself from the mother, Adonis, as a puer, continually returns to the mother and so must be born again and again. His final death is simply his permanent rather than temporary return to her. It is the culmination of his past returns rather than a break with them. Previously, he had been strong enough to resist the mother temporarily. Now he can no longer do so.

Put another way, Adonis' cycle of death and rebirth constitutes neurosis: his weak ego compulsively returns to the mother. His final death represents psychosis: in returning forever to the mother, his ego dissolves altogether.

Adonis as a Greek Eternal Child

If Adonis is an instance of the puer archetype, he is a distinctively Greek instance. To begin with, the analogy between humans and plants is remarkably, though not uniquely, Greek. Frazer may reduce human and divine life to a metaphor for plant life, but, as Detienne elaborates, the Greeks themselves deem plant life a metaphor for human life. They symbolize the puer archetype botanically: the gardens are symbolic of Adonis.

Furthermore, the Greeks link the puer not only to plants but, more significantly, to the polis. The puer's psychological retardation entails political retardation: to fail to become an adult is to fail to become a citizen. A puer is suited for precisely that form of government which involves no responsibility and therefore permits, if not requires, political infancy: tyranny. Adonis' submission to the mother may be associated with what has been called "the myth of matriarchy," a vision of a society tyrannized by females.[41] He lives in a society in which males are neither

40. Jung 1967.343, n. 79.
41. On the concept of matriarchy in Greece and elsewhere see Zeitlin 1978; Bachofen 1967; Fromm 1949; Campbell 1964; R. A. Segal 1990.84–103.

rulers nor even citizens. Having experienced only smothering females, he projects those qualities onto all females and thereby submits unquestioningly to them. Females are able to tyrannize him because he projects the smothering side of the mother archetype onto them. For Jung, a female tyrant serves as the object for the mother archetype, just as a male tyrant like Hitler serves as the object for the shadow archetype.[42]

The family constitutes the link between personality and the polis. The opposition that Herodotus, among others, draws between the polis of Greece, in which even the ruler is subject to the law, and the tyranny of Persia and the East, in which the ruler is above the law, holds for family life as well.

Herodotus catalogs the violations of familial mores by Eastern potentates to demonstrate their tyranny. King Candaules of Sardis orders Gyges, his bodyguard, to look secretly at the queen as she disrobes. She then forces Gyges to kill her husband (Herodotus 1.8–13). Solon tells King Croesus of Lydia that the happiest man he has known was an obscure Athenian who had fine sons and lived to see them raise children in turn. Croesus himself has two sons, one deaf and dumb, the other killed—like Adonis, while hunting boar—by a friend who had accidentally killed his brother and been banished by his father for it (Herodotus 1.29–33). King Astyages of Media orders Cyrus, his grandson, killed at birth to prevent his usurpation of the throne. In revenge for Harpagus' failure to carry out the deed, Astyages serves him up his son. Cyrus subsequently does topple, though not kill, his grandfather (Herodotus 1.117–119). King Cambyses of Persia, Cyrus' son and successor, marries two of his sisters, murders one of them, and murders his brother as well. He goes insane and dies childless (Herodotus 3.31–32). King Xerxes of Persia, having failed to seduce his brother's wife, arranges a marriage between his son and his brother's daughter, whom he then manages to seduce instead. In revenge for her daughter-in-law's getting her robe, Xerxes' wife has the daughter-in-law's mother, her own sister-in-law, mutilated. Xerxes then offers his brother his own daughter in marriage as a substitute for his mutilated wife. Declining the offer, the brother goes off with his sons to foment revolt. Xerxes has all of them killed.

42. Hitler, says Jung in 1939, refers to his "Voice," which is "nothing other than his own unconscious, into which the German people have projected their own selves." Their projection onto him of the shadow archetype "is what makes him powerful. Without the German people, he would not be what he seems to be now" (McGuire and Hull 1977.119–120). On the political implications of Jung's psychology, see Odajnyk 1976.

As for the domestic lives of Greek tyrants, whom Herodotus acknowledges but deems an aberration, Periandros of Corinth murders his wife, deposes his father-in-law, and dispossesses his one talented son (Herodotus 3.50.3–3.52.6). Peisistratos of Athens refuses to have "normal" sex with his second wife because he fears a curse upon her family (Herodotus 1.61.1).

Adonis is incapable of citizenship because he, like the tyrants, is incapable of settled family life. On the one hand he fosters no family: he never marries, has no children, and dies young. On the other hand he is born into no family: he is the child of incest, not marriage, and his father tries to kill his mother. He is thus barred doubly from citizenship: he lacks not only maturity but also a pedigree, itself the result of the immaturity of his puella-like mother. If Herodotus testifies to the political necessity of siring a family, the Aristotelian *Constitution of the Athenians* testifies to the political necessity of descending from one: "the right of citizenship belongs to those whose parents have been citizens" (*Constitution of the Athenians* 42). The individual family had a place and a context in the social unit of the kinship group.

Until Kleisthenes changed the basis of citizenship from kinship to locale, membership in a phratry was prerequisite. Even after the deme, which was a matter of locale, replaced the phratry as the prime political unit, the phratry remained important. Though a fourth-century Athenian, for example, could be a citizen without belonging to a phratry, his position would be both "uncomfortable and questionable."[43] Moreover, membership in the deme was itself hereditary. Consequently, citizenship remained a matter of birth, as the *Constitution of the Athenians*, referring to the time after Kleisthenes, states.

The tie between humans and plants itself furnishes a metaphor for the tie between humans and politics. *Hubris* 'excess' is related to 'exuberance in plants'. For Hesiod, Theognis, and others, loyalty to the polis yields political fruit and disloyalty political barrenness.[44]

The Greeks link the puer not only to plants and politics but also to hunting. Adonis' haplessness at hunting symbolizes his haplessness at adulthood. He fails utterly as a hunter not just because he becomes the hunted instead but, even more fundamentally, because he has no conception of hunting. He succumbs to the hunt for the same reason that

43. Andrewes (1971.92) points out that, despite the territorial basis of the system instituted in 507 B.C., a man who went to live elsewhere did not change his deme.

44. See G. Nagy 1985.60–63.

he succumbs to the goddesses: blindness. Just as he thinks that all loving females are the Great Mother, so he thinks that the world itself is. In primitive fashion, he deems himself one with the world. More accurately, he either thinks the world loving or thinks himself protected from it by the Great Mother. He ignores Aphrodite's warning not because he valiantly dismisses ordinary caution but because he does not comprehend the danger. In Ovid's version Aphrodite tells him that the dangerous animals respect neither youth nor beauty, but he is deaf to her pleas. He assumes that all animals are either tame or easy prey.

A true hero would be aware of the danger but bold enough to face it. His heroism would *presuppose* his recognition of the true nature of the world. By contrast, the pseudo-hero Adonis is oblivious to any danger and so need muster no bravery to face it. He is oblivious to the nature of the world. He is less effeminate than blind—less unwilling or even unable to hunt than unaware of what hunting, of what killing and getting killed, means. He dies not because he is a poor hunter but because he is none at all.

Yet Adonis' case is even more severe. So enveloped is he in the Great Mother that he actually wants to be killed in order to return wholly to her. Consciously, he is blind to the danger of the hunt, but unconsciously he courts it. To say that Adonis courts danger is certainly to say that he chooses it. Even though he is unaware of the nature of what he is choosing, he still chooses to hunt. He is not, therefore, reducible to an impersonal force like corn for Frazer. He remains a personality, however lopsided a personality. One can, then, invoke him as a model, negative or positive, for life in society.

Like the tie between human and plant, the tie between human and hunter becomes a metaphor for the tie between human and citizen. Pierre Vidal-Naquet suggests that hunting was a key aspect of the two-year military stint which, according to the *Constitution of the Athenians* (42), Athenian youths were required to undergo before citizenship. Following not only Lévi-Strauss but even more Arnold van Gennep, Vidal-Naquet argues that those years were a rite of passage and therefore involved a break with the life that the youths, or ephebes, both had known until now and would know afterward. The ephebes thus spent their years at the frontier rather than in the city and spent them with one another rather than with their families.[45]

45. Vidal-Naquet 1981.147–162.

Above all, claims Vidal-Naquet, the ephebes engaged in a brand of hunting that was the opposite of the brand that, as hoplites, they would soon be undertaking. As ephebes, they hunted individually, in the mountains, at night, and armed only with nets—thereby relying on trickery to capture their prey. As hoplites, they would be hunting in a group, on the plain, during the day, and armed with spears—thus relying on courage and skill to kill their prey. Vidal-Naquet cites texts in which these two kinds of hunting are sharply contrasted: adult hunting, by day and with the spear (in keeping with the hoplite ethos), and hunting by night, a "black hunt" based on the use of the net. Following again van Gennep and Lévi-Strauss, Vidal-Naquet contends that the contrast between the hunting of ephebes and the hunting of hoplites served to inculcate hoplite values in the ephebes.

Vidal-Naquet's evidence for the link of the *ephebeia* with hunting is twofold. He appeals, first, to the myth associated with the Apatouria, the festival at which Athenian fathers registered their sixteen-year-old sons as citizens, as members of phratries, and as ephebes for two years. Vidal-Naquet asserts that the subject of the myth, the Athenian Melanthos, or "Black One," is—like Adonis—a negative model for the ephebes: he is an ephebe who never becomes a hoplite. Even as an adult he resorts to deceit rather than courage or skill to defeat his opponent, the Boeotian King Xanthos (the "Blond One").

Vidal-Naquet appeals, second, to the figure of Melanion, the Black Hunter, as described by Aristophanes:

μῦθον βούλομαι λέξαι τιν' ὑμῖν, ὅν ποτ' ἤκουσ'
    αὐτὸς ἔτι παῖς ὤν.
    οὕτως ἦν νεανίσκος Μελανίων τις,
ὃς φεύγων γάμον ἀφίκετ' ἐς ἐρημίαν,
    κἀν τοῖς ὄρεσιν ᾤκει·
    κᾆτ' ἐλαγοθήρει
    πλεξάμενος ἄρκυς,
    καὶ κύνα τιν' εἶχεν,
κοὐκέτι κατῆλθε πάλιν οἴκαδ' ὑπὸ μίσους.
    οὕτω τὰς γυναῖκας ἐβδελύχθη
    'κεῖνος, ἡμεῖς τ' οὐδὲν ἧττον
    τοῦ Μελανίωνος οἱ σώφρονες.

Aristophanes Lysistrata 781–796

I wish to tell you a story I once heard
    when I was still a boy:
    how there was once a youth, by the name of Melanion,

who, eschewing marriage, went away to live in the mountains.
> He spent the time hunting hares,
> for which he set snares,
> and he had a dog,

and he hated women so much that he never went home again.
> Melanion loathed women, and so, no less than he,
> do we, the wise.

The connection between Melanion and the *ephebeia* is both that Melanion, as a fellow black character, has all of the dark associations of Melanthos, and that Melanion is an ephebe-like hunter who never marries. To Vidal-Naquet, Aristophanes depicts Melanion "as an ephebe, but a sort of ephebe *manqué*." The chorus provides a version of "the widespread myth of the gloomy solitary hunter who is either a misogynist or who tries to insult Artemis, and who, in either case, flouts the social rules."[46]

The severity of Adonis' failure at hunting makes him truly a puer rather than, like Melanthos and Melanion, merely an adolescent. If one extrapolates from Melanthos as fighter to him as hunter, both he and Melanion succeed at hunting of only an adolescent variety. By contrast, Adonis fails at hunting of any kind. One can scarcely imagine his defeating an animal or human foe not just by courage or skill but even by trickery. One can scarcely imagine his recognizing who his foes are or even what a foe is. Adonis is thus not, like Melanthos and Melanion, just an adolescent who never advances to adulthood but an infant who never advances to adolescence—or even to childhood. His infantilism takes adolescent form, but infantilism rather than adolescence it really is. The severity of his failure as a hunter means the severity of his failure as a citizen. The myth of Adonis represents, then, the negation of practices without which the polis cannot be conceived: exogamy and reproduction. The myth dramatizes the consequences of rejecting those practices: barrenness and death. Myth can teach by negative as well as positive models.

46. Vidal-Naquet 1981.161. For a discussion of the argument, see Knox 1983.28–30.

CHAPTER 5

Antigone: Kinship, Justice, and the Polis

John D. B. Hamilton

In Sophocles' *Antigone* the conflict between the two main antagonistic characters (Kreon and Antigone) seems so radical, the distance between them so abysmal, that there is great temptation to interpret the drama simply as the clear-cut antithesis of two principles, family and polis. This play has been cited, since Hegel's time, as a perfect example of the conflict between two equal rights, the collision between familial love and the law of the nether gods on one side and the right of the state on the other. Both sides attain injustice just because they are one-sided, but both have validity.[1] This play has been studied from many angles and with diverse approaches, yet its interpretation has been rather consistently informed by such a view. The fall of both characters, who succumb because they cannot yield, is seen as an illustration of the essential antagonism between the polis and the early kinship systems in ancient Greece—thought to imply the inherent instability of the polis, with city and citizen always latently at war with each other, and with a corresponding body of myth that depicted the inevitable demise of the polis and did not offer mechanisms for mediation and evolution.

In this chapter I offer an alternative to such a view. I explore the striking and paradoxical figure of Antigone, taking into account the anthropological dimensions of her tale. Since funeral practices and their connection with kinship systems are prominent in Sophocles' play, I examine them with close attention, in the light of the social and political developments that gave rise to the fifth-century polis. The understanding of the Sophoclean heroine that we may gain in this manner

---

1. Hegel's actual analysis is more complex; see Steiner 1984.19–42.

offers us a new perspective from which to look at the role of myth in the context of the polis. To anticipate my conclusion, Antigone appears as the very embodiment of *dikē* 'justice' *in the polis*, and I argue that her act of disobedience in fact reconciles the values of *genos* and polis. Kreon, on the other hand, is simply wrong and tyrannical.

Before examining archaic Greek burial rites and their connection with the *Antigone*, I must take a brief but careful look at the concept of kinship, for it has a crucial role in this play, in the Antigone myth, and in all the Theban tales that precede it. As Meyer Fortes puts it, members of kinship groups are bound by axiomatic rules of amity that are rooted in the domain of the family. This is the principle of "prescriptive altruism." In his fieldwork among African tribes of the Gold Coast, Fortes observed that members of a kin group perceive their social universe as divided into two opposed spheres of moral alignment. On the one side is the sphere of kinship and the familial domain; on the other, the sphere of non-kinship. When kinsmen seize bows and arrows in a quarrel, it is the equivalent of war, and warfare between kin of any degree is considered a heinous crime.[2] An example of such a "heinous crime" in the Theban saga is the confrontation between Eteokles and Polyneikes and their death at each other's hands. In turn, Antigone carries out a religious duty and observes the principles of kinship morality as she performs a symbolic burial rite for Polyneikes, defying Kreon's prohibition. In Fortes' terminology, Antigone becomes an "actor." She exercises *kēdos* 'care' or 'concern'. This word had two specialized meanings in ancient Greece: (1) the grief or mourning—and honors—given to the dead; (2) a union or relationship based on marriage or compact.[3] The first is within the scope of Fortes' concept of prescriptive altruism.

Antigone was produced in Athens in 442 B.C., an age of "enlightenment" in which a succession of institutional and legislative reforms culminated in what is known as the Greek *dēmokratia* 'democracy'. The reforms of Solon and Kleisthenes had led to the creation of a system of demes (*dēmoi*) which undercut and cut through the old aristocratic political structures, the "royal families" or "lineages," the *genē*. There is much controversy concerning the origin, nature, and relationships of the *genē*, the *phulai,* and the *phratriai*.[4] I translate the term *genos* (plural *genē*) as 'lineage'.

2. See Fortes 1969.231–232.
3. See *DELG* II.522–523.
4. See Bourriot 1976, Jones 1980, Nagy 1990a, chap. 2, Roussel 1976, and Snodgrass 1980.

Antigone justifies her act of disobedience of the civic law in this famous passage:

KP. καὶ δῆτ' ἐτόλμας τούσδ' ὑπερβαίνειν νόμους;
AN. οὐ γάρ τί μοι Ζεὺς ἦν ὁ κηρύξας τάδε,
 οὐδ' ἡ ξύνοικος τῶν κάτω θεῶν Δίκη
 τοιούσδ' ἐν ἀνθρώποισιν ὥρισεν νόμους·
 οὐδὲ σθένειν τοσοῦτον ᾠόμην τὰ σὰ
 κηρύγμαθ', ὥστ' ἄγραπτα κἀσφαλῆ θεῶν
 νόμιμα δύνασθαι θνητὸν ὄνθ' ὑπερδραμεῖν·
 οὐ γάρ τι νῦν γε κἀχθές, ἀλλ' ἀεί ποτε
 ζῇ ταῦτα, κοὐδεὶς οἶδεν ἐξ ὅτου 'φάνη.

Antigone 449–457

KREON. Did you dare transgress these laws [*nomoi*]?
ANTIGONE. Yes, I did. For to me it was not Zeus who made that proclamation, nor did that Justice who dwells with the gods below ordain such laws for mankind. And I did not believe that your edicts were so powerful that you, a mortal, could override the gods' unwritten and unshakable customs [*ta nomima*]. For these laws are not of today nor are they yesterday's, but they live forever, and no one knows when they first came to light.

Bernard Knox finds in these words of Antigone allusions to customs and beliefs "older than the polis." Her reverence for the family dead and her belief in their continued existence seem to have belonged to the earliest religion known to man. Similar beliefs are suggested by archaeological remains of humans who long preceded the coming of the Cro-Magnons to Europe.[5] Knox, along the lines of the traditional interpretation, sees Kreon as a representative of the polis. His prohibition against funeral rites for Polyneikes is not a violation of an individual conscience— Antigone's—but an "age-old practice or custom," part of *ta nomima* 'established customs'.[6] Antigone, then, pitted against the polis, is seen to represent ancient—perhaps even mesolithic—practices and beliefs that Kreon can neither understand nor integrate into his political view as *turannos* 'tyrant'. Yet, as I anticipated above, I submit that it is Antigone who represents the polis, and that Kreon is the unjust ruler who would destroy the very foundation of the body politic, the family.

5. See Knox 1964.98 and Levy 1948.6 (cited by Knox).
6. See Knox 1964.97.

The Greek word *genos* 'lineage' bears further examination. It is certainly a pre-civic, or better, pre-polis term. Mythmaking creates genealogies; the *genos* of Oedipus goes back to Kadmos and eventually finds its origin in Zeus. The term *genos*, as Louis Gernet suggested, was as anachronistic in the fifth century as some terms we still use today are to us, for example, the "gentry" of Virginia or the "brahmins" of Boston.[7] And yet, tragedy—no less than epic—was constantly representing before fifth-century Athenian audiences *genē* 'lineages' of the most undemocratic sort. In the *Antigone*, as in Greek tragedy generally, the heroic myths that provide the plots are connected with royal lineages, noble *genē* which, in terms of social practice, values, and forms of religion, represent for the polis of the fifth century the very things that it often had to reject—or at least confront—in order to establish itself.[8]

The rite Antigone performs for her dead brother Polyneikes, minimal as it is (*Antigone* 429–431), does not just provide evidence of a belief in an afterlife (though such a belief may be part of ancient Greek tradition). Her act is based on *kinship*, on a duty belonging to that which Fortes calls "the general principle of kinship morality." It is a form of *kēdos*. Antigone, carrying out funeral rites for her brother, is acting as a member of a *genos*, as a kinswoman.

On the other hand, this compliance creates a terrible conflict, an *agōn* 'contest', between her and Kreon. Their opposition seems akin to the struggles over the bodies of heroes represented in the *Iliad*.[9] There is evidence that there were two kinds of funerals, two (proper) manners of treatment of the dead in ancient Greece. One is the domestic or familial funeral; the other, the public or grand one. Even today there are examples of both. There is the small graveside scene with relatives, friends, and the officiating religious figure. And there is the massively orchestrated funeral, that of a John Kennedy, a Mountbatten; it is a pageant, a public event, often disruptive, and not without some resemblance to what we find in the *Iliad*'s description of the funeral of Patroklos.[10]

Two observations are relevant in regard to the deaths of heroes. First, the death of the warrior in battle is a beautiful death; on vases the body of the dead hero is often larger than those of the living.[11] Homeric

7. Gernet 1968.279–288.

8. See Vernant and Vidal-Naquet 1988.26–27.

9. Consider, for instance, the battle over the bodies of Amphios (*Iliad* V 620–627), Hypsenor (XI 257–262), and Sarpedon (XVI 502–525); for Patroklos, see XVII 121–129 and Bradshaw in chap. 6.

10. *Iliad* XXIII.

11. See Brelich 1958.232–249, Loraux 1977.109–137, and Vernant in Gnoli and Vernant 1982.45–76.

warriors (*hērões*) contest over the dead either to appropriate the armor or mutilate an alien corpse, or to honor a *philos* 'comrade', 'one who is near and dear'. Why does Sophocles choose a young woman to be the spokesman, the "actor," in a battle over a corpse? Is this not a form of behavior proper, rather, to the great heroes in the *Iliad*? Very early in the play, Antigone's sister, Ismene, says,

ἀλλ' ἐννοεῖν χρὴ τοῦτο μὲν γυναῖχ' ὅτι
ἔφυμεν, ὡς πρὸς ἄνδρας οὐ μαχουμένα.

Antigone 61–62

We must remember that we are two women, not born to contend [verb *makhomai*] with men.

Breaking her ties with her sister, Antigone enters the world of *makhē* 'battle', a man's world.

The second observation is even more important. The heroic funeral was a grand event. In the description of Patroklos' funeral in *Iliad* XXIII, the fundamental ideology of the burial ritual becomes apparent. Christiane Sourvinou-Inwood argues that, on the basis of the Homeric nexus of death attitudes and representations of death rituals (a conflation of elements originating in different societies and periods), it is possible to reconstruct actual Dark Age and eighth-century attitudes and rituals.[12] It is important to note that Greek death rituals, even in their earliest and most public forms, were not conducted by professional priests, but by the kinsfolk of the deceased, aided by other members of the community. Sourvinou-Inwood distinguishes two dominant action plots: mourning and burying. When reference is made to mourners, these are mostly women; when to burial, they are men—a neat division of tasks in which women play a key role, yet one that is only preliminary in the context of the grand funeral.[13] She refers to three phases of death rituals, which I reproduce here in a simplified manner.

a. Preparation of the body and expressions of violent grief. Separation is emphasized. The kinswomen fling themselves on the corpse, shriek and wail, give expression to grief. They wash the corpse, anoint it, and clothe it before it is laid out on the bier. This is a "familial" stage of the funeral, and the women carry the ritual weight. But men too (rela-

---

12. See Sourvinou-Inwood 1983.34.
13. *Odyssey* iii 260, *Iliad* XI 394–395, XXII 82–89, XVIII 339–340, and XVI 674–675. See Sourvinou-Inwood 1983.37–38.

tives and close friends) either inflict wounds on themselves or defile themselves with dirt. It is interesting to note that Patroklos' corpse is washed by his comrades, the Myrmidons (*Iliad* XVIII 343–355). Men rather than women perform this function; an anthropologist would call the Patroklos episode an inversion wherein the exception proves the rule. Sarpedon's case is quite different; he is a Lycian and the otherness of his postmortem is duly stressed.[14]

b. Wake (πρόθεσις) and lamentation. Here the roles seem to converge, and these rituals are carried out equally by females and males. The community visits to view the corpse and pay its respects, and a formal lament is performed by two choruses, one of professional male singers and another of kinswomen.

c. Burial ceremony, comprising the procession (ἐκφορά), the cremation and/or rites at the grave, and the burial of the bones or corpse. Here the public or social dimension predominates, and men are performers of these rituals. The massive public funeral takes place: speeches, libations, the funeral pyre, the games—the memorialization of the hero. The death rituals for Patroklos in the *Iliad* are a model for this stage, in which the community, represented by the males, predominates. And *Iliad* VII 427–438 (Priam forbids loud wailing at the funerals of the Trojan warriors) may reflect, Sourvinou-Inwood argues, an incipient eighth-century trend to restrict the encroachment of funerals upon normal communal life. This trend continued in the Archaic age, as the development of the polis brought about the imposition of extramural burials and the custom of family groupings of graves; generally speaking, a shift in attitudes concerning death occurred.[15]

In her act of honoring her brother, Antigone performs the function of woman and warrior at once. Her ritual may not resemble the heavily structured ceremony we see in the epic texts, whereby a society of warriors is disrupted (the funeral of Patroklos lasted at least eleven days; see *Iliad* XXIV 31), but it contains the overtones of the epic funeral. Antigone does not only what a kinswoman would, should, and could do, but what a warrior, a *philos* or *hetairos,* would do.

But why does Antigone so act, creating a conflation of tasks in which one cannot clearly distinguish sexual roles? We must look carefully at her words to Kreon and understand them in the light of kinship amity:

14. See Nagy 1990a, chap. 8.
15. Nagy 1990a.38–41.

οὔτοι συνέχθειν ἀλλὰ συμφιλεῖν ἔφυν.

Antigone 523

I was born not to share in hatred [*sunekthein*], but in 'nearness and dearness' [*sumphilein*].

She was, in her own words, born to share in *philotēs* 'nearness and dearness'. What does it mean for this young woman to be a *philē* (the feminine of *philos*)? The Greek word *philos* suggests proximity. Martin
Schwartz has pointed out that the Indo-European root *phi-* means 'by', as
in the phrase "by the sea"; to be *philos* to someone is to be 'near and
dear' to him.[16]

There are scales of affection and there is a hierarchy of *philoi* 'those
who are near and dear' to a hero. A fine example of this is found in the
ninth book of the *Iliad*, where Phoinix, in order to persuade Achilles to
return to battle, tells "the best of the Achaeans" a story that is paradigmatic for all heroes who must gain *kleos* 'fame' (*Iliad* IX 524–605). It is
the tale of Meleager, who, just as Achilles, becomes angry and withdraws
from battle; his city is under attack and he is, again like Achilles, the *sine
quo non* for his people. Without him the city would perish. Delegation
after delegation comes to him; they beg him to return and to save the
city, and they offer him gifts of enormous value. Kakridis spotted the
ascending scale of affection in the delegates' relationship to Meleager.[17]
First the priests, then his father, followed by his sisters, his mother, and
his fellow warriors (*hetairoi philtatoi*) appeal to him—but all to no avail.
The last suppliant is Meleager's wife, and *she* is successful. How does she
persuade this stubborn warrior to save the city? She laments (*oduromai*)
the death of warriors, the fall of a city; she rehearses for her husband the
terror of defeat, the enslavement of women and children. She performs
a lament before the fact. Meleager, moved by his wife's supplication,
reenters the battle and saves the city.

It is for this reason that Meleager is famous, though Phoinix is making quite another point: Meleager entered the battle too late and so lost
the prizes promised him by earlier suppliants. Achilles could find himself in Meleager's position. There are at least two messages encoded in
Phoinix' admonitory tale: heroes should be flexible and take gifts, and
heroes are moved only by the one who is most "near and dear."
Meleager's wife's name, Kleopatre, shows precisely why Meleager has the

16. See M. Schwartz 1982.
17. Kakridis 1949.21–24.

kleos 'fame' of his *pateres* 'fathers', a fame bestowed upon him within praise poetry. Achilles too will be famous because of his most "near and dear," his *philtatos hetairos* Patroklos, whose function and name parallel those of Kleopatre.[18]

Why would Antigone earn *kleos* 'fame'? We must examine her scale of affection and follow the concept of "nearness and dearness" (*philotēs*) to its logical but in her case complex conclusion. Before Antigone goes to her death, Sophocles has her utter a perplexing valediction (905–912). Some say it is spurious; others deem it fanatical or at least inconsistent.[19] Yet if we examine it closely we see that it expresses in rather lucid tones Antigone's scale of affection; it tells us who is *philos* 'near and dear', or rather, who is *philtatos* '*most* near and dear' to her.

> οὐ γάρ ποτ' οὔτ' ἂν εἰ τέκνων μήτηρ ἔφυν,
> οὔτ' εἰ πόσις μοι κατθανὼν ἐτήκετο,
> βίᾳ πολιτῶν τόνδ' ἂν ᾐρόμην πόνον.
> τίνος νόμου δὴ ταῦτα πρὸς χάριν λέγω
> πόσις μὲν ἄν μοι κατθανόντος ἄλλος ἦν,
> καὶ παῖς, ἀπ' ἄλλου φωτός, εἰ τοῦδ' ἤμπλακον
> μητρὸς δ' ἐν Ἅιδου καὶ πατρὸς κεκευθότοιν
> οὐκ ἔστ' ἀδελφὸς ὅστις ἂν βλάστοι ποτέ.
>
> *Antigone* 905–912

If I had been the mother of children or if my husband's body were wasting away, I would not have chosen this labor, going against the citizens. For the sake of which law [*nomos*] do I speak thus? One husband dead, I might have found another, or a child from a new husband, had I lost the first. But with my mother and father both hidden away in the land of Hades, no brother [*adelphos*] could ever be engendered.

Antigone's scale of affection is clear. The origin of kinship amity is in the womb; this is *genos* talk, the language of bloodline or lineage. The Greek word for "brother" is *adelphos* 'from the same womb' and, for Antigone, the most "near and dear" is the one from the same womb.

The language of the womb dominates in the vocabulary of this play. Several examples should suffice here.

a. Antigone addresses Ismene in the prologue thus: ὦ κοινὸν αὐτά-δελφον Ἰσμήνης κάρα "O common sharer of the same womb, Ismene"

18. See Benveniste 1969.I.338–353 and Nagy 1979.102–103.
19. See Whitman 1951.92–93.

(*Antigone* 1). The line may seem tautological, yet here is the opening theme of the symphony in this Sophoclean play.

   b. Haimon, who loves Antigone, pleads with his father for her life:

ἐμοὶ δ᾿ ἀκούειν ἔσθ᾿ ὑπὸ σκότου τάδε,
τὴν παῖδα ταύτην οἷ᾿ ὀδύρεται πόλις,
πασῶν γυναικῶν ὡς ἀναξιωτάτη
κάκιστ᾿ ἀπ᾿ ἔργων εὐκλεεστάτων φθίνει.

Antigone 692–695

But I can hear how the entire city mourns secretly for this young girl, saying that of all women none has ever deserved less to die, nor for a deed more worthy of *kleos*.

Antigone, says Haimon, would not leave her fallen brother (*autadelphos*) unburied, a prey for birds and hungry dogs (696–699). We must note that Haimon speaks here for the polis, and the polis is honoring Antigone in terms reserved for heroes. No longer is she a child (*pais*). Through what seems a genuine rite of passage, she has become a woman (*gunē*) whose deeds rival those of warriors: she now possesses *kleos* 'fame'. Haimon's name is cognate with *haima* 'blood', and we are led to suspect that the combination of *haima, autadelphos,* and the lamentation of the polis is highly significant. Antigone represents, in the eyes of the polis, the values of kinship amity.

   c. Antigone says to Kreon (511), οὐδὲν γὰρ αἰσχρὸν τοὺς ὁμοσπλάγχ-νους σέβειν "There is nothing shameful in the reverence (*sebein*) of those sharing the same inner parts (*homosplankhnoi*)." Here the formulation of kinship amity is even more strikingly physical.

   d. In 191–210, Kreon attempts to justify his treatment of Eteokles and Polyneikes, the rival *adelphoi* 'from the same womb'. Eteokles will be honored, Polyneikes will not. Kreon calls Polyneikes a "blood sharer" (*sunaimos*), and he describes his edict concerning funeral honors as "akin" (*adelpha*) to his interpretation of a ruler's duty (191), but he does not understand the significance of either term, in his aberrant conception of a just city.

   Antigone's scale of affection is based on *philotēs* 'nearness and dearness', a form of kinship amity where the womb, the *delphus*, is the touchstone. In honoring Polyneikes, she honors the womb. She also honors her father Oedipus, who is also her brother and thus doubly *philos* through the womb of Jocasta. She is *adelphē* (feminine form of *adel-*

phos) to her father; her father is *adelphos* to her. Oedipus, Antigone, Polyneikes, Eteokles, and Ismene are all *autadelphoi* 'from the same womb'; it is kinship of the deepest kind. Part of the Theban saga, as is well known, involves an incredible violation of blood bonds: two *adelphoi* kill each other. Part involves the crime of incest, what Lévi-Strauss calls "an excess of kinship."[20] Antigone faces an extraordinary situation. One sharer of the womb is excessively dishonored, another excessively honored. She is, in a real sense—since Ismene refuses the role—the last member of the *autadelphoi*, of the womb sharers, who can establish any equilibrium.

Antigone's name reveals her function. *Anti-* can mean 'opposed to' *or* 'in compensation for'. The *gen-/gon-* root is cognate with *genos* 'lineage', and *gonē* can even mean 'womb'.[21] Antigone's action validates kinship based on the womb in compensation for its being dishonored; she restores an equilibrium of honor to "those from the same womb." The polis approves of her, honors her, and honors her scale of affection. We might say that Antigone, to use Fortes' terms, has given value to kinship amity as "actor"; tribal values have been reshaped as polis values. These values, as expressed by Antigone and as accepted by the polis, are axiomatically valid, and they are based on "blood," on the *genos*. Thus Antigone honors the *genos* and all *genē* relationships. Her act of honor, this *kēdos*, is compensatory.

In another sense, however, she opposes the *genē* 'lineages', bloodlines. She is indifferent to Haimon, chooses virginity in death, and opposes in her simple ritual for a dead kinsman the massive burial associated with the funerals of the royal *genē*. Could the democratic polis tolerate the disruption of massive *genē* funerals? Athens had enough difficulty coping with the presence of dynamic aristocrats. We know that the legislation of Solon and Kleisthenes set limits on funeral rites: the πρόθεσις 'wake' had to take place indoors, harsh mourning practices were forbidden, the ἐκφορά 'funeral procession' was ordered to occur before sunrise the day after the laying out of the body, the participation of women was limited to close relatives and those over sixty years of age.[22] One could point to many other examples, but it is clear that there was a gradual and deliberate domestication or limitation of death rituals in the Athenian polis. Some might suggest that the polis destroyed the

20. Lévi-Strauss 1972.81–106, esp. pp. 89–90.
21. See LSJ and Euripides *Phoenician Women* 1597; see also Hesiod *Works and Days* 733, where *gonē* means 'seed'.
22. See Sourvinou-Inwood 1983.47.

old aristocratic ways, but is it not just as plausible to suggest that the polis slowly integrated them into its own life? Rituals for the dead were not suppressed; they became "familial." Surely Antigone stood for such with her deep regard for kin, and the polis justly honored her. The play of Sophocles is her *kleos*. But the city despised the likes of Kreon. Sourvinou-Inwood has said that the funerary legislation of Solon revealed an increasing desire to push death away, "to restrict death's encroachment on community life by limiting the disruption and lowering the emotional tone, of the death ritual."[23] Antigone's life, virginity, and death enlarge the values attached to kinship, setting before the fifth-century Greek audience a woman who does not destroy but preserves and even reestablishes a just polis. Antigone represents the kind of civic and pre-civic justice that does justice to kin. She bravely transgresses Kreon's prohibition of burial, not with a massive funeral, but with a handful of dust, a triple libation—all based on a scale of affection grounded in the womb and evoking the pre-polis, what we might call the tribal values, the world of the *genē*. In a strange way, then, she is heroic in stature, an image of equilibrium and *dikē* 'justice', but she also puts all women in their proper ritual place within the new polis—and proclaims the power of the womb.

The image of the just virgin or maiden (*parthenos*), the Athena-like patroness of the just city, is traditional. It appears in much earlier texts than Sophocles' *Antigone*. In Hesiod's *Works and Days*, for example, *dikē* 'justice' is personified as a maiden whom men assault and drag from her path for their own evil purposes.[24] Hesiod portrays justice as an incorruptible *parthenos*. When she is dragged off, there is a *rhothos* 'murmur of protest' that spreads among the people. West notes that in the *Antigone* Kreon describes the reactions of those who resist him in precisely this way:

> ἀλλὰ ταῦτα καὶ πάλαι πόλεως
> ἄνδρες μόλις φέροντες ἐρρόθουν ἐμοί,
> κρυφῇ κάρα σείοντες, οὐδ' ὑπὸ ζυγῷ
> λόφον δικαίως εἶχον, ὡς στέργειν ἐμέ.

Antigone 289–292

Some men in the city murmured [*errothoun*] against me from the beginning, chafing at this edict, wagging their heads in secret. They did not

23. Ibid., and Alexiou 1974.14–23.
24. Hesiod *Works and Days* 220–221, 256; see West 1978 on these lines.

keep their necks loyally under the yoke, like men contented with my rule.

Sophocles' theme of *dikē* 'justice' evokes imagery and diction from Aeschylus' *Seven against Thebes*, in which the *autadelphoi* Eteokles and Polyneikes kill each other. Two passages in the *Seven* are particularly suggestive. One belongs to the extraordinary scene that pairs successively six Argive enemies and six Theban defenders, to culminate in the encounter of the two brothers at the seventh gate. A scout arrives to tell Eteokles that he has seen his brother: Polyneikes, he reports, is a formidable foe. The scout describes the shield of Polyneikes; it is a *diploun sēma* 'a double-meaning sign'.

ἔχει δὲ καινοπηγὲς εὔκυκλον σάκος
διπλοῦν τε σῆμα προσμεμηχανημένον·
χρυσήλατον γὰρ ἄνδρα τευχηστὴν ἰδεῖν
ἄγει γυνή τις σωφρόνως ἡγουμένη·
Δίκη δ' ἄρ' εἶναί φησιν, ὡς τὰ γράμματα
λέγει· "κατάξω δ' ἄνδρα τόνδε, καὶ πόλιν
ἕξει πατρῷαν δωμάτων τ' ἐπιστροφάς."

Seven against Thebes 642–648

He carries a shield, well rounded and newly fashioned, with a double sign [*diploun sēma*] cunningly fixed on it. A woman is advancing in modesty, and she leads a warrior, all in gold. She declares that she is *Dikē* 'Justice', as the writing shows [*hōs ta grammata legei*]: "And I will bring back this man and he shall have the city of his forebears and shall range in his father's halls."

Froma Zeitlin has explored the system of meanings signified by the pairings of champions, shields, and names.[25] Two codes, she says, are delineated: that of the city and that of the family in its genealogical extension. The fortunes of the city have been interwoven with those of Laios' family ever since the response he received from the oracle. The death of Eteokles and Polyneikes ultimately fulfills Apollo's prophecy.[26] The brothers, born from a union that violated the rules of kinship and doomed by their father's curse, pose a threat to the safety of Thebes. They have identical claims to hegemony and they inevitably destroy one another.

25. Zeitlin 1982.
26. See Thalmann 1978.22.

Dikē figures prominently on the shield and plays a key role in the semantic system of the shield scene. Eteokles proclaims *dikē* for himself (662, 667, 670–671). He decides to stand against Polyneikes as one with more *dikē* (*endikōteros,* 673). But Polyneikes, by the device on his shield and the message that it bears, now appropriates it. Thus *diploun* 'double', which on one level refers to the double figuration on the emblem, on the other serves as a sign of the double claim to *dikē*. Yet it is the *Erinus* 'Fury' or curse of family retribution, not *dikē*, that stands brother against brother in their will to mutual destruction (681). The *kleos* 'glory' in Eteokles' name (= "truly full of *kleos*") is thus undermined, and he proves the equal of Polyneikes (= "much strife").[27]

In the second passage, the chorus of women use the word *autadelphos* as they offer a last opportunity for mediation. The chorus ask Eteokles, ἀλλ' αὐτάδελφον αἷμα δρέψασθαι θέλεις "Will you harvest blood from the same womb [*haima autadelphon*]?" (*Seven against Thebes* 718). Eteokles, of course, will, thus violating the bonds of kinship. The line seems almost proverbial, with the implication that harvesting blood from the same womb is a "heinous crime." As Zeitlin points out, it is not *Dikē*, even though the two *autadelphoi* claim her, but her chthonic counterpart, *Erinus* 'Fury', that compels the sons of Oedipus to repay their nurture, as it were, as citizens of Thebes to the mother earth by dying for the city in order to defend her from an external enemy. The play of Aeschylus draws the story to the fratricide that is its inevitable conclusion.[28] Sophocles shows Antigone, in the aftermath of the mutual slaying, redressing Kreon's error and offering herself in sacrifice (as a ritual substitute of *Dikē*) in order to reestablish the balance of justice in the polis.[29] Herodotus (1.60.3–5) tells of the sixth-century Athenians who could conceive of the woman Phye (*phuē* 'flourishing stature') as the image of Athena leading her protege Peisistratos back from exile. Athenians of the fifth century, similarly, conceived Antigone in the image of *Dikē* who leads the polis to a new appreciation of kinship amity.

27. Zeitlin 1982.135–153. See also Nagy 1979.130, 262.
28. Now *genos* and polis, adds Zeitlin, can interact again. See Zeitlin 1982.153–168.
29. See Pozzi 1989.

CHAPTER 6

The Ajax Myth and the Polis: Old Values and New

David J. Bradshaw

In Sophocles' dramatic re-presentation of the Ajax story, the relationship of myth to polis has traditionally been seen in terms of antithetical models of heroism. Ajax himself exercises a rigid virtue incompatible with the hierarchy of values dominant in the fifth-century polis; the figure of Odysseus, meanwhile, demonstrates a flexibility that Ajax lacks, the very flexibility that makes him the consummate political animal. The *aretē* 'excellence' of the individual epic warrior whose egocentric absolutism is almost nonhuman is set over against the *aretē* of the community-oriented pragmatist whose relativism may prove essential to humane interaction among civilized individuals.[1] Such a juxtaposition comprises an interesting adaptation of myth to the concerns of Sophocles' Athens, establishing as inappropriate to a modern age the warrior ethos that had been, through the selective appropriation and propagandizing efforts of the aristocrats, received as paradigmatic for the city-state.[2] Ajax's singleminded pursuit of individual honor issues in violence and pollution, thereby revealing the anarchic threat implicit in his heroic mode, which makes that mode unacceptable within the polis; yet his terrible obsession, his pollution, and his volatile violence endow Ajax with the stature of tragic agonist, as once they must have established him

---

1. Jebb 1896, Whitman 1951, Brown 1951, Adams 1955, Knox 1961, Stanford 1963, Rosenmeyer 1963, Kirkwood 1965, and Segal 1981 all subscribe, with varying emphases, to the synthetic summary offered above.

2. Although the Homeric poems did not advance a single set of values as normative, aristocratic emphasis upon certain aspects of a warrior ideal would have given a particular slant to the reception and understanding of these poems, which were regarded as canonical.

as the hero of cult.[3] Like Oedipus or Orestes, he is a liminal figure who has transgressed boundaries yet therefore may become the *daimōn* 'divinity or hero' who protects boundaries.[4]

Such a traditional reading of *Ajax* appears generally sound. That Odysseus exercises a necessary virtue and is not simply a craven time server whose opportunism only limns Ajax's integrity is as clear as the fact that Odysseus' characteristics are those celebrated as quintessentially Athenian by Thucydides' Pericles, who in the great funeral speech, notes that the citizen appears μετὰ χαρίτων μάλιστ' ἂν εὐτραπέλως ... αὐταρκὲς παρέχεσθαι "to exhibit himself as sufficient by means of his graces and with surpassing versatility" (2.41.1–2). According to this view, as Bernard Knox asserts, Ajax's death implies that the Homeric individual ethos (represented in the epic by Achilles), after prevailing for centuries as an ideal of human nobility and action, had come to an end, challenged and superseded successfully in the fifth-century polis. The most developed form of this new outlook was reached in democratic Athens.[5]

More, though, passes with great Telamonian Ajax than heroic individualism of an old order; he is more than a *pharmakos* 'scapegoat'[6] upon whom Athenians might lay communal guilt for a violent self-assertiveness that was as outmoded as it was excessive. Sophocles presents situations that are problematic; he confounds rather than confirms the too ready conceptual antinomies by which people may understand matters. Without doubt, Ajax does, to some degree, embody an ethic that may be admired but not emulated; but Sophocles presents through this hero certain elements of the noble nature whose loss touches upon a spiritual imbalance with which his Athens was decidedly confronted. One might argue that Ajax is not, in all respects, the easy counter to Odysseus that an ancient spectator—or a modern reader—might be tempted to make him, that the Ajax figure, in the pre-Sophoclean tradition and in the drama, is not so monolithic as he is sometimes thought to be. A reconsideration of Ajax, and particularly of the Homeric virtue of *aidōs* 'shame to be thought dishonorable' that Ajax both champions and violates, may

3. Burian 1972 indicates clearly which aspects of cult ritual are and which are not pertinent to Sophocles' drama.

4. Concerning Ajax as protective *daimōn*, see Herodotus 8.121 and Pausanias 1.35.3. Adams 1955.93–95, Rosenmeyer 1963.187–189, and Segal 1981.142 all find the status of Ajax as *daimōn* important in considering the play.

5. Knox 1961.20.

6. Bremmer 1983 offers helpful clarification of this term.

lead to a better understanding of why and how Sophocles would choose this myth to adapt for presentation to the polis.

A major irony confronting the Sophoclean Ajax is his reversal from ally to enemy of the other Greeks. This irony, of course, keenly felt by modern readers of the two Homeric epics, provides a clear illustration of the intertextual referencing that binds *Iliad* and *Odyssey* together. In *Odyssey* xi the antagonism between Odysseus and Ajax resulting from the contest for the arms of Achilles illuminates passages of the *Iliad* in which the two heroes are somehow related. Consider, for example, *Iliad* XI 459–501, wherein Odysseus, wounded and set upon by Trojans, is rescued by Menelaos and Ajax. A characteristic action of Menelaos, in Homer, is to recognize the plight of a fallen comrade and to call for the rescue of the warrior, while one of Ajax's characteristic actions is to effect such a rescue by shielding the fallen and warding off Trojan attacks.[7] The general episode at XI 459–501, then, seems unremarkable, yet the simile describing the affair leads to some reflection upon the antagonism which subsequently develops between Ajax and Odysseus.

εὗρον ἔπειτ' Ὀδυσῆα Διῒ φίλον· ἀμφὶ δ' ἄρ' αὐτὸν
Τρῶες ἕπονθ' ὡς εἴ τε δαφοινοὶ θῶες ὄρεσφιν
ἀμφ' ἔλαφον κεραὸν βεβλημένον, ὅν τ' ἔβαλ' ἀνὴρ
ἰῷ ἀπὸ νευρῆς· τὸν μέν τ' ἤλυξε πόδεσσι
φεύγων, ὄφρ' αἷμα λιαρὸν καὶ γούνατ' ὀρώρῃ·
αὐτὰρ ἐπεὶ δὴ τόν γε δαμάσσεται ὠκὺς ὀϊστός,
ὠμοφάγοι μιν θῶες ἐν οὔρεσι δαρδάπτουσιν
ἐν νέμεϊ σκιερῷ· ἐπί τε λῖν ἤγαγε δαίμων
σίντην· θῶες μέν τε διέτρεσαν, αὐτὰρ ὁ δάπτει·
ὥς ῥα τότ' ἀμφ' Ὀδυσῆα δαΐφρονα ποικιλομήτην
Τρῶες ἕπον πολλοί τε καὶ ἄλκιμοι, αὐτὰρ ὅ γ' ἥρως
ἀΐσσων ᾧ ἔγχει ἀμύνετο νηλεὲς ἦμαρ.
Αἴας δ' ἐγγύθεν ἦλθε φέρων σάκος ἠΰτε πύργον,
στῆ δὲ παρέξ· Τρῶες δὲ διέτρεσαν ἄλλυδις ἄλλος.
ἤτοι τὸν Μενέλαος ἀρήϊος ἔξαγ' ὁμίλου
χειρὸς ἔχων, ᾗος θεράπων σχεδὸν ἤλασεν ἵππους.

Iliad XI 473–488

[Menelaos and Ajax] found Odysseus beloved of Zeus, and around him
the Trojans crowded, as bloody scavengers in the mountains

---

7. Notably, Menelaos and Ajax assume the same roles in recovering the body of Patroklos that they have played in rescuing Odysseus.

crowd on a horned stag who is stricken, one that a hunter
shot with an arrow from the string, and the stag has escaped him, running
with his feet, while the blood stayed warm, and his knees were springing
    beneath him.
But when the swift arrow has beaten him, then
the bloodthirsty [ōmophagoi 'eaters of raw meat'] scavengers begin
    to feast on him in the mountains,
in the shaded glen. But some spirit [daimōn] leads that way a dangerous
lion, and the scavengers scatter in terror, and the lion eats it;
so about wise much-devising Odysseus the Trojans
crowded now, valiant and numerous, but the hero
with rapid play of his spear beat off the pitiless death-day.
Now Ajax came near him, carrying like a wall his shield,
and stood forth beside him, and the Trojans scattered one way
    and another.
Then taking Odysseus by the hand warlike Menelaos
led him from battle, while his henchman drove the horses close up.[8]

The components of action on the metaphoric level prove congruent with those on the narrative level with a single exception whose prominence suggests a deliberate rather than an infelicitous breakdown of metaphor. Odysseus the wounded stag, hampered in his retreat by the congealing of blood and stiffening of limbs, seems about to succumb to encircling Trojan jackals when the lionlike Ajax scatters them; in the simile, however, the lion devours the stag, while, notably, on the narrative level Ajax rescues Odysseus. Is there implicit in the simile a sense of radical antagonism between the two heroes that could not, with propriety, be part of the narrative text?

If the foregoing passage does suggest the adversarial relationship of Ajax and Odysseus, it projects, of course, an outcome that never develops, that of Ajax easily destroying a hapless Odysseus.[9] Such an unfulfilled projection is distinctly countered by the aptly prophetic failure Ajax meets in the competitions of the funeral games in *Iliad*

---

8. Throughout this essay I employ Richmond Lattimore's translation of the *Iliad*, adapting his rendering of Homer at some points in order to underscore concerns about specific terms.

9. I doubt that there is any connection between the image of Ajax as the devourer of the stag and the description of the slaughter of the cattle by Ajax in Sophocles. It may, however, prove instructive to keep in mind this matter of devouring one's enemies. As we see later, it proves crucial to Odysseus' envy of Ajax in Pindar. So, too, Thucydides condemns the *phthonos* 'envy' that unleashes appetitive desires which, in turn, lead to political and ethical *anomia* 'lawlessness'.

XXIII.[10] Here Ajax fails to win a wrestling match with Odysseus, and besides suggesting the specific result of later competition between the two, the match could be interpreted as defining the nature of the forces opposed to one another: *megas Telamōnios Aias* 'great Telamonian Ajax' is pitted against *Odusseus polumētis* 'Odysseus of many wiles' (708–709), and the traditional juxtaposition of strength (*biē* 'physical force, violence') against cunning (*mētis*) may appear operative. Certainly the physiques of the two heroes reinforce this notion: Ajax, it should be recalled, is taller by a head than the other Argives (III 225–227), whereas Odysseus is shorter by a head than Agamemnon (III 191–194). And, pointedly, Odysseus wins by a trick, a *dolos*; "not forgetting his *dolos*" (δόλου δ' οὐ λήθετ' XXIII 725), he trips Ajax in spite of the other's superior size and strength.

It does simplify matters to understand Ajax as a hulking giant who lacks the guile that ensures success to Odysseus. Certainly Pindar, in *Nemean* 8, advances the opposition between the two somewhat along these lines. The figure of Ajax poses a disturbing question for Pindar: why, since he is acknowledged as best of the Achaeans after Achilles (*Iliad* II 768–769), should not Ajax be awarded Achilles' armor? As Pindar relates the myth, Odysseus is a personification of *phthonos* 'envy, greed', an opportunist whose calculating duplicity and facility with phrase enable him to deprive Ajax of deserved honor; Ajax, meanwhile, is projected as dumb (*aglōssos*), lacking the verbal ability that serves as a register of *mētis*.[11]

ὄψον δὲ λόγοι φθονεροῖσιν,
ἅπτεται δ' ἐσλῶν ἀεί, χειρόνεσσι δ' οὐκ ἐρίζει.

10. Whitman 1958.263–264 suggests that "the panorama of the *Games* foreshadows the future in certain details, and draws into the scheme of the *Iliad* hints of the traditional events later told in the *Little Iliad, The Sack of Troy,* and the *Returns.*" It should be noted that, besides the wrestling match examined above, Ajax fails to win two other competitions. Polypoites bests him in throwing the pig iron. More significant, Diomedes defeats him in one-to-one combat. This loss is important because it is a contest over the armor of Sarpedon and may foreshadow the later loss of the arms of Achilles. It may also, if Whitman is correct about the predictive nature of the games, adumbrate the grisly end that awaits Ajax as he falls on the sword given him by Hector: Achilles requires that, in order to win the arms, the contestants must continue spearplay until one "shall get through armor and dark blood and reach to the vitals of the other" (ψαύσῃ δ' ἐνδίνων διὰ τ' ἔντεα καὶ μέλαν αἷμα, XXIII 806), and the Achaeans call a halt to the contest when it appears that Ajax will indeed be successfully attacked in this fashion by Diomedes.

11. Detienne and Vernant 1978.25 and Nagy 1979.45–48 assert that *phrazomai* 'tell, give counsel, devise' is a verb associated with *mētis*.

κεῖνος καὶ Τελαμῶνος δάψεν υἱόν,
   φασγάνῳ ἀμφικυλίσαις.
ἦ τιν᾽ ἄγλωσσον μέν, ἦτορ δ᾽ ἄλκιμον, λάθα κατέχει
ἐν λυγρῷ <u>νείκει</u>· μέγιστον δ᾽ αἰόλῳ ψεύ-
   δει γέρας ἀντέταται.

Nemean 8.21–25

Words are a morsel for those who have *phthonos* 'envy, greed'.
He [one who has *phthonos*] grabs at the noble rather than have
   eris 'discord' with the inferior.
That one [Odysseus] even devoured the son of Telamon [Ajax],
   skewering him on the sword.
One who is unversed in speech but stout at heart is held down
   by Neglect on the occasion of a baneful *neikos* 'quarrel, blame'.
And the biggest honorific portion is handed over to intricate Deceit.[12]

The Pindaric Ajax is victimized by an ignoble intriguer before whose schemes he is powerless because speechless.[13] Pindar here seems deliberately to exploit the recollection his audience would have had of the silence with which the shade of Ajax, in *Odyssey* xi 541–565, receives Odysseus' plea for amity. Longinus (*On the Sublime* 9.2) later pronounced this silence among the shades to be "more sublime than words" in that it indicated the high-mindedness of Ajax. It remains uncertain, though, how much the speechlessness of Pindar's subject partakes of sublimity; his is an inability rather than a refusal to speak, a noble defect that is the natural expression of an almost too simple integrity devoid of cunning. The envious plottings of Odysseus, on the other hand, seem the essence both of base cunning and of appetitive desire, as the envious one literally devours Ajax, feeding his ego on his adversary's substance. The straightforward *aretē* of the greathearted warrior succumbs to the treachery of a designing malevolence; *mētis*, in its vilest manifestation, overcomes *biē*, as the two aspects of human strength remain disparate, being revealed in opposed figures.

Although there may be a dignity to Ajax's being without speech in Pindar, it is a pathetic dignity. If he is too noble to indulge in cleverness of words, Pindar never expressly says so. The poet attributes to him strength of heart (*ētor d' alkimon*), but couples this with his being

12. The translation is that offered by Nagy 1979.225. I have added the glosses on the basis of his discussion of the passage.
13. Martin 1989.71–72 supplies interesting comment concerning the strategy of remaining silent when challenged in a *neikos*.

tongueless (aglōssos), what in Latin is communicated by stupiditas and in English by dumb: the inability to speak or to speak well is looked upon as evidence of intellectual primitivism. Such characterization accords with a possible interpretation, which I have discussed above, of the opposition between *megas Telamōnios Aias* and *Odusseus polumētis* in the funeral games. Indeed there is a temptation to regard Ajax in epic and drama very much as he must be regarded in Pindar's epinician poetry. Doing so satisfies one's own predisposition to see matters in binary categories of polar opposition (might versus wit); doing so does not disrupt a consideration of the main action of the *Iliad,* and it may allow for a readier categorizing of the plot of drama. And yet, however apt a consideration of Pindar's Ajax as unwittingly stouthearted may be, it is inappropriate both for the Homeric and the Sophoclean hero. Homer presents Ajax as perceptive, tersely eloquent, a man of strategy quick of mind and of limb. Sophocles, inheriting the Homeric tradition, fashions his own hero also as a man who, though raw, has foresight, exercises strategy, and, most significant, apprehends his agony as an intellectual and spiritual affair. Properly assessing the Ajax of epic allows for the better comprehension of Iliadic themes and characters. More to the point of our initial concern, however, gauging the depths of the Sophoclean protagonist enables one better to appreciate the dynamics of the tragic enactment, to ascertain why the Ajax myth would have proven particularly suitable to the concerns of Sophocles' Athens in the 440s B.C.[14] Accordingly, let us touch briefly upon certain passages in the *Iliad* to explore the contention that Ajax is, fundamentally, a man of balance who exercises *mētis* as well as *biē*. Let us then turn to examine the tragic Ajax, proposing that he is consistent with the epic figure, and that his betrayal both of others and of himself would have confronted Athens with an image of that dissolution of loyalties which defined the malaise of the imperial polis.[15]

By uncritically associating extraordinary size and strength with slowness of wit, one may neglect to appreciate all that Ajax does and says in the *Iliad*. Of course, the adjective formulaically associated with his name is *megas* 'huge, great', and his physical might appears superior to that of other Greeks as well as all the Trojans. Himself ἕρκος Ἀχαίων "the wall

14. This approximate dating of *Ajax* is probable but not certain. Easterling 1985.296 says, "Most scholars would put *Ajax* before *Antigone* (probably late 440s) . . . though the evidence is not conclusive." See also p. 765.

15. On the reaffirmation of the ideals of Homeric epic in the plays of Sophocles, see Callen King 1985.47–66.

of the Achaians," he is described as φέρων σάκος ἠΰτε πύργον "carrying like a wall his shield," the latter phrase suggesting as much about the power of the shieldbearer as it does about the specific nature of the shield.[16] Such strength, though, is complemented by an alert agility evidenced in physical action and also in intellectual discernment and decision-making.[17] Ajax is a man of balance; the consistency with which he conducts himself as the Greek defense disintegrates reveals the equanimity of the well-disposed soul. Notably, too, he is singled out for his remarkable physical balance in one of Homer's most arresting similes:

οὐδ' ἄρ ἔτ' Αἴαντι μεγαλήτορι ἤνδανε θυμῷ
ἑστάμεν ἔνθα περ ἄλλοι ἀφέστασαν υἷες Ἀχαιῶν·
ἀλλ' ὅ γε νηῶν ἴκρι' ἐπῴχετο μακρὰ βιβάσθων,
νώμα δὲ ξυστὸν μέγα ναύμαχον ἐν παλάμῃσι,
κολλητὸν βλήτροισι, δυωκαιεικοσίπηχυ.
ὡς δ' ὅτ' ἀνὴρ ἵπποισι κελητίζειν εὖ εἰδώς,
ὅς τ' ἐπεὶ ἐκ πολέων πίσυρας συναείρεται ἵππους,
σεύας ἐκ πεδίοιο μέγα προτὶ ἄστυ δίηται
λαοφόρον καθ' ὁδόν· πολέες τέ ἑ θηήσαντο
ἀνέρες ἠδὲ γυναῖκες· ὁ δ' ἔμπεδον ἀσφαλὲς αἰεὶ
θρῴσκων ἄλλοτ' ἐπ' ἄλλον ἀμείβεται, οἱ δὲ πέτονται·
ὣς Αἴας ἐπὶ πολλὰ θοάων ἴκρια νηῶν
φοίτα μακρὰ βιβάς, φωνὴ δέ οἱ αἰθέρ' ἵκανεν,
αἰεὶ δὲ σμερδνὸν βοόων Δαναοῖσι κέλευε
νηυσί τε καὶ κλισίῃσιν ἀμυνέμεν.

Iliad XV 674–688

Nor did it still please great-hearted Ajax to stand back
where the other sons of the Achaians had taken position;
but he went in huge strides up and down the decks of the vessels.

16. Ajax's shield is older in style than those of his fellow warriors; it is larger than the typical round shield, being oblong in shape and designed to cover the entire body. See the note to *Iliad* VII 219 in Willcock 1976.

17. Ajax is early on advanced as having this complementarity of virtues. He appears initially as the Greek champion who responds to Hektor's challenge to single combat; here he declares that he will be beaten by neither *biē* 'force' nor *ideia* 'craft' (VII 197–199), and his subsequent success validates his boast. Hektor, after having narrowly escaped death at Ajax's hands, defines his opponent as the ideally balanced figure, declaring him to have divine gifts of *megethos*, *biē*, and *pinutē*, 'stature', 'strength', and 'wisdom' (VII 288–289). This initial characterization of Ajax is never violated or altered in any subsequent description but is instead developed further; it is this understanding of Ajax's nature that Sophocles adopts.

He wielded in his hands a great pike for sea fighting,
twenty-two cubits long and joined together by clinchers.
And as a man who is an expert rider of horses
who when he has chosen and coupled four horses out of many
makes his way over the plain galloping toward a great city
along the travelled road, and many turn to admire him,
men or women, while he steadily and never slipping
jumps and shifts his stance from one to another as they gallop;
so Ajax ranged crossing from deck to deck of the fast ships
taking huge strides, and his voice went always up to the bright sky
as he kept up a terrible bellow and urged on the Danaans
to defend their ships and their shelters.

Far from being a stolid Antaeus-type whose merit consists only in his
intractability, Ajax displays impressive alacrity and finesse. Moreover,
that his nimble defensive action, distinguishing him from the rest of the
Achaeans who have hung back somewhat, receives comparison with a
specialized variation of charioteering is significant: controlling yoked
horses so as to command a coordinated effort is a standard trope for
self-mastery, for personal harmony or dynamic equipoise.[18]

Ajax's defense of the ships against Hektor's onslaught is but one
revelation of him as an able tactician and strategist. For while he is usually not one of the chiefs involved in war councils, he is nevertheless
chosen for the embassy to Achilles—and *his* (not Odysseus', not
Phoinix's) is the speech that moves Achilles to modify his intention of
sailing away immediately with his Myrmidons.[19] Ajax is usually, though,
described in the action of fighting, where he proves himself an astute
commander as well as a fierce warrior. Frequently he is presented as the
hero who, often by himself, conducts a rearguard action in order that
others might retreat, yet note the emphasis Homer supplies when he
recounts the struggle over the body of Patroklos:

σάκεσσι γὰρ ἔρχατο πάντῃ

ἑσταότες περὶ Πατρόκλῳ, πρὸ δὲ δούρατ' ἔχοντο.
Αἴας γὰρ μάλα πάντας ἐπῴχετο πολλὰ κελεύων·
οὔτε τιν' ἐξοπίσω νεκροῦ χάζεσθαι ἀνώγει
οὔτε τινα προμάχεσθαι Ἀχαιῶν ἔξοχον ἄλλων,
ἀλλὰ μάλ' ἀμφ' αὐτῷ βεβάμεν, σχεδόθεν δὲ μάχεσθαι.

18. For chariot racing as a paradigm for *noos*, see Nagy 1990a, chap. 8.
19. See Martin 1989.40 for consideration of Ajax's words to Achilles as "authoritative
speech." Martin, curiously, regards Ajax's speech as only minimally effective.

ὡς Αἴας ἐπέτελλε πελώριος, αἵματι δὲ χθὼν
δεύετο πορφυρέῳ, τοὶ δ' ἀγχιστῖνοι ἔπιπτον
νεκροὶ ὁμοῦ Τρώων καὶ ὑπερμενέων ἐπικούρων
καὶ Δαναῶν· οὐδ' οἳ γὰρ ἀναιμωτί γε μάχοντο,
παυρότεροι δὲ πολὺ φθίνυθον· μέμνηντο γὰρ αἰεὶ
ἀλλήλοις ἀν' ὅμιλον ἀλεξέμεναι φόνον αἰπύν.

Iliad XVII 354–365

for they, standing about Patroklos,
fenced him behind their shields on all sides, and held their spears
   out-thrust.
For Ajax ranged their whole extent with his numerous orders,
and would not let any man give back from the body, nor let one
go out and fight by himself far in front of the other Achaeans,
but made them stand hard and fast about him and fight at close quarters.
Such were the orders of gigantic Ajax. The ground ran
with red blood, the dead men dropped one after another
from the ranks alike of Trojans and their mighty companions
and Danaans also, since these fought not without bloodletting,
but far fewer of them went down, since they ever remembered
always to stand massed and beat sudden death from each other.

That the Greeks lose fewer men than the Trojans is clearly the result of Ajax's discernment and his superintendence of discipline in the ranks. Indeed, that the Greeks prove able to retreat with Patroklos' body is attributed not simply to Ajax's power as a fighter but also to his *mētis*. It is he, after all, who calls upon the Greeks, saying ἀλλ' ἄγετ' αὐτοί περ φραζώμεθα μῆτιν ἀρίστην "let us deliberate with ourselves upon the best *mētis*" to recover the fallen comrade *and* conduct a safe retreat (XVII 633–639).[20] Then it is he who suggests that word of Patroklos' death be sent to Achilles in order that Achilles might ensure the success of the rescue, even naming the appropriate messenger, Nestor's son Antilochos, who has inherited some of his father's ability to manipulate people with words (XVII 640–655).[21] Having given such directives to elicit Achilles' assistance, Ajax provides the protective counterattack against the Trojans necessary for others to begin carrying Patroklos' body to the rear; yet Achilles' potential return to battle, following Antilochos' arrival with

20. Again there is the correspondence of *mētis* and *phrazomai* pointed out earlier.
21. For an example of Antilochos' perspicacity and his persuasiveness, consider his confrontations with Achilles and with Menelaos over awarding of prizes for the chariot race (*Iliad* XXIII 539–613).

news at the ships, is finally necessary to rout the Trojans and guarantee successful retreat. That Patroklos' body is not defiled is thus due to Ajax's *biē* as a defender but also to his *mētis*, his foresight or counsel as commander.

Similar in certain respects to Ajax's possession of *mētis* is his aptitude for perceiving the will of the gods, his informed apprehension of the reality before him. This sensitivity is not uncommon among the Iliadic heroes, but it may be important to note its presence in Ajax's personality, for he is sometimes regarded as insensitive or mindlessly combative. Often the crucial insight into the significance of events is expressed in Homer by the word *noos* 'perceptive intelligence' or the corresponding verb *noein*.[22] On occasion, as in the narrative of the embassy to Achilles, Ajax is specifically noted as involved in actions of *noos*.[23] But more frequently Homer simply asserts that the hero comes to recognize what supraphysical reality lies behind the events of battle. Thus when he is informed by Teukros that a new bowstring has broken in his hands even as he was about to shoot Hektor, Ajax correctly assesses an adversity of divine will and calmly counsels modified resignation about the given setback with continued effort to repulse the Trojans (*Iliad* XV 471–477).[24] Related to such perspicacity is the all-unwelcome understanding that comes to Ajax when Hektor, at length, lops the spearhead from the long pike with which Ajax had been defending the ships against Trojan attacks:

γνῶ δ' Αἴας κατὰ θυμὸν ἀμύμονα, ῥίγησέν τε,
ἔργα θεῶν, ὅ ῥα πάγχυ μάχης ἐπὶ μήδεα κεῖρε
Ζεὺς ὑψιβρεμέτης, Τρώεσσι δὲ βούλετο νίκην·
χάζετο δ' ἐκ βελέων. τοὶ δ' ἔμβαλον ἀκάματον πῦρ
νηὶ θοῇ· τῆς δ' αἶψα κατ' ἀσβέστη κέχυτο φλόξ.

Iliad XVI 119–123

22. For detailed study of the term *noos* in Homer, see von Fritz 1943.79–93. See also Frame 1980 and Nagy 1990a, chap. 8.

23. Perhaps surprisingly, it is Ajax rather than Odysseus who assesses the appropriate time to commence the exhortations to Achilles, signaling to Phoinix, and Odysseus follows Ajax's lead (IX 222–224). So, too, it is Ajax who recognizes from Achilles' instructions about preparations for Phoinix's lodgement that it is appropriate to leave, and he so informs Odysseus just prior to delivering remarks that convince Achilles to alter his purpose of sailing away with his men on the subsequent day.

24. The poet has already indicated that Zeus specifically countermands the intention of Teukros to slay Hektor (XV 461–465).

Ajax recognized, and shivered for knowing it,
that this was the work of the gods, that Zeus high-thundering had
        always cut short
his plan to do battle, and had willed that the Trojans should win.
He drew away out of the missiles, and the Trojans threw weariless fire
on the fast ship, and suddenly the quenchless flame streamed over it.

The image is one of great pathos as, with regret and against his better
will, Ajax sees the futility of further opposition; his insight and his resignation are all the more evocative because of his reluctance to accept
what he knows of the disparity between his own hopes and the overarching will of the gods.

Not in apprehension of reality alone but in his articulation of ideals
as well does Ajax prove himself quite able. Far from being the *aglōssos*,
the tongueless hero of Pindar, the Homeric Ajax gives, not infrequently,
effective endorsement of the value and necessity of commitment to
those with whom one fights. The Homeric term for such a sense of loyalty, or shame to be thought disloyal or ignoble or cowardly, is *aidōs*.[25]
Consistently, Ajax calls upon the faltering Achaeans to recall *aidōs*, and
his appeals have a stern eloquence. One such exhortation may serve to
illustrate how Homer distinguishes Ajax as a fighter endowed with strategic intelligence and also with a keen sense of responsibility to honor
which he renders with grim wit and telling force:

Αἴας δ' αὖθ' ἑτέρωθεν ἐκέκλετο οἷς ἑτάροισιν·
"αἰδώς, Ἀργεῖοι· νῦν ἄρκιον ἢ ἀπολέσθαι
ἠὲ σαωθῆναι καὶ ἀπώσασθαι κακὰ νηῶν.
ἢ ἔλπεσθ', ἢν νῆας ἕλῃ κορυθαίολος Ἕκτωρ,
ἐμβαδὸν ἵξεσθαι ἣν πατρίδα γαῖαν ἕκαστος;
ἢ οὐκ ὀτρύνοντος ἀκούετε λαὸν ἅπαντα
Ἕκτορος, ὃς δὴ νῆας ἐνιπρῆσαι μενεαίνει;
οὐ μὰν ἔς γε χορὸν κέλετ' ἐλθέμεν, ἀλλὰ μάχεσθαι.
ἡμῖν δ' οὔ τις τοῦδε νόος καὶ μῆτις ἀμείνων,
ἢ αὐτοσχεδίῃ μεῖξαι χεῖράς τε μένος τε.
βέλτερον, ἢ ἀπολέσθαι ἕνα χρόνον ἠὲ βιῶναι,
ἢ δηθὰ στρεύγεσθαι ἐν αἰνῇ δηϊοτῆτι
ὧδ' αὔτως παρὰ νηυσὶν ὑπ' ἀνδράσι χειροτέροισιν."
ὣς εἰπὼν ὄτρυνε μένος καὶ θυμὸν ἑκάστου.

Iliad XV 501–514

---

25. Redfield 1975.113–119 offers concise, thorough, and clear explication of the use of
aidōs in Homeric contexts.

But Ajax on the other side called to his companions:
"Have shame [*aidōs*], you Argives; here is the time of decision, whether
we die, or live on still and beat back ruin from our vessels.
Do you expect, if our ships fall to helm-shining Hektor,
you will walk each of you back dryshod to the land of your fathers?
Do you not hear how Hektor is stirring up all his people,
how he is raging to set fire to our ships? He is not
inviting you to come to a dance. He invites you to battle.
For us there can be no *noos*, no *mētis*, better than this one,
to close in and fight with the strength of our hands at close quarters.
Better to take in a single time our chances of dying
or living, than go on being squeezed in the stark encounter
right up against our ships, as now, by men worse than we are."
So he spoke, and stirred the strength and spirit in each man.

Aware of the need for *mētis* and *noos* which will be serviceable, Ajax is yet
more conscious that this need must relate to the proper disposition of
individual warriors acting in concert with one another in order to avoid
shameful defeat. As he later says with gnomic understatement, αἰδομέ-
νων δ' ἀνδρῶν πλέονες σόοι ἠὲ πέφανται "more come through alive when
men recall *aidōs*" (XV 563). Sparing of words Ajax may on occasion be,
at least when compared with the voluble Nestor[26] or Odysseus; yet when
he speaks, he speaks with strength and consciousness informed by frater-
nal social responsibility. He can stir Achilles by referring to forsaken loyalty to friends, and he can motivate his men with calls to redeem an
almost lost honor. No "beef-witted lord," Ajax uses words that appeal to
judgment and to desire; if his speech is spare, the very economy contributes to its effectiveness.[27]

Even more than his words, Ajax's actions establish him as the Iliadic
figure most consistently associated with *aidōs*. He is the hero who
delights that his lot is to champion all the other Greeks in single combat
against Hektor; who never abandons his companions in battle but
instead moves to rescue them; who takes control of defensive retreats to
prevent their becoming utter routs; who leads the resistance against

26. It is instructive to compare Nestor's call to remember *aidōs* at XV 661–666 with those
of Ajax, especially with Ajax's exhortation at XV 733–741. The supposedly tight-lipped warrior is given much the same speech as is the venerable counselor whom Pope somewhat
querulously glossed as "narrative with age."
27. The Shakespearean phrase (from *Troilus and Cressida* II.i.11) and the Shakespearean
portrayal of Ajax have been in mind for many modern scholars writing about the Homeric
and the Sophoclean hero and may account for a somewhat skewed reading of the character
of Ajax.

Hektor at every point; who proves most resolute when the Achaean cause seems most endangered. That he is the object of others' loyalty is indicated not only by their turning toward him for leadership but also by their common concern at the funeral games that his duel with Diomedes be halted before he comes to harm and that, though he has been bested, he share in the prize equally; he inspires loyalty as well as demonstrating it. In large measure, Ajax, whose personal interest and sense of individual honor find expression in furthering the common enterprise at Troy, stands in sharp contrast to Achilles, whose consuming self-interest and obsession with individual honor find expression in negating this common goal.[28] Aidōs will not allow Ajax the Achillean exaltation of personal worth which entails the destruction of one's comrades.

Ajax also is juxtaposed with Hektor, of course, who is the hero of aidōs among the Trojans. In the battle before the ships and again in the battle over Patroklos' corpse, they consistently parallel one another, alternately calling their men to remember honor and loyalty and fight for their countrymen.[29] Yet, as he did on a simple physical level when they met in arranged combat, Ajax here emerges as superior, if not in arms yet in honor. Consider the pointed contrast between the two which is established just after Patroklos enters battle:

> Αἴας δ' ὁ μέγας αἰὲν ἐφ' Ἕκτορι χαλκοκορυστῇ
> ἵετ' ἀκοντίσσαι· ὁ δὲ ἰδρείῃ πολέμοιο,
> ἀσπίδι ταυρείῃ κεκαλυμμένος εὐρέας ὤμους,
> σκέπτετ' ὀιστῶν τε ῥοῖζον καὶ δοῦπον ἀκόντων.
> ἦ μὲν δὴ γίγνωσκε μάχης ἑτεραλκέα νίκην·
> ἀλλὰ καὶ ὧς ἀνέμιμνε, σάω δ' ἐρίηρας ἑταίρους.
>
>   Ἕκτορα δ' ἵπποι
> ἔκφερον ὠκύποδες σὺν τεύχεσι, λεῖπε δὲ λαὸν
> Τρωικόν, οὓς ἀέκοντας ὀρυκτὴ τάφρος ἔρυκε.

Iliad XVI 358–363, 367–369

28. Whitman, who asserts that "more than any other figure on the Greek side, Ajax is the man of *aidōs*" (1958.171–173), stresses the artistry of Homer's offering a description of Ajax doggedly fighting a battle against superior odds immediately after Achilles utters his wish that, in order to augment his glory the more, all Trojans *and* all Greeks except for himself and Patroklos might meet death before the walls of the citadel. Certainly this passage (XVI 97–111) emphasizes sharply the juxtaposed ideals of heroism entertained by the two warriors.

29. The frequency with which Ajax and Hektor are counterpointed in their speeches and actions is remarkable: XV 415–419, 484–517, 552–564, 685–695; XVI 101–121, 358–376; XVII 125–131, 210–245.

But the great Ajax was trying forever to make a spearcast
at bronze-helmed Hektor, but [Ajax] in his experience of fighting,
with his broad shoulders huddled under the bull's-hide shield, kept
watching always the whistle of arrows, the crash of spears thrown.
He knew well how the strength of the fighting shifted against him,
but even so stood his ground to save his steadfast companions [hetairoi].

                            while his fast-running horses
carried Hektor away in his armour; he abandoned the people
of the Trojans, who were trapped by the deep-dug ditch unwilling, . . .

Ajax behind the very shield that has so often protected the Greeks, patiently waiting the opportune moment which, for him, never comes, endangered and at a disadvantage himself now that he is engaged in offensive rather than defensive fighting, yet holding his position in order to preserve his *hetairoi* 'companions': this is the normative image of *aidōs*, and it is pointed by Hektor's abandonment of his people, careening off with armor he will soon exchange for that which, foolhardily, he will strip from Patroklos' corpse.[30]

The Homeric Ajax, then, is somewhat an exemplary figure, associated with *mētis*, with *noos*, and, most strongly, with *aidōs*. And this hero would, naturally, have been of special interest to Athenians, for he is the closest proximation to an Athenian epic hero, since Menestheus, the nominal Athenian leader, remains a minor figure in the *Iliad*. Ajax, though, from the island of Salamis, which lies a mile from the coast, is certainly not minor, and his genealogy, cult worship, and status as the progenitor of one of the ten tribes (Aiantis) all establish him as Athenian. Ajax is the son of the hero Telamon and the Megarian princess Periboia; Telamon himself is the son of Aiakos, whom the sea nymph Aegina bore to Zeus.[31] W. B. Stanford, summarizing the geneal-

30. The detail that Hektor flies σὺν τεύχεσι 'in his armor' may be significant in developing the theme that concern with spoils and personal honor leads Hektor to forget *aidōs*. Consider how Glaukos upbraids Hektor for retreating with Achilles' armor rather than fighting to take Patroklos' corpse and thereby effect an exchange for the fallen Sarpedon's body (XVI 140–168). This speech is similar in tone and intent to the rebuke administered by Apollo (in the form of Mentes) when Hektor abandons more pressing concerns to chase vainly after the prize of Achilles' horses (XVI 69–81). Hektor yearns after spoils that may not, properly, be his, even as he has desired, improperly, to be deathless and honored as Athena and Apollo are (VIII 538–541). This wish for personal exaltation is often at odds with better judgment needed to preserve the safety of the group; the point is made most clearly in Hektor's dismissal of Poulydamas' observation that the upcoming battle with Achilles will be for city and family and so must preclude any self-indulgent quest for individual glory in battle (XVIII 249–313).

31. On this genealogy, see Wickersham in Chap. 1.

ogy and its significance, notes that "as great-grandson of the nymph Aegina, and son of the king of Salamis and a princess of Megara, [Ajax] embodied Athenian aspirations to lordship over the islands and coast of the Saronic Gulf."[32] Without doubt, Ajax's heritage would have made him most attractive to expansionists within the imperial polis, for it does seem to embrace much of the territory that eventually came under the domination of Athens. This matter of genealogical background carried important implications for issues of jurisdiction, so much so that the Megarians accused the Athenians of actually interpolating into the Iliadic canon the brief passage that associates Ajax's ships with those of Menestheus.[33] Whether such tampering took place is perhaps a moot issue with respect to Ajax's connection with Athens; in any case, the Athenians appropriated Ajax—and Salamis—on the grounds of this juxtaposition in the Catalogue of Ships. Certainly by the fifth century Ajax was a cult figure in Athens, associated in worship with Athena.[34] Pausanias records that there remained a temple of Ajax as well as a statue and asserts that Ajax's son Eurysakes was also honored in ritual at Athens (1.35.3). Of comparable significance is the fact that the Aiantis tribe traced itself to Ajax, and Herodotus (6.35), Pausanias (1.25.2), and Plutarch (*Solon* 10) record the tradition that Ajax's son (or grandson) Philaios became an Athenian citizen, thereby consigning suzerainty over his forebears' islands to Athens. Indeed, it was only natural that Athenians turn to Ajax, since they had firmly embodied in their civic myths his associations with *their* polis.[35]

In the Homeric Ajax, moreover, Athenians of the mid-fifth century might see qualities which, without willful distortion, they could associate with virtues of their own historic-heroic past, the period of the Persian wars. Athens had orchestrated the Greek defense, drawing up the battle plans and holding the various allied forces to disciplined commitment to established strategies. If it is an exaggeration to say that Athens rallied the other city-states to the cause of Greek independence from Persian control, it is not a great exaggeration (see Herodotus 7.131). Athenian

32. Stanford 1963.xii–xiii. Here and elsewhere I am indebted to Stanford's edition and commentary.

33. Whitman 1958.67–86 examines the nature and discredits the validity of these accusations and offers additional comment about Athens in relation to Iliadic myth and to Iliadic times.

34. Ajax's relations to Athena may prove another instance of the pattern wherein a god is antagonistic to a hero in myth yet associated with the hero in ritual. See, in this regard, Nagy 1979.289–300.

35. See Wickersham in Chap. 1.

resistance to Persian hegemony involved insistent appeals to others to share in this struggle. Athens' inflexible determination to endure, to recall honor and fight to preserve itself as well as those other city-states leagued with it—these attitudes characterize Athenian action in the wars. That Athenians *could* regard Ajax as exemplifying those very virtues which they, too, had practiced is certainly a possibility, especially in view of the fact that the Persian war was often regarded as parallel to the traditional Trojan conflict. That Athenians who fought the Persians *did* regard Ajax as somehow responsible for their victory is clear from their having supplicated Ajax (as *daimōn*) before the battle of Salamis (Herodotus 8.64.2),[36] and from their subsequent sacrifice to Ajax at Salamis following the victory (Herodotus 8.121.1).

The Ajax whom Sophocles introduced onto the tragic stage, then, would have been regarded as a protective *daimōn* of the polis, a figure revealing an admirable balance of physical prowess and intellectual discretion, and, above all, a hero distinguished by his consistent espousal of the honor one secures and maintains through loyalty to one's allies. Sophocles' tragic agonist is quite similar to this figure from earlier myth. The concern in the drama with his burial pertains not simply to the vindication of an individual but more tellingly to the legitimation of a cult hero: that Ajax receive appropriate interment is essential to his exaltation to heroic status and his functioning as tutelary *daimōn*, and Athenians would have had particular interest in the story of a challenge to proper burial.[37] So, too, the Sophoclean character is a bold strategist recognized for his prudent forethought; though he may be raw-minded, he is not simply a physical giant slow of wit, and his suffering is most pointedly a mental or spiritual agony. Moreover, as Teukros and the chorus clearly establish, this Ajax, too, is noted for his courageous loyalty to his comrades—both his own men and the other Greeks. What complicates the Sophoclean Ajax, of course, is that he violates the very ideal of *aidōs* he has championed, and his intellectual and spiritual struggle concerns his grappling with the dynamics of this violation. In his betrayal of this ideal, in the perplexed search for self-understanding and self-definition that follows such betrayal, Ajax holds the mirror up to a

36. They also sent to Aegina for the bones of Aiakos and his sons; since Ajax was considered to have been buried in Troy (Pausanias 1.35.4–5), his relics could not have been requested, but both he and Telamon were specifically invoked at Salamis.

37. Adams 1955.93–95 stresses the relationship of burial to status as a hero-*daimōn*, seeing the issue of proper burial to be central to the concerns of Sophocles' presenting the play for the tragic enactment in Athens.

polis troubled by similar confusion concerning values and identity. As Sophocles shapes the myth, he re-presents an Ajax who symbolizes not only a heroic past but also a present radically at odds with this past.

Sophocles takes pains that his audience not mistake the distinctive character traits of his protagonist. Even as the deluded Ajax leaves Athena to dispatch the animal he has been made to see as his enemy, she asks Odysseus whether he had ever discovered anyone *pronousteros* "with greater forethought,"[38] or δρᾶν ἀμείνων ... τὰ καίρια "more judicious in acting at the right moment" (*Ajax* 119–120). Emphasized here are those qualities that distinguish the sagaciously disciplined warrior of epic myth; Odysseus' pitying acknowledgement of Ajax's excellence in these regards would but have confirmed an established Homeric understanding of Ajax and would have intensified perception of the disparity between the hero's previous career and his present actions. That Ajax suffers from *nosos* 'disease, derangement of mind' is all the more terrible because he has been noted for his considered intelligence and his intuitive aptitude for seizing the propitious moment.

So, too, other terms employed early on in the action to characterize Ajax are consonant with the portrayal of the perceptive and resolute hero of Homeric epic rather than with the image of the passive victim advanced by Pindar. He has engaged in a *bouleuma* 'deliberated plan' (44) in moving against the Greek leaders. His intended ventures are termed *tolmai* 'daring actions' (46). The word may carry the suggestion of excessive (hence self-defeating) boldness, but it should be recalled that in both the *Iliad* and the *Odyssey* the adjective *tolmēeis* 'strong-hearted, enduring' is used positively, frequently being employed to describe Odysseus. That Ajax's intentions were not foolhardy in nature is indicated by Athena's observation that, except for her vigilance, he would have succeeded in his attack (45). His being described in terms associated with Odysseus, moreover, receives further development: his action is described by Athena as *dolios* 'crafty or cunning' (47), and his night foray may recall the deadly nocturnal stealth displayed by Odysseus in the *Doloneia*.[39] Establishing him as having such Odyssean qualities reinforces the point that Ajax himself commands no mean intelligence but rather is formidable as a strategist, not simply as a fighter.

38. The comparative *pronousteros* has as its base *noos*, suggesting the insight or foresight which is aligned to the will of the gods.

39. Segal 1981.110 notes the similarity of Ajax's venture to Odysseus' exploit in *Iliad* X.

Perhaps most important, though, is the fact that Ajax endures a mental agony to which only the greatminded hero could prove susceptible. His tragedy is bound up with his loss of control over his intellectual powers.[40] Always the warrior whom both comrades and enemies respect for his discerning purposiveness and self-command, Ajax has, through the *nosos* Athena has visited upon him, been made to act in a fashion that robs him of the very respect that comprises his personal identity. Ability to direct planned action resolutely and effectively, indeed, simple self-command and self-consciousness, have been taken from him, and he has been made to play the fool. He has engaged in actions that are the very antitheses of the heroic exploits that define his being, and, accordingly, he finds the essence of his heroic nature threatened with negation. Consciousness of what he has done constitutes his agony, as Tekmessa makes strikingly clear:

και νῦν φρόνιμος νέον ἄλγος ἔχει·
τὸ γὰρ ἐσλεύσσειν οἰκεῖα πάθη . . .
          μεγάλας ὀδύνας ὑποτείνει.

Ajax 259–260, 262

          now sane, he has new anguish,
for to see suffering brought on by oneself . . .
intensifies great distress.

Ajax is freed from derangement of mind only to discover that he has brought *aiskhron* 'disgrace' upon himself, and he refuses to live with disgrace, to continue without the self-respect and the respect from others which would make life meaningful. Ajax initially realizes that he has lost the respect of others when he learns that the arms of Achilles have been awarded to Odysseus. Here is a judgment that he is *not* the one preeminent in battle and council, but it is a judgment that might be regarded as false. The night attack is Ajax's attempt to deny the validity of this assessment of his merit. The failure in the attack, however, especially the disgraceful nature of the failure, corroborates, before others and himself, that he has acted ignobly and not as the supremely capable warrior should act. No longer may his shame be attributed to the twisted

40. Knox 1961.5 offers the traditional view that Ajax's madness pertains only to the visual delusion that the livestock he slaughters are the Greek leaders. Simpson 1969.89–92 regards the optical confusion as integrally connected with a madness manifested in the design against the Atreidai.

judgment of others; the evidence of the slaughtered cattle makes real for Ajax as well as for others an evaluation of himself as unworthy.

Maintaining respect, the bonds of *aidōs*, of course, is what had always characterized the figure of Ajax. Teukros makes clear reference to this tradition of Ajax as the fighter loyal to the cause in his repudiation of Agamemnon, rehearsing in extended detail those significant actions of the Homeric Ajax known to the audience: his rescuing those fallen in battle; his preventing the destruction of the ships by fire; his championing the Greeks in single combat as well as in pitched battle against Hektor (1266–1289). The chorus of Salaminian sailors also recreate the understanding of Ajax as the chief exemplar of *aidōs*. They, too, recall the hero's loyal and courageous actions undertaken on behalf of the Atreidai (616–620). Because his reputation has been impugned, they express great anxiety about their own fate (134–140), acknowledging their dependence upon his protective strength, which has heretofore sustained them most reliably (158–161, 1211–1213). Ajax himself stresses his special bond with these men when he addresses them as *philoi* 'near and dear', those who are bound by the closest of non-familial ties (349–350). Worth noting in this context also is Ajax's devoted commitment to Tekmessa and Eurysakes, as well as his intense bonding with the stern father Telamon awaiting him at Salamis. He has continued loyal in affection to Tekmessa though she is a concubine rather than his wife (211–212), and his overriding personal relations seem to be with the son who will continue to validate his heroism and with the father whose heroic career he has tried to emulate. Honoring such family ties is most characteristic of the type of loyalty implicit in the term *aidōs*, and Sophocles gives repeated emphasis to the importance and depth of Ajax's familial relations. It is interesting to note that the two heroes to whom Ajax is traditionally opposed, Hektor of the *Iliad* and the Odysseus of the *Odyssey*, are also distinguished by their orientation to the family.

The emphasis given to the honorable loyalty that *had* distinguished his hero allows Sophocles to augment the irony inherent in the conclusion of Ajax's career. Suffering at first from what he regards as a breach of loyal faith on the part of those who refuse to award him Achilles' arms, Ajax acts himself to violate his most fundamental commitments. Bound by honor to protect his comrades, he moves, not simply to abandon, but to destroy them. If, as we have seen, in the epic poem he has served as the consistent foil to an Achilles who forsakes his duty to friends, in the tragic drama Ajax assumes a markedly Achillean temperament: stung by others' failure to engage in reciprocal exchange of loyalty and recognition, he deliberately reverses his relationship with the Greeks, basing his tergiversation on theirs. Because of the miscarriage of his intended revenge, moreover, Ajax also comes, perversely, to fail in his continuance of family tradition and in his very protection of family: with acute awareness of disparity, Ajax juxtaposes his father's earlier success in securing honor at Troy with his own present failure (434–440), while Tekmessa outlines in pathetic imaginings her own future victimization, the vulnerability of Eurysakes, and the heart sorrow of Ajax's parents, all of which would derive from Ajax's resolution to die because he has been shamed (492–524). Through his actions Ajax turns to live a lie, for he becomes the thing he is not: an isolated self-seeker rather than one bound with others to champion their common interests; a betrayer rather than a preserver of *philoi* and *hetairoi* 'friends' and 'comrades'; a man almost incapacitated by doubt about values and first principles rather than a man whose secure sense of self in relation to others had provided the necessary basis for determining values.

Confusion about absolutes and a reluctance to entertain any notion of personal or moral relativism together determine the intellectual quandary in which Ajax finds himself. He yearns for a world wherein strength and accomplishment yield similar portions of honor from one generation to the next. He is radically disturbed that his father had won at Troy *eukleia* 'honorable fame' while, with comparable heroic exploits, he finds himself *atimos* 'dishonored' (434–440; see also 470–472, 845–851). The consistency that *would* provide motivation for human endeavor is not apparent in fact, and heroic reward seems accidental rather than earned. In a world governed by such capricious chance, it is shameful for the nobleman, reflects Ajax, to search for happiness when the round of days is only προσθεῖσα κ' ἀναθεῖσα τοῦ γε κατθανεῖν "prompting toward then pulling back from death" (473–476). Fluctuating uncertainty Ajax sees as the operative principle in his universe, and he is accordingly dismayed and perplexed, resisting the insecurity, the injustice, in cosmic ordinance.

What is most deeply troubling to Ajax is that he recognizes this mutability not only as a principle external to man but also as a law of human nature, ruling even himself. If he admits to a not unattractive instance of inconstancy in his firm temperament's being softened by Tekmessa's appeal to him (650–653), he also touches upon a thoroughly disquieting illustration of impermanence with respect to human loyalties.

ἐπίσταμαι γὰρ ἀρτίως ὅτι
ὅ τ' ἐχθρὸς ἡμῖν ἐς τοσόνδ' ἐχθαρτέος,
ὡς καὶ φιλήσων αὖθις, ἔς τε τὸν φίλον
τοσαῦθ' ὑπουργῶν ὠφελεῖν βουλήσομαι,
ὡς αἰὲν οὐ μενοῦντα.

Sophocles *Ajax* 678–682

for I have lately learned that
an enemy is to be hated by us only so much,
because he too will hereafter become a *philos*, while to the *philos*
I shall resolve to offer only so much help,
because he will not always remain [a *philos*].

Friendship is ephemeral, transitory. Certainly Ajax has in mind the disloyal actions of the other Greeks toward him, yet in himself he represents that very relativity of commitment he bemoans. *Both* he and the Atreidai have proven unstable in their alliances. What once was the straightforward ideal of helping friends and hurting enemies becomes self-contradictory when friend turns to act as enemy.[41] Ajax has been inconsistent in his own actions. His integrity has been challenged, for he has changed, changed from his commitment to *aidōs* and, as a result, altered also in the certainty of his actions: no longer loyal, he is no longer effective in sustained execution of the well-chosen strategy, but instead engages in actions with *duslogiston . . . khera* "an unwitting hand of violence" (40) and *phrenes diastrophoi* "disordered wits" (447). Aware of his subjection to time conceived as an agent of unavoidable vicissitude, he takes the one recourse that can put him beyond time, beyond the instability of human existence in time: he kills himself.[42] In this way

41. Knox 1961.3–10, 14–18 offers a thorough analysis of this traditional maxim of heroic ethos (*tous men philous eu poiein, tous d' ekhthrous kakōs*) and of the perplexity that confronts Ajax when the maxim can no longer apply to his life. Simpson 1969.89–92 explores how the contradiction Ajax apprehends is related to his *nosos* or mental derangement.

42. Simpson 1969.96–99 offers a much needed clarification of the rationale behind Ajax's decision to take his life. Other commenters have been disturbed that Ajax resolves upon suicide even though he has noted and seemingly reconciled himself to mutability in the world: (ἡμεῖς δὲ πῶς οὐ γνωσόμεσθα σωφρονεῖν; / ἔγωγ' "and should not we likewise learn to be wise? / I shall learn" (677–678). Simpson emphasizes that it is not a cyclic or heuristically dialectic mutability that Ajax perceives, but rather one in which absolutes give way to absolutes. Yielding does not mean, to Ajax, "continuing to live in the world with a flexible and quiescent attitude." Simpson points out that "Ajax . . . likens himself to these phenomena which . . ." rather than "alter their nature and coexist with their successors . . . *disappear* and *cease to exist*." Brown 1951.22–23 touches upon but neglects to develop an interpretation similar to Simpson's.

alone he can restore his absolutism and unconditioned character, reasserting his integrity even as he countermands the possibility of its ever again being violated.

Without doubt, his final actions, terrible, irrevocable, make Ajax, from the modern perspective, an existential hero for his refusal to endure life on any terms other than those he himself finds acceptable. How a fifth-century audience in Athens would have responded to this resolute intransigence is less easily ascertained. Clearsighted recognition of the limitations of human existence paradoxically combined with a refusal to accept such limitations as just or as personally valid: this is a pattern that Athenians saw and, in some way, approved in the Sophoclean Philoktetes, Deianeira, and Oedipus, particularly the Oedipus of *Oedipus at Colonus*. Refusal to act as a human, a mortal, was bound up with seemingly inevitable destruction, yet also essentially linked to such assertiveness was a recognition of the transcendent nature of the individual. The audience of the *Ajax* might well have responded as would a contemporary audience to Ajax's unflinching determination to assume control of his own destiny. For those Athenians, however, other considerations might also have been in order; if the *Oedipus at Colonus* presented citizens of 401 with a most positive image of a polis governed by a wise and generous Theseus and protected by an apotheosized Oedipus, the *Ajax* offered to citizens of the 440s a more problematic image of their polis. The figure of Ajax could, as I have noted, underscore the heroic nature of the Athenian past; he could also, though, reflect back to Athens questions about current issues and troubles.

In the period after mid-fifth century, Athens was engaged in ongoing ideological turmoil, striving to achieve clear self-definition and—what was much the same thing—a serviceable conception of its proper relationship to other city-states, especially those nominally joined with it in the Delian League. Founded initially to meet Persian aggression and consistently led by an Athens more powerful than other members, this defensive alliance had lost most of its reason for existing in or about 449 when a pact with Persia—or a less formal mutual cessation of hostilities—had effectively ended the threat of invasion from the East. Even before that time, there had been attempts by various poleis to secede from the confederation by refusing to supply their required quotas of arms or taxes; Athens had dealt firmly, severely, with such recalcitrance, insistent upon holding together an alliance essential to countering a formidable and still active enemy (Thucydides 1.97–99). As the Persian threat became increasingly remote, however, what had been seen as justifiable actions of maintaining disciplined commitment to a common goal assumed the nature of blatantly imperialist maneuvers of aggrandizing a strong central power at the expense of smaller, outlying groups. Athens was determined to sustain the league, increasing the number of league members who fulfilled obligations by paying tribute rather than supplying men and ships; in this fashion Athens could ensure its own strategic power relative to that of its allies (Thucydides 1.19, 99). Meanwhile, possibilities for a land empire, which had seemed promising as Athenians exerted expanding hegemony over those areas of north-central Greece which they had conquered in a series of related campaigns, were shattered when Athenian forces suffered a major defeat at Koroneia in 447; consequently, Athens turned even greater attention to solidifying control over those maritime poleis of the Aegean which indeed desired, or were convinced that they needed, protection within the Delian League. In 454, too, Athenians had actually arrogated control over the league treasury, moving it from Delos to Athens, and soon they began to use tribute money to finance construction of the Parthenon and other civic projects. As other city-states grew restive under increasing domination by Athens, citizens within the imperial democracy questioned the morality and practical wisdom of positions the polis had assumed.

Plutarch provides commentary that historians have drawn upon for their knowledge of what transpired between the Persian and Peloponnesian wars, and though the accuracy of his accounts is often blurred by his distance from the events and by his polemical purposes, there is a general consensus that his appraisal of the tensions in Periclean Athens is valid. Plutarch (*Pericles* 12) recounts a resistance to imperial expansion and a particular opposition to the use of Delian League funds for public projects. Thucydides, son of Melesias, the leader of the group opposed to the new imperialism, came to prolonged and sharp controversy with Pericles during 444; the points of contention were simple—Athens was accused of betraying faith and acting hubristically as an oppressor of former allies rather than as their defender, while the concern to build and adorn the Parthenon was assessed as a vain obsession for externals which made Athens appear no better than an extravagant woman. The upshot of this conflict was that Thucydides came, the following spring, to suffer under the process of *ostrakismos* 'banishment' and he went into exile.[43] Evidently most Athenians favored the developing role of their

43. See Bury et al. 1927.474.

polis against other Greek city-states, for Pericles' party carried the day. Nonetheless, that there was a pronounced opposition to growing Athenian ascendancy and a sympathy with the oppressed allies in 444 may be significant in assessing the topicality of the *Ajax* and the ways in which playwrights used myth.

Considered in conjunction with the crucial issues of the 440s, the *Ajax* may appear as pertinent to the ideology of the polis as Aeschylus' *Oresteia* had been in 458. The Aeschylean trilogy is clearly related to juridical reforms that made Athens the legal center for trying all homicide cases, indeed, all capital cases involving members of the confederacy (eventually the Athenian courts took jurisdiction over all disputes between league members). A deeper relevance of the trilogy to the polis consists in an enactment of myth that brings the political structure to the very brink of destruction and then refounds it.[44] Sophocles' play has a similar relation to the polis, for Ajax can be seen as the Athenian agonist, not only in that he embodies traditional values but also in that he confronts the problems of redefinition which the contemporary polis was addressing. Faced with situations wherein allies failed to give what citizens regarded as just recognition of longstanding Athenian protection, Athens turned to reduce such allies, warring against the very groups it was pledged to protect. Seeing themselves as betrayed, deserted, their own commitment abused by self-serving confederates unwilling to engage in reciprocal loyalties, Athenians reversed their relationship toward their partners in the league, and in so doing they came to question their own identity and purpose. Clearly, Ajax, like Athens, is distinguished by commitments broken to him and then by him. His outrage at not being honored for good services rendered to the other Greeks would have been well apprehended by an Athenian audience in 444, as would his decision to revenge himself. He had served as the "bulwark" or "wall of the Achaeans" against the Asian enemy, and his efforts had come to be unappreciated, almost contemned; Athens, whom Pindar had called the "bulwark of Greece" (F 63 Bowra),[45] had also assumed major responsibility for defending against the Asian threat and, like Ajax, could consider her efforts ignored, forgotten.

Of course, most notable in Ajax's career is the failure of his intended revenge and the clear indication that it is wrongheaded. In establishing

44. See Fagles and Stanford 1975.
45. This point is noted by Brown 1951.2, although he neglects to connect Pindar's phrase with the Homeric epithet for Ajax, perhaps because it would undermine his argument that Ajax represents the subjugated island of Aegina rather than Athens.

parallels between the polis and a hero traditionally associated with the polis, what might Sophocles have had in mind with respect to the hero's destruction? The question becomes more problematic, perhaps, when one recalls that Sophocles, in 443, served as treasurer for the Delian League, collecting for Athens the tribute of the confederated poleis.

I suggest that, by submitting the Ajax myth for consideration on the tragic stage, Sophocles set before Athens the challenge of ordering her present and her future in relation to her past. Certainly an understanding of the play should not be limited to such a particular interpretation of its intrapolitical significance. There is without question a universality of theme or mytheme which makes the *Ajax* important to modern as well as to classical times. Here there is the story of what happens all the time as though it happened once upon a time, or, to employ a more traditional definition of myth, ταῦτα δ' ἐγένετο μὲν οὐδέποτε, ἔστι δ' ἀεὶ "while these things never happened, they always are" (Sallustius *Of the Gods* 4.9). Notwithstanding this transtemporal aspect of the myth and of the play, though, it is instructive to remark the dimension of this fifth-century drama which is very much of that time, of that place. Ajax was *the* Athenian hero from the epic tradition. In adapting the heroic-age myth to the concerns of the polis, however, Sophocles avoids the extremes of simplistic chauvinism and of satire. The figure associated with Athens he presents as noble yet mistaken, an exemplar of virtue yet one whose loss of virtue leads to his destruction. There is, then, the possibility of viewing the play as a tract advocating that Athens, unlike Ajax, should not forsake the traditional protective loyalty to allies that has comprised her distinctive *aretē* 'excellence'.

Such a thinly allegorical understanding of the drama does not, however, seem to do full justice to its complexity and depth; although it is obvious that Ajax ought not have attempted to prosecute his revenge, it is also clear that some among the Greek leaders (Menelaos and Agamemnon) are so ignoble and obsessively self-interested as to warrant Ajax's enmity. Indeed, as Sophocles has developed the story, it is impossible for Ajax to act without in some way contradicting his own virtue: he may neither ignore the spurning of his faithful commitment and service to the other Greeks nor, properly, exact vengeance for their failure to respond to him with appropriate gratitude and recognition. His position, like that of Athens with her allies, could admit of no straightforward resolution of difficulties, for Ajax, like Athens, has been confronted with a world characterized by a transvaluation of values. How greatly Ajax or Athens contributed to such transvaluation may be issues subject to disagreement, yet the circumstances in which both hero and city-state had to operate were ones in which confusion concerning normative virtues was a critical precondition inhibiting simple, virtuous action.

Thucydides was to describe the actual fifth-century malaise in writing about the Corcyraean revolt, which transpired less than twenty years after the *Ajax* was staged, and he notes that the deteriorating moral situation in Corcyra soon became typical of circumstances throughout Hellenic civilization. What he relates is a sordid tale of a society wherein conceptions of virtue were arbitrarily changed and indeed completely inverted to accord with individuals' self-interested desires (3.82.1–4).[46] The motivating principle behind such sophistical undermining of absolutes Thucydides records as *to phthonein* 'the malicious envying of others' (3.84.2–3). The similarity of the state of affairs described by Thucydides to the world of the *Ajax* is striking. Not simply is envy apparent in all four of the major Iliadic figures in the drama, as well as a subject for choral comment (148–161), but more—the confusion with which Ajax must contend and to which he contributes is generated by an inversion of the most fundamental of valuations, that involving friends and enemies and how one should act toward them. The *Ajax*, in a sense, predicts the *anomia* that was to ensue upon that ongoing dissolution of loyalties within the Delian League which was bound up with the erosion of traditional virtues.

What Sophocles has done, then, in the drama, is to define a problem that his Athens proved unable to solve. The Ajax myth Sophocles selects and adapts so that it serves, in part, as a reflection of historical conditions pertinent to the interests of the contemporary polis. Ajax represents the *aretē* that had ensured the heroic nature of the Athenian past and guaranteed the success of the polis. His problem is, somehow, to keep that virtue operative in a world indifferent, even hostile, to the maintaining of such honor; and this is the very challenge set before the polis by the dramatist. The tragedy of the Athenian hero is that, almost against his will, he betrays the very ideals that were his greatness; such betrayal was also the tragedy of Athens itself.

46. See Edmunds 1975 for lucid analysis of that inversion of values criticized by Thucydides, and also for comment concerning the relationship of Thucydides' ethics to earlier tradition.

CHAPTER 7

The Polis in Crisis

Dora C. Pozzi

Hamilton suggests in Chapter 5 that the figure of Antigone, in the play of Sophocles named after her, personifies *dikē* and dramatizes the foundational role of *genos* in the polis; in Chapter 6 Bradshaw proposes that the Sophoclean *Ajax* recaptures the genuine Homeric *aretē* of its hero, tragically alien to the world of the new imperial polis. In this chapter I ask once again, more generally, how Greek drama conveyed its messages and explore some of the functions of this new enactment of myth ocurring in Athens in the second half of the fifth century.[1]

Myth, Drama, and the Polis: Tragedy

The theater of Dionysos furnished Athens with a medium that reached massive audiences of its own citizens as well as foreigners. Performances that might have evolved into full-fledged theatrical phenomena had existed in other parts of the Greek world; yet Athens was the only city that successfully set up a festival with pan-Hellenic audience and unchallenged authority.[2] Dramatic festivals were *agōnes* 'con-

1. With this volume already submitted to the press when Gregory Nagy's *Pindar's Homer: The Lyric Possession of an Epic Past* (1990b) was published, I could not do justice to all the provocative ideas that book offers concerning the Athenian state theater. I was able, however, to add a few footnotes with reference to Nagy's arguments.

2. Choral songs in honor of Dionysos, known as dithyrambs, had certainly been performed elsewhere, perhaps since a very early date. Herodotus 1.23 tells how Arion, arriving in Corinth after a mythical journey, performed the dithyramb there (according to the Suda *s.v.*, Arion invented tragedy). Kleisthenes of Sikyon is said to have "returned" to Dionysos the tragic choruses performed earlier in honor of Adrastos (Herodotus 5.67.5). Thespis is credited with having brought to Athens his troupe from Ikaria or Sikyon (Themistius *Orations* 27.337b and Suda *s.v.* Thespis). Thespis is possibly a generic name: *Odyssey* i 328; viii 498; xvii 385 (see *DELG s.v.* θεσπέσιος and θέσπις 1968.I.432). An early plurality of dramatic traditions is suggested also by Aristotle's references (*Poetics* 1448a28–b3) to the claim of the Dorians and "others in the Peloponnesos" to have originated tragedy, and to

tests' in which the playwrights competed for prizes; in turn, the plays enacted oppositions, conflicts often unsurmountable between characters, their ideas, and their values. To deploy those oppositions, fifth-century drama imitated the dialectic form of debate exercised in the forum of the polis at large, which at the same time was being developed and refined by the sophists. But the theater of Dionysos came to be the scene of another, less visible but continuous and important form of *agōn*: the confrontation of different clusters of allegiances, values, and traditions. Athens was the locale and the ideological center of fifth-century theater. We must remember that the speeches and the lyrics conveying such oppositions were contrived by Athenian poets; that a state official chose the plays to which a chorus would be granted, that is, which would be produced; and finally, that a committee of Athenian citizens evaluated the performances and adjudicated prizes. Fifth-century Athenian theater was *the theater of Greece*, in the city that, to believe Thucydides, Pericles called "the school of Greece" (Thucydides 2.41.1–2).

The space that the theater of Dionysos occupied lay on the southern slope of the Acropolis, at a higher level than the grounds of incessant civic activity in the *agora* 'place of assembly' but lower than the temples devoted to the worship of the gods that crowned the city on the Acropolis. The spatial symbolism is instructive, for the theater was a locus of encounter and mediation between the two.[3] There the polis enacted both its own constitutive myths and those that represented threats to its lasting stability and its power. Tragedy negotiated the oppositions by enacting myth in a forum of the polis and as part of a public solemn ceremony. As they gathered in the theater to participate in the festival, the *politai* 'citizens' were at the same time reaffirming their sense of communality and national identity.[4]

To appreciate fully the role of drama in the fifth-century polis we must consider its roots. I use the plural "roots" intentionally, to skirt the vexed question of the "origin of tragedy." I am referring to the diverse performative traditions and to the cultic and mythic nonliterate traditions that, mingling, converged in the phenomenon we know as the

---

the beginnings of comedy in Megara and Sicily.

3. On the tensions and ambiguities latent in the dramatic enactment and its function as an institution of the polis, see Vernant and Vidal-Naquet 1988.23–48.

4. The terms "national" and "nationalistic" are extended here to apply to the Greek *poleis* insofar as they were, despite their size, politically autonomous and thus equivalent to modern nations. They interacted with one another in a way that one would describe today as "international."

Greek theater of the fifth century. The long-established classification of
literary genres should be applied with caution to the multiple forms and
functions of song—usually associated with dance—and poetry that
existed in Archaic and Classical Greece.[5] In the course of their development, song and poetry entertained various relationships with myth and
ritual, but they are likely to have been related always to at least one or
the other. And as we see below, performative traditions, especially
choral ones, had sociopolitical implications of paramount importance.
With such qualifications, then, let us turn our attention to some examples of performative predramatic or early dramatic traditions. Greek
poetry existed in performance, as "song," long before it took the form in
which we know it today, that of a text, that is, "poetry."[6] When the epic
lays were crystallized in the monumental poems that we possess, the *Iliad*
and the *Odyssey*, the text thus constituted served as a pan-Hellenic canon
that continued to be performed.[7] Lyric, both choral and monodic, was
performative as well. Some of these performances probably involved
dramatizations.[8]

It is worth noting that among the earliest mentions of performative
poetry other than epic there is evidence of the connections those songs
had with religious and ceremonial occasions. In addition to the dithyrambs, or songs in honor of Dionysos (Archilochus F 77D.117 T) there
were paeans, or hymns sung to Apollo (*Hymn to Apollo* 514–519 and *Iliad*
I 472–474), *humenaia* 'wedding-songs' (*Iliad* XVIII 491–495 and *Shield of
Herakles* 273–285), and *thrēnoi* 'dirges' (*Iliad* XXIV 720–722); the "Linos

5. See Harvey 1955, Rossi 1971, and Calame 1977.22–27. For a new model that accounts
for the emergence of the modes denoted by traditional genres and subgenres from an
early fundamental contrast between singing and speaking, see Nagy 1989.1–77, esp. 39–46,
and 1990b.1–115.

6. I use the terms "song" and "poetry" in the sense proposed by Nagy 1989.4–8 and
1990b, chap. 1. For Nagy, "song" is a suitable designation for the choral performances
associated with special occasions of ritual and myth; it is distinguished from ordinary
speech by its wide variety of patterns. Early Greek lyric song (= song in a narrower sense),
nonlyric poetry, and prose emerged from one another in this order by a process of gradual
differentiation. "Poetry" is marked by being restricted to recitation in a limited number of
metrical patterns (dactylic hexameter, elegiac distich, and iambic trimeter).

7. For the poetics of the process of pan-Hellenization leading to a "Homeric" canon of
epic poetry, see Nagy 1979, esp. chaps. 9–10, and Nagy 1989. Nagy 1990b investigates
(beyond its title, *Pindar's Homer: The Lyric Possession of an Epic Past*) not only "the epic
past" of lyric but also the "lyric" remote precursors of epic.

8. Herington 1985 surveys the artistic environment within which Attic tragedy as we
know it arose. He emphasizes "the long-obscured fact that Greece was essentially a song
culture well into the fifth century B.C." For a detailed discussion of the available evidence
concerning the performance of pre-tragic Greek poetry, see esp. chaps. 1 and 2.

song" in the description of the shield of Achilles (*Iliad* XVIII 561–572) is a harvest song. Tyrants, who had a stake in promoting the worship of Dionysos, were prone to instituting dithyrambs.[9]

Yet dithyrambs were at times devoted to other gods, such as Apollo.[10] These early processional dithyrambs evolved into a literary genre—one of the few lyric genres recognized as such by the end of the sixth century B.C. When Herodotus (1.23) says that, under the tyrant Periander, Arion "composed, named and taught a dithyramb in Corinth" (see note 1), he marks not the invention but the transformation of the dithyramb into a public spectacle held during the festivities of Dionysos.[11] Whenever and wherever that happened, through the agency of a poet whose mythic model may have been Arion, the dithyramb was, as I argue for the choruses of tragedy in fifth-century Athens, partially desacralized. These public choruses became eventually the heirs of almost all other choral forms.[12]

Lyric fragments dated as early as the seventh century B.C. attest to the multiple functions of choral performances, not only ritual but also sociopolitical and pedagogical. Claude Calame, studying the fragments of Alcman known as his *Partheneia*, concludes that the *partheneion* 'maidens' song' did not exist as a distinct lyric genre in the Archaic period. Songs performed by female choruses, most commonly of young girls, were composed for a variety of occasions, and the "morphology" of the performance varied accordingly. Those occasions, normally associated with a goddess (but also with Dionysos), were of the sort known since van Gennep's work as "rites of passage." Calame's review of a large number of such choruses of female adolescents shows that, although they offered a ritual frame for divine intervention in human life, from a sociological viewpoint they were the counterpart of male adolescent initiation groups.[13] The earliest form of tragedy may have had similar functions. John Winkler, on the basis of an impressively arrayed corpus of

9. Privitera (1977.29) notes that the cult of Dionysos found favor with tyrants because it was shared by the whole community and did not pertain to groups such as the ancient aristocratic families, not simply because it was "popular," as is often assumed. The Dionysiac religion and other equally communal cults were suited to the role of sociopolitical mediation that the tyrants undertook. Privitera mentions as an example Peisistratos, who founded civic institutions in Athens: the theater and also the important Panathenaic celebration in honor of Athena. See also Privitera 1970.36–42.

10. See Pickard-Cambridge 1968.3–4.

11. Privitera 1977.

12. Ibid.

13. Calame 1977.I, esp. pp. 15–47, 361–455.

evidence concerning the festival, the audience, the texts, and pictorial representations of tragic performances, proposes the theory that these were "by, for, and about ephebes."[14] *Ephēboi* (male adolescents), who reenacted the advent of Dionysos in the opening ceremonies of the festival, were seated, Winkler conjectures, in the central wedge of the auditorium, in a configuration that cut across the ten rows seating members of the ten *phulai*.[15] Therefore their group represented the ephebic class of the entire polis. When tragic, dithyrambic, and comic contests were formalized in Athens as parts of the dramatic festival, the word *tragōidoi*, according to Winkler, referred to the ephebes who continued in the tragic choruses the tradition of dances performed in rank and file in rectangular formation. Such features of the performance suggest to Winkler that "the audience's experience of tragedy was built on a profoundly political core, and that Athens' youngest citizen-soldiers occupied a central (though in various ways masked) role in this festival of self-representation."[16]

In the surviving plays, and in the summaries of lost plays, motifs related to initiation are prominent.[17] The dramatic personality of tragic choruses, representing groups of male or female adolescents, old men, or foreigners, that is, groups that were marginal with respect to the Athenian sociopolitical structure, is compatible with Winkler's statements.[18] The texts of Greek tragedy bear out his conclusions. The experience of the theater in fifth-century Athens was one of initiation and learning (of this Euripides' *Ion*, discussed below, offers an example). I would add to Winkler's remarks that the tragic choruses impersonated the polis in two ways, as a group of those to be initiated and as the voice of those who would accept them in their midst, as those who must learn and those who embodied the principles to be learned. The tragic chorus is able to shed its dramatic character and become a choral voice representing the wisdom of tradition, the cogency of the laws, the precepts of religion—in sum, the codes of value that lie at the heart of the polis. The chorus and the tragic performance inherited such authority from the religious experiences in connection with which, as we have seen above, song and dance originated. Even though tragedy expanded

14. Winkler 1985.49. For the concept of ephebe, see Vidal-Naquet 1981 and 1986a.
15. For the difficulties in translating *phulē* as 'tribe' with reference to the divisions of the polis, see Nagy 1990a, chap. 12, esp. pp. 277–278.
16. Winkler 1990.62.
17. For allusions to ritual initiation in the texts of drama, see Seaford 1977–1978.
18. See Winkler 1985.32–38.

and diversified the referential scope of ritual drama (as it adopted the multiforms of myth for its enactment), tragedy never dissociated itself totally from the religious experience. I began this chapter with a question concerning tragedy's messages. Let us now take a closer look at the religious foundations of tragedy, to see how the authority that enabled it to express such messages emerged.

In a famous passage, Aristotle connects the beginning of tragedy with the dithyramb.[19] Scholars of the "Cambridge school" posited the origin of tragedy in a ritual dance in honor of Dionysos as god of vegetation. In our time Walter Burkert and others recognize ritual as the fountainhead of tragedy. Burkert points to the ritual of sacrifice as "the most important ritual complex . . . which constitutes the realm of the sacred." Tragedy, he says, is "close to the ideology of sacrifice." Drama incorporated into its own vocabulary some words clearly related to the ritual of sacrifice. For instance, the Greek verb *draō* is most frequent in fifth-century tragedy with the meaning 'do, accomplish', especially in contrast to *paskhō* 'suffer'. But in other inscriptions and texts (see LSJ) it means 'offer a sacrifice' or 'perform mystical rites'.[20]

The vehicle of the sacrality of drama was the chorus. The choruses of fifth-century drama, notably those by Aeschylus and Sophocles, often articulate and reflect upon this religious significance. The following passage in Sophocles' *Oedipus the King* offers an example:

εἰ δέ τις ὑπέροπτα χερσὶν
    ἢ λόγῳ πορεύεται,
Δίκας ἀφόβητος οὐδὲ
    δαιμόνων ἕδη σέβων,
κακά νιν ἕλοιτο μοῖρα,
    δυσπότμου χάριν χλιδᾶς,
εἰ μὴ τὸ κέρδος κερδανεῖ δικαίως
καὶ τῶν ἀσέπτων ἔρξεται
ἢ τῶν ἀθίκτων θίξεται †ματάιζων†,
τίς ἔτι ποτ' ἐν τοῖσδ' ἀνὴρ †θυμῷ† βέλη
ἔρξεται ψυχᾶς ἀμύνειν;

19. γενομένη δ' οὖν ἀπ' ἀρχῆς αὐτοσχεδιαστικῆς—καὶ αὐτὴ καὶ ἡ κωμῳδία, καὶ ἡ μὲν ἀπὸ τῶν ἐξαρχόντων τὸν διθύραμβον "[Tragedy] originated, even as comedy, from improvisations . . . from the leaders of the dithyramb" (*Poetics* 1449a9).

20. Burkert 1966a; see also Seaford 1981 and Nagy 1990b.387–388. For an exploration of the metaphor of sacrifice in Euripidean drama, see Foley 1985. The metaphor of ritual sacrifice is present in other forms of early Greek poetry, such as the victory odes of Pindar; see Svenbro 1984.218 and Freiert in Chap. 2.

εἰ γὰρ αἱ τοιαίδε πράξεις τίμιαι,
τί δεῖ με χορεύειν;

Oedipus the King 883–895[21]

If a man goes haughtily
    in deed or word,
with no fear of *Dikē* and no reverence
    for the shrines of the gods,
may an evil doom take him,
    as the gift his luckless pride has earned him;
if he reaps unfair gain
    and does not refrain from impious actions,
if he lays wanton hands on things untouchable!
What man, having done that, will ward off the arrows of the gods
from his *psukhē* 'life'?
If such actions are held in honor,
why should I join the sacred dance?[22]

The odes that framed and punctuated the moments of the tragic enactment continued the traditions of religious choral performances. Thus the tragic chorus inherited a privileged voice, felt to open a channel of solemn communication with the deities.

    Yet, as we have seen, dithyrambs and other religious choruses were forms of public, collective ritual instituted by the poleis. And for that reason a natural separation from the purely religious sphere took place gradually, and diverse modes of experience associated with ritual song and dance acquired growing emphasis and autonomy. The sacrality of the origin was diminished in the diverse forms the choral performances adopted and adapted to various communal purposes. Initiation may have been one of the earliest functions underlying the institution of dramatic performances. The fifth-century theater, in turn, represents the conclusion of a long process of political appropriation of religious choruses. In the form the dramatic enactment eventually took, ritual was desacralized. I submit that this desacralization, however, was limited. The performance of tragedy retained some of the authority and the solemnity of its sacral origin.

    21. This text is cited as in Dawe 1984.
    22. This poignant question expresses also ethical and political concerns, intimately connected to religion—a link of which drama serves as the best witness.

Paradoxically, it was the reference to an objectively enacted plot, that is, to myth, that drew the tragic enactment away from the sphere of the sacred. For while ritual per se is relatively stable and may change its signified without altering the signifier (consider the many diverse applications of the ritual act of prayer, or that of sacrifice),[23] the *mimēsis* 'imitation' of divine, heroic, and human actions that the spectators watched in the theater was "open," it enacted pluralistic mythic traditions, reshaping them in novel ways. It related to the spectators as individuals under the burden of a common human fate and as representatives of their society, the polis. That men from other poleis were present only made the message more cogent for all.

It is the reference to a plot that gives unique projections to the tragic play. In drama the plot drawn from the lore of myth becomes symbolic as the chorus, referring to a singular chain of events and singular heroic characters as paradigms, interprets them while impersonating a plurality, be it a social group, an age group, or a fictional community; at the same time, the chorus draws to itself the spectators, and it represents them as members of the audience, the polis, or humankind. Its authority comes from the poet chosen by the polis to "teach a chorus"; that is, the poet authorizes the choral statements before performance; then he yields to the chorus' collective voice.[24] The chorus may invoke, pray, thank the gods, lament, rejoice, or even threaten— all the while evoking myth. It addresses the deities, but men as well; it is impersonal but profound and solemn, since it is formalized by song and dance. In the dramatic performance the reflections inherited from the proverbial tradition confer upon the plot and the entire play the sense that its message is the vehicle of important values. The polis celebrates the festival as a rite in which the symbolic enactment of myth affirms communal values.

I mentioned earlier the ideological nature of fifth-century Athenian drama. It seems pertinent now to ask, how were Greek myths and ideologies related? In the famous ode that celebrates and also explores the limits of human resourcefulness, Sophocles mentions men's *astunomoi*

23. See Burkert 1985.54–55.

24. *Didaskein* 'teach' and other related words were used as technical terms related to the functions of the poet-producers of fifth-century plays and dithyrambs. A wider use for poet-producers of other kinds of choral lyric is suggested by the title of *didaskalos* given to Alcman in Sparta. See Herington 1985, esp. pp. 24–25. For the tradition of choral authority, its models in cult and myth, and the function of choral performance in the constitution of society, see Nagy 1990b, esp. chaps. 2 and 12.

orgai "impulses governing political life" (*Antigone* 354–356). Such impulses (both positive and negative) directed a constant process of reformulation and reencoding of myths. Simultaneous differentiation and syncretism diversified their referential scope, relaxing their earlier associations and often tying them with stronger bonds to new ones. As the communities where myths had emerged evolved, developing antagonistic fields of forces, myths appeared able to convey conflicting systems of values, or ideologies, with increasing intensity of definition. The mythic tradition was constantly reformulated as it was evoked to affirm new values in the increasingly complex society of each polis.[25] Myths were not, to be sure, the only ideological modes of discourse, for the scene of ideologies was the polis at large. Ideological *agōnes* 'contests' took place in the theater as well as in the *agora* 'place of assembly', in the courts of law, everywhere, in sum, where men gathered and acted "politically."[26]

Upon reaching the playwrights, myths were therefore endowed with multiple and often divergent sets of values. Greek drama, continuing in its own enactment the association of myth and ritual, reencoded myths and ideologies in its own structure, which collapsed text and action. The ideological discourse of Greek drama was inscribed in the setting of the theater, both a religious and a political institution. In the latter part of the fifth century, Athens put a vigorous ideological system to the service of the hegemony and the imperial expansion it was seeking unabashedly. The dramatists, however, availed themselves of the rich symbolic diction, the intertextual net that drama had in turn created as it evolved, and the plastic nature of the mythic narrative to critique and reevaluate the ideological tradition of Athenian myths.[27]

25. In Chap. 1 Wickersham describes some of the mechanics of this process in the Archaic and Classical Greek world.

26. The nature of ideologies is dual: on the one hand, they are inherent in sociopolitical frames; on the other, they belong to linguistic and discursive contexts. On myth and ideology, see Barthes 1972.116; on ideology and power, Foucault 1978, esp. I.97–98. On Athenian ideologies in Greek drama, see Loraux 1981 and Zeitlin 1986.

27. Segal 1983 defines the role of Greek myth as the "semiotic and structural system" of Greek tragedy.

Euripides' Ion

Euripides' *Ion* reformulates several mythic traditions in a novel manner and as a result this play conveys new, complex, and important ideological values. Overtly, *Ion* exalts Athens while integrating references to several myths and cults (Ion, son of Apollo and the Erekhtheid Kreousa, comes to Athens to be crowned king and thus continue the autochthonous race), but the subtext of the play undercuts and supplements its text by further integrating the myths of Apollo with references to Dionysiac myths and to rituals of the Dionysiac cult.[28] I argue that Ion's arrival in Athens represents a symbolic advent from Delphi not only of Apollo but at the same time of a civilizing, beneficent Dionysos, a god to inspire the city's mythic history the play retrospectively creates, just as he inspires the dramatic festival at which the play is performed.

The following myths are primarily relevant to the story of *Ion*:[29] the birth of Erikhthonios from the earth; the story of Xouthos, an ally of early Athens, and his son Ion;[30] Ion as the son of Apollo;[31] the myth of the four *phulai* 'tribes'.[32] *Ion* also relates to the Delphic and pan-Hellenic oracle of Apollo and to rituals of Athenian cult connecting Delphi and

28. Burnett 1970.4 mentions the similarity between the birth stories of Ion and Dionysos as a parallel that "sounds from within the plot . . . Delphi is his [Ion's] Nysa." But with the exception of Müller (1975) scholars have not recognized the important role that Dionysiac themes have in this play of Euripides. He discusses primarily the theological implications of the references to Dionysos and Iakkhos. See Zeitlin 1990.

29. For the equally important role of the Eleusinian myth and cult in this play, I refer the reader to Loraux 1981, esp. pp. 33–153 and 197–253, and to Zeitlin 1990.

30. Apollodorus (1.7.3 and 3.15.1) says that Xouthos married Kreousa; Xouthos is the father of Ion and Akhaios (1.7.3). Herodotus (7.94 and 8.44) refers to Xouthos as the father of Ion. According to Strabo 8.7.1 C383 and Pausanias 7.1.2, Xouthos, son of Hellen, married the daughter of Erekhtheus and had from her two sons, Akhaios and Ion.

31. Euripides is our earliest source for the genealogy of Ion as son of Apollo, which is mentioned later by Plato *Euthydemus* 302d and by Arrian *Anabasis of Alexander* 7.29. Again, outside this play there is no evidence of a connection of this myth with the cult of Apollo Patroos. See Owen 1939.xii–xiii and Walsh 1978.311, n. 45.

32. In Hesiod F 9 MW, Hellen is the father of Doros, Aiolos, and Xouthos, and Xouthos is the father of Ion. Achaea inhabited by Ionians appears in Pausanias 7.1.4 (Ion was king of Aigialos in Achaea and gave his name to its inhabitants, called Ionians), but in Strabo 8.7.1 C383 Athens sent a colony to Aigialos at the time of Ion. Ion, says Strabo, having conquered the Thracians, and having been made king of the Athenians, divided his people into four tribes. According to Herodotus 1.145, the Achaeans drove the Ionians from Achaea and they emigrated to Asia Minor. In Herodotus 5.66.2, Ion institutes *phulai* ("tribes"); Herodotus says the Athenians were called Ionians after their *stratarkhēs* 'army commander' Ion, son of Xouthos. See Nilsson 1951.65–68 and Nagy 1987b. For the mythical foundations of Greek society and *phulai* as divisions of the polis, see Nagy 1990a, chap. 12.

Athens such as the cult of Apollo Patroos[33] and the *Orgia* 'Secret Rites' of the Thyiades at Delphi in honor of Dionysos.[34] The Athenian festival known as Arrhephoria, where a basket plays a prominent part, is echoed in the abandonment at birth and in the final recognition of Ion.[35] Euripides combines the story of Erikhthonios with the story of Ion as the putative son of Xouthos whose real father is revealed to be Apollo. His version of the traditional genealogies concerning the four tribes is not found elsewhere. By making Apollo the father of Ion, Euripides substantiates aetiologically the cult of Apollo Patroos.

Ion enacts, in the symbolic mode of the theater, a new "foundation" of Athens by a hero who inherits the privileges of autochthony and also descends from a highly revered god whose pan-Hellenic prestige the Athenians therefore share.[36] From the point of view of the polis, Ion is "he who journeys,"[37] one who will arrive as a king. Just as in other tales of foundation (e.g., the myths of Kadmos or Apollo), the ultimate test consists in overcoming a chthonic threat, which (from Ion's point of view) appears to be embodied in Kreousa. Like other heroes, Ion has been exposed as an infant and saved; the polis first expels, then wel-

33. See Jacoby 1944.72–75, Nilsson 1957.34–35, and Burkert 1985.255–256.

34. Every two years women initiates of Dionysos, called *Thuiades* 'Women in a ritual hurry', went up to the high meadows above the Delphic shrine to celebrate Dionysos with torches. Women were sent by the Athenian state periodically to assist in these celebrations. See Henrichs 1978. For the view that the late testimonies available (Plutarch, Pausanias, and others) are not applicable to earlier Thyiadic associations and rituals, see Villanueva Puig 1986.

35. According to Pausanias 1.27.3, the Arrhephoroi were two young girls who, after a year of priestly service to Athena on the Acropolis, descended at night to a sacred precinct of Aphrodite in the Gardens with a basket containing a secret object, unknown to them as well, and came back up after substituting another equally secret object. The ritual evokes the myth of the daughters of Kekrops, the Aglaurids, who received from Athena the infant Erikhthonios in a covered basket. When, disobeying the prohibition of the goddess, they opened it, the view of the snake-child Erikhthonios terrified them and they hurled themselves from the north rock of the Acropolis. See also Aristophanes *Lysistrata* 641. The details and the location of the ritual are controversial. Robertson (1983.228) argues that this ceremony was not connected to Aphrodite or an initiation ritual but was rather "concerned with ... the taking of omens for the general safety and prosperity." Harrison 1890.xxvi–xxxvii is still useful; see also Burkert 1983.150–154; 1985.228–229, 264; 1966b; also Parke 1977.141–143.

36. Walsh 1978 points to the ironic treatment of the racial doctrine of Athenian autochthony, which is, he says, "consistently and subtly undermined" throughout *Ion*. On autochthony in *Ion,* see also Wolff 1965, Loraux 1979 and 1981, and Parker 1986. In an essay published after this chapter was written, Saxonhouse 1986 discusses the critique of autochthony implicit in *Ion.*

37. *Ion* 661 is a pun on the name *Iōn*, of obscure etymology (see *DELG* 1968.II 475 *s.v.* Ἴωνες), as if it were the participle of εἶμι 'come or go'.

comes the hero. On the other hand, the transit of Ion resembles an initiation, a rite of passage leading to recognition and adulthood. Ion's journey in search of his own identity is comparable to that of Theseus, and it also resembles, in some ways, the journey of Oedipus in Sophocles' *Oedipus the King*.[38] The recognition of Oedipus, however, culminates in the destruction and utter confusion of the family relationships and in his self-blinding and exile. By putting out his eyes, Oedipus cancels symbolically the excess of knowledge that he now has. Oedipus cannot live as son of Laios and Jocasta and at the same time as king of Thebes. Now that he knows his parentage, only the role of scapegoat befits him. Ion, on the contrary, learns without guilt; he finds and refounds his family. He goes from being *amētōr* 'without a mother' and *apatōr* 'without a father' (109) to the recognition of his mortal mother and the knowledge that he is not just the servant of Apollo but rather the son of the Olympian god.

Thus *Ion* appears as an ingenious and dramatically powerful synthesis of traditions. Even though doubt is cast at first on the truth of the oracle, it turns out to be fulfilled, and the drama, developing in leaps and bounds, reaches a satisfactory conclusion with the appearance of Athena "from the machine." The wicker basket collapses the birth stories of Erikhthonios and Ion.[39] The final scene glorifies both Athena and Apollo; mother and son are reunited; the new king will be the ancestor of a strong race. The rearrangement of traditional genealogies in *Ion* achieves the important purpose of putting Athens at the head of the Ionians (1575–1588). The play also connects Doros and Akhaios, eponymous ancestors of other Greek *phulai*, with the Athenian Ion (1589–1594).

All of that said, there are, however, passages in *Ion* that resist interpretation stubbornly. They contain puzzling clues leading to Dionysos and they invite us to connect Apollo and Dionysos; there is a strange association of the two gods in this play, as strange as was their actual alternance in cult at Delphi. Let us review some of these passages.

The description of the colonnade in the parodos (190–218) includes, as Zeus's helpers in the battle against the giants, not only Athena but also Dionysos wielding his "peaceful wands" (ἀπολέμοισι βάκτροισι,

38. See Whitman 1974.79.
39. For the parallel between the births of Erikhthonios and Ion, see Loraux 1981 and *Ion* 1427–1429.

216–218).[40] The benign aspects of Dionysos, as we see below, are evoked in *Ion*.

In the first stasimon Euripides mingles Apollonian and Dionysiac rituals, placing around the Delphic tripod the song and dance of the Thyiades on Parnassos:

> Φοιβήιος ἔνθα γᾶς
> μεσσόμφαλος ἑστία
> παρὰ χορευομένῳ τρίποδι
> μαντεύματα κραίνει . . .

Euripides Ion 461–464

where the hearth of Apollo at the central navel of the earth utters unfailing prophecies near the tripod surrounded by dancing . . .

The scene of the Thyiadic *Orgia* is also evoked by the chorus of Kreousa's attendants, who mention in the second stasimon "Parnassos . . . where Bakkhos . . . dances nimbly at night with the Bacchants" (714–717). (They are praying for the death of Xouthos' supposed son, for they believe he does not belong to the Athenian royal house.) Ion's birth and recognition are persistently associated with Dionysos. The place where Apollo took the girl (whose identity the maidens of the chorus do not know yet), and where she later abandoned the child born from the union, is said to be the cave of Pan rather than Apollo's cave (492–494).[41] There were two sacred caves on the north slope of the Acropolis; why did Apollo not draw Kreousa to his own cave? Again, the cave is Pan's ἄδυτα 'sacred precinct' at 938, with the obvious parallel of the Delphic ἄδυτον. The Arcadian Pan (worshiped in Attica) was a god in his own right, a deity of unbridled nature and an embodiment of the power of procreation, but at the same time a follower of Dionysos.[42] There are references to Pan in the plural, perhaps as member of a society similar to those of the satyrs and silens of Dionysos in whose resemblance he is portrayed. As a musician, Pan is antagonistic with respect to Apollo and his lyre. The satyr Marsyas is the traditional musi-

40. On this imaginary description, see Müller 1975.25–28. For Dionysos aiding the Olympians in the battle against the Giants (Γηγενεῖς 'Earth-engendered') in the Siphnian treasury at Delphi, see Vian 1952.206–207 and Segal 1982.153.

41. We should also note that at 1400 (see *Iphigenia in Tauris* 1125–1131) Kreousa makes the cave "Kekropid."

42. For the connection of Dionysos with Pan, see Lucian *Dialogues of the Gods* 22.3 and Ovid *Metamorphoses* 1.689–712, 11.153–171. See Burkert 1985.110, 173.

cal rival of Apollo, but so also is Pan, who invented and played the double pipe. Xouthos thinks he sired Ion when he lay with a Thyiad (545–554). Wishing to celebrate, belatedly, the birth of Ion, he goes toward "the double Dionysos rock where the πῦρ βακχεῖον 'Bacchic fire' leaps" (1125–1126). This is another reference to the Phaidriades, the two peaks on Parnassos traditionally known as "the peaks of Apollo and Dionysos," the Thyiadic landscape. Furthermore, the wicker basket of Erikhthonios / Ion in the recognition scene (1320–1444) may have reminded Euripides' audience also of some forms of the myth of the infant Dionysos lying in a winnowing-fan.[43] Dionysos' place of privilege and authority in an orderly cosmos is symbolized in the description (mentioned earlier) of the Gigantomachy in the parodos. In the third stasimon, rejecting the intrusion of a stranger in the Athenian royal house, the chorus (ironically) deplores the shame they would feel before "the god celebrated with many songs" (1074–1075).[44] They are alluding to Dionysos / Iakkhos, invoked in the Eleusinian mysteries of Demeter.[45]

The play alerts us to the presence of its message also with other signposts. Its overarching dramatic structure offers a symmetric frame[46] within which a striking number of duplications occur: mountains, caves, gods, temples, and even oracles appear in pairs. For example, the women of the chorus, contemplating the colonnade where the Gigantomachy they will soon describe is supposedly sculpted, marvel at the διδύμων προσώπων καλλιβλέφαρον φῶς "the beautiful-eyed light of double faces" (189). This expression has been explained variously: as two facades, east and west, of the temple; as two temples; as two statues; or (the most plausible realistic counterpart) as the two pillars on either side of the door of the classical temple. Doubling is not uncommon in the discourse of myth and it has in the theater a wide range of effects which cannot be discussed here; I merely suggest that the constant pairs in *Ion* may serve to point to the fundamental pair of antagonistic and complementary gods, Apollo and Dionysos.[47] The contrast between them comes

43. Even though the ritual of Dionysos Liknites ("Dionysos of the winnowing-fan") is attested only in Hellenistic times (Plutarch *Isis et Osiris* 35.365a; see Nilsson 1957.38–45), the myth may be ancient, as Henrichs 1978.153 points out.

44. See *Homeric Hymn to Dionysos* 26.7.

45. See Euripides *Bacchae* 723–726. Müller 1975.43 refers us to Sophocles *Antigone* 1146–1152, 1084 for similar representations of the starry sky (*aithēr*) in connection with the nocturnal Greater Eleusinian Mysteries.

46. Burnett 1970.16, 1971.101–129.

47. On doubling in Euripides' *Bacchae*, representing the duality of Dionysos, see Segal 1982.27–54; Detienne 1989.24–26 and n. 94.

through as the play develops a sharp critique of Apollo. I am not referring here to the vexed question, did Euripides "the atheist" intend to
discredit the god and the oracle? but to a poetic and dramatic questioning of the relationship of god to man.[48] Is Apollo cruel, swift to punish
but reluctant to come to the aid of mortals for whose plight he is responsible (Ion, Kreousa)? Does his oracle lie to men (Xouthos)? Just as in
Aeschylus' *Eumenides*, the end of *Ion* will prove the distant god to be caring and protective after all.

As the play begins, Ion is an eternal adolescent (like the god he
reveres), devoted to Apollo and to the service of his temple.[49] His passion for total purity drives him to ridiculous extremes (102–135). Ion's
harshness is shown later, when he threatens to have Kreousa thrown
from a cliff (1268) for having attempted to poison him. The Delphians
too are ruthless: they condemn her to be stoned to death by a considerable majority, "not by one vote" (1223)—an allusion perhaps to the vote
in Aeschylus *Eumenides* 735. The music of Apollo is related to cruelty
again and again. In the just mentioned monody by Ion it is with the
"songs of his bow," the twangs of Apollo's weapon, that he wants to kill
the birds that profane the altar (171–173). In turn, the parallel monody
by Kreousa at 859–922 is a song of blame, mixed however with some
lighter notes that suggest the ambiguity of the figure of Apollo. As has
been noted, the language and the symbols create the vision of a divine
rape.[50] In the prologue Hermes had said that Apollo took her "by force"
(βίᾳ, 11). She cried, "Mother!" just as Persephone when she was raped
by Hades. Even Delos, the island of Leto, says Kreousa, hates Apollo.
Musical vocabulary is appropriate to discuss this piece because it is a song
and because the metaphor of music serves in it as the main vehicle (the
other is color) to communicate Kreousa's vision of the male god, remote
and indifferent to woman's plight.[51] The tunes of Apollo's golden lyre
symbolize a harmonious but distant order, the Olympian transcendence

48. It would hardly be necessary to recall Verrall's 1895 ultrarationalistic view that Euripides defies logic in order to prove the absurdity of the traditional religion had it not been
revived recently by critics who argue against it, and who one hopes have laid it now
definitively to rest. See Michelini 1987, Yunis 1988, and Lefkowitz 1989, who reads
Verrall's views into current criticism.

49. See Burkert 1975. Compare Robert Segal's study in Chap. 4 of the figure of Adonis
as a *puer aeternus*.

50. See Loraux 1981.197–253; Burnett 1970.83–87 notes the representation of rape in
Kreousa's monody yet perceives in it also "covert praise."

51. The utterances of the Delphian Pythia were interpreted and set in hexameter form.
Song and prophecy are identified when the chorus asks τίν' ... ἔχρησας ὑμνῳδίαν "What
prophecy did you sing?" (681–682); see also 905–906.

that men are reminded to compare with their mortal condition by the two pillars at the entrance to the Delphic temple, inscribed "Know thyself" (γνῶθι σεαυτόν) and "Nothing in excess" (μηδὲν ἄγαν) (*SIG* 1268).

In contrast, dancing is often associated with Dionysos. At 499–500 the three Aglaurids (or the girls who acted out their myth) dance ὑπ' αἰόλας ἰαχᾶς ὕμνων "to the wavering tunes" of Pan's pipes.[52] And in the ode at 1048–1150 Dionysos is evoked by the chorus with images of song and dance on Parnassos. In the Bacchic dancing—be it of the mythic Maenads descending from the mountains into the city or of the Thyiades mimicking that descent and dramatizing the approach of the god—the distance between god and man is bridged. Dionysos, in his epiphanies, brings dancing into the spaces of men (see Sophocles *Antigone* 1140–1152).

The journey of Ion toward the double recognition, the revelation by Athena that Apollo is his father and Kreousa his mother (1553–1605), enacts his transit from adolescence to full adulthood, to kingship, and to the honors pertaining to a heroic founder. At its end he gains at once a father and a mother, a fatherland, and a kingdom. Autochthony is a dead end, for, as has been noted repeatedly, it cancels sexuality and makes the reproductive function of the female superfluous.[53] In *Ion* the mythic model of a single autochthon is supplemented by a familial paradigm, and sexual reproduction ensures the continuity of the founder's lineage. Kreousa exclaims at 1465, having recognized Ion as her son and the heir to the throne of Athens: ἀνηβᾷ δ' Ἐρεχθεύς "Erekhtheus grows young again!"

We must note that, while at first he lacks a father and a mother (109), Ion soon accepts the false paternity of Xouthos. The recognition of the father takes place in two stages, separated by a long dramatic time, leading from a false father (Xouthos) to a true father (Apollo). But a false mother (Pythia) mediates in the recognition of the true mother in a single scene that brings about the conclusion of the drama. So, throughout the play, Ion remains motherless and laments having been deprived of the bliss of maternal nourishment. The motifs of birth and nurture may be followed through the text of *Ion*. The Delphic temple and its priestess nourished Ion: τοὺς θρέψαντας Φοίβου ναούς "the

---

52. I have in mind here only the enactment of the myth of the daughters of Kekrops in the annual ceremony of the Arrhephoria (see n. 35). In connection with the enactment of myth in the dramatic performance, Nagy 1990b, chap. 12, offers a provocative theory on *mimēsis*.

53. See Loraux 1981.132–147 and Segal 1982.182 and n. 38.

temple of Apollo that nourished me" (318–319), τὸν βόσκοντα ... τοὺς βόσκοντας "he who fed me ... they who fed me" (137, 183). A mother's breast he has not known; the Pythia nurtured him instead. Ion yearns to see his natural mother: ὦ φίλη μῆτερ, πότ' ἄρα καὶ σὸν ὄψομαι δέμας; / νῦν ποθῶ σε μᾶλλον ἢ πρίν, ἥτις εἶ ποτ', εἰσιδεῖν "O dear mother, when shall I lay my eyes on your countenance, too? Whoever you are, now I long to see you even more than I did before" (563–565). Ion has been deprived of motherly embrace and nourishment:

> χρόνον γὰρ ὅν με χρῆν ἐν ἀγκάλαις
> μητρὸς τρυφῆσαι καί τι τερφθῆναι βίου,
> ἀπεστερήθην φιλτάτης μητρὸς τροφῆς.

Ion 1375–1377

For when I should have enjoyed in my mother's arms
the soft pleasure of my life,
I was deprived of my own dear mother's nurture.

Coming out of the mother's womb is symbolically represented both by the basket of the Erikhthonios myth and by the cave where Kreousa gave birth to Ion. And again, Ion's journey involves his "coming out" from the enclosed space of the sacred precinct of Apollo to the world outside, and it symbolizes also birth or rebirth.

To arrive at the double recognition Ion must overcome his excessive zeal for purity and his fear of woman. The image of the evil female, represented primarily by Kreousa, recurs in this play several times. She is the daughter of Kekrops, the snake-man, and she has received two drops of the earthborn Gorgon's blood; one is beneficial, the other poisonous (998–1015, 1054–1057).[54] When the recognition comes about, Kreousa takes the place of the longed-for absent mother, the nourishing mother. Only when the positive qualities of nourishment and shelter are transferred to her can Ion recognize her as his mother.[55]

54. Identities overlap and attributes are exchanged notably in this tale in which Perseus does not have a role: Athena decapitates the Gorgon, draws two drops of blood (one beneficial, the other poisonous), and gives them to Erikhthonios. He in turn hands them over to Erekhtheus, who entrusts the two drops to Kreousa. (In a more common form of this myth, the two drops are given to Asklepios; see Apollodorus 3.120.) In the beginning of the choral ode at Ion 1048–1105 an invocation of Persephone underscores Kreousa's possession of chthonic powers; that they were bestowed upon her through the mediation of Athena serves the purpose of ideological appropriation that is apparent in the myth.
55. At 1324 Ion addresses the Pythia thus: "I greet you, my own dear mother, even though you did not give me life." It is not the lack of a "clue" (328) that prevents Ion from

Then she can assure Ion that when she exposed him she did not do it without tears (1458–1459). She uses a birth metaphor, ἐκλοχεύω 'give birth', as if in abandoning him she had expelled him from the womb again (921). The movement is reversed now, when she draws him to herself in affectionate embrace.

Ion, then, comes to terms with father and mother, and so the realm of the female is dissociated from the chthonic threat, and god and mortal are reunited as the parents of the youth who is finally ready to assume his role as a man. All of this has been made possible, Euripides leads us to conclude, because Athens has allowed a "foreign intrusion" (ξενικὸς ἐσβολά, 722).[56] Xouthos is a foreigner, and he will ensure the continuity of the royal rule. Ion, thought to be one, is proven to descend from the autochthon Erikhthonios. But also, and most important, it is Dionysos, the foreign god, who has entered the city.[57] The god associated in this play of Euripides with Demeter and her rituals, represented as the leader of song and dance on Parnassos and as Zeus's helper in a cosmic victory over violent disorder, is clearly a benevolent deity, the "Athenian Dionysos" that Marcel Detienne describes as a "civilizing power."[58] That is one of the faces of the god shown in the magnificent total study of Dionysos that Euripides left us in his *Bacchae* (see, for example, 274–285, 381–385, 770–774). In that play Dionysos, being the son of Semele, is a god of dark and frightening subterranean powers; yet being also the son of Zeus, he mediates between the chthonic and the civilized worlds.[59] In *Ion*, however, the chthonic aspects of Dionysos do not come to the fore. Dionysos is linked with Erikhthonios, the beneficent autochthon; he is associated with the good powers of the earth and not with its destructive aspects. These are impersonated by Kreousa insofar as she

---

finding his real mother; it is his disposition that impedes it.

56. The theme of xenophobia is persistent in *Ion*: 673–675, 721–722, 1057–1060, and 1069–1073. It recurs too in other plays of Euripides: *Herakles, Medea, Heracleidae,* and *Suppliant Women.*

57. The mythic history of the religion of Dionysos constantly speaks of his cult or his effigy being brought into a community, and of the god entering the space of a city. Often these beginnings are preceded by the rejection of Dionysos by a group that is therefore severely punished and finally adopts his cult. See Detienne 1989.5. Well-known variants, in addition to Euripides *Bacchae*, are the persecution of the Maenads by Lycurgus (*Iliad* VI 130–140) and the rejection of Dionysos by the Proetids (Apollodorus 2.2.2) and by the Minyads (e.g., Antoninus Liberalis 10). For the story of the rejection of the god at Eleutherai (recorded in Hyginus *Fabulae* 225 and the scholia to Aristophanes *Acharnians* 243), see Nagy 1990b.397, on the "iambic" nature of early drama.

58. Detienne 1989.45–65.

59. See *Bacchae* 101, 698, 704–711, 766–768, 1019; see Segal 1981.125–126, 137.

is portrayed as an evil mother and identified, in Ion's perception, with the Gorgon with whose poison she threatens his life.

The girls who performed the Arrhephoria ritual went down with one secret thing in the basket, then came up again with another, equally secret; so Ion, who will go to Athens as the putative son of Xouthos but is really the son of Apollo, also represents Dionysos. The arrival of Ion in Athens, then, points to Dionysos' advent as much as to Apollo's. And the praise of Dionysos still resounds when, in the last scene, Apollo is justified and praised by Athena and Kreousa. Honoring Dionysos, as the chorus of *Bacchae* assures Teiresias (328–329), Athens will not slight Apollo. No other god was as fit as Dionysos to remedy the sexual impasse of autochthony, its inability to perpetuate the race.[60]

It is time now to ask, how do the explicit and implicit messages of *Ion* relate to the ideology of fifth-century Athens? The patriotic inspiration of this play's message is especially clear in the recognition scene. A garland made from leaves of the olive tree has not withered with time; neither has the wicker basket that contains the tokens (1432–1435). The olive tree, the mythically indestructible and self-restoring gift of Athena, is a symbol of the city (1479–1480).[61] In 1580–1594 there is a hint of imperialistic Athenian ambitions, yet the nationalistic zeal is tempered by the Dionysiac message. The Dionysos of *Ion* is a benign god, one who vanquishes his enemies with peaceful wands. A stranger, he should be admitted into the city, for his music is varied, not distant and monotone like the tunes of Apollo's golden lyre (see Euripides *Bacchae* 126–134, 155–165).[62] Whereas the stories of his arrival in other cities are tales of the doom suffered by those who resisted him, Athens seems to be priding itself in this play on its generous welcome of the foreign god.

Myth, Drama, and the Polis: Comedy

In the beginning of this chapter I referred to tragedy's roots in earlier performative traditions and to its new, unique conjunction of myth and ritual. Before turning now to Aristophanes' *Birds*, I address similar issues in reference to comedy. To judge from the extant plays of Aristo-

60. First the cave of Pan and the strains of his music (492–502) and then Dionysos as leader of the Parnassian Orgia (714–718) are invoked in choral odes where the central theme is a prayer for εὐπαιδία 'successful procreation'.

61. See Frazer's commentary on Pausanias 1.27.2.

62. See Segal 1982.23–26, and the examples he cites.

phanes that represent this genre, the performance of Greek Old Comedy pertained to the vaster phenomenon, by no means exclusively Greek but cross-cultural, syncretic, and remarkably enduring, that Mikhail Bakhtin and others call "carnival."[63] During carnivalistic festivals, rules and limitations valid in the everyday world are suspended. Oppositions based on sex and status are commonly inverted; often those normally subordinate establish a parody of normal hierarchy in exercising ritual authority over their superiors, as carnival creates a new manner of relationship between them in a middle ground between reality and fantasy. Such a world is eccentric and not governed by logic. It mingles the sacred and the profane, the high and the lowly, wisdom and folly. Bringing in a lore of experiences that includes performance and spectacle, carnival has been able to exert a powerful formal, genre-forming influence upon literature. Applying Bakhtin's language, I suggest that in the Greek tradition literature was "carnivalized" when Old Comedy arose from carnival as a formalized performance and assumed its function. Aristotle observes (*Poetics* 1449b2–4) that at the date from which the record of comic poets begins, Attic Comedy had already "certain definite forms" (σχήματά τινα). Old Comedy, as we know it, is a part of the dramatic festival in the theater of Dionysos, and it presupposes tragedy, as is shown by the abundant *paratragōidia* 'mock-tragedy' in Aristophanes' plays and the sophisticated critique of tragedy in the *Frogs*.

The spatial symbolism that helped us visualize the function of tragedy is again instructive. Comedy was brought from the periphery (the countryside) and from below (the marshes and the *agora* 'place of assembly') to the middle ground of the theater of Dionysos, to the center where the polis had established earlier a locus of mediation through tragedy.[64]

If, looking for the beginnings of comedy, we turn once more to Aristotle's *Poetics*, we find statements which, in the absence of his book on comedy, remain difficult and controversial. In a famous division of (dramatic) poetry into tragedy and comedy, he says:

διεσπάσθη δὲ κατὰ τὰ οἰκεῖα ἤθη ἡ ποίησις· οἱ μὲν γὰρ σεμνότεροι τὰς καλὰς ἐμιμοῦντο πράξεις καὶ τὰς τῶν τοιούτων, οἱ δὲ εὐτελέστεροι τὰς τῶν φαύλων,

63. See Bakhtin 1984.1–58 and Nagy 1990b.397–398.

64. See Aristophanes *Acharnians* 247–283. Nagy 1990b, chap. 12, see esp. 388–391, citing Pickard-Cambridge 1968.1–25, 51, and Seaford 1984.118, discuss the references to the Rural Dionysia as testimonies of an undifferentiated form of drama urbanized during the time of Peisistratos.

πρῶτον ψόγους ποιοῦντες, ὥσπερ ἕτεροι ὕμνους καὶ ἐγκώμια. τῶν μὲν οὖν πρὸ Ὁμήρου οὐδενὸς ἔχομεν εἰπεῖν τοιοῦτον ποίημα, εἰκὸς δὲ εἶναι πολλούς, ἀπὸ δὲ Ὁμήρου ἀρξαμένοις ἔστιν, οἷον ἐκείνου ὁ Μαργίτης καὶ τὰ τοιαῦτα. ἐν οἷς κατὰ τὸ ἁρμόττον καὶ τὸ ἰαμβεῖον ἦλθε μέτρον—διὸ καὶ ἰαμβεῖον καλεῖται νῦν, ὅτι ἐν τῷ μέτρῳ τούτῳ ἰάμβιζον ἀλλήλους.

Poetics 1448b24–32

Poetry now was divided into two kinds, according to the particular nature [of the poets]. For while the more serious poets imitated noble actions and the actions of noble men, the more ordinary ones imitated the actions of meaner men, at first composing invectives [*psogoi*] (just as those composed hymns to the gods and praises [*enkōmia*] of men). We cannot speak of any such poem earlier than Homer, but it is likely that there were many. From Homer onwards we have examples, such as his *Margites* and other similar ones. In these, as was appropriate, the iambic meter also was introduced, and for this reason even now it is called iambic, because they "lampooned" [*iambizon*] one another in iambic metre.

We should note that Aristotle associates comedy with the "iambic" tradition (1449b8), with a burlesque "Homeric" epic, *Margites*, which may have been precisely an example of *iambos*, and with the *kōmoi* 'revels, celebratory groups of singers-dancers' (see also 1449a11).[65] That the Dorians, according to Aristotle, argue against such etymology serves actually to attest to it.

Recent studies of both epic and non-epic texts confirm Aristotle's division of "mimetic" (that is, performative) poetry into two kinds, of praise (*ainos*) that confers glory (*kleos*), and of blame (*psogos*). Although it is possible to say that tragedy inherited primarily the first function and comedy the second, it would not be accurate to consider either of these functions exclusive of either form of drama.[66] Hamilton in Chapter 5 and Bradshaw in Chapter 6 showed how Sophocles' *Antigone* and *Ajax* set forth the *kleos* of their main heroic characters; I have argued in this chapter that Euripides' *Ion* enhances the *kleos* of a mythical Athenian king. Further on, I submit that the object of *psogos* in the *Birds* is the polis itself, its ills, and its immoderate desire for power.

65. For *iambos* as a ritual and a literary "genre" and for *Margites,* see Dover 1964.183–222, West 1974.22–39, and Nagy 1979.259–264. For the *kōmos,* see Pickard-Cambridge 1968.132–162, West 1974.3, and Nagy 1979.241–242 and 249–251.
66. For a review of traditional theories concerning the origin of comedy, see Sifakis 1971.15–22 and West 1974.35–36. Seaford 1984, and especially Nagy 1990b, chap. 12, resolve the issue of a separate "origin of comedy."

In the same passage in which he defines the origin of tragedy, Aristotle also points to a traditional Dionysiac origin of comic performances:

γενομένη δ᾽ οὖν ἀπ᾽ ἀρχῆς αὐτοσχεδιαστικῆς—καὶ αὐτὴ [sc. ἡ τραγῳδία] καὶ ἡ κωμῳδία, καὶ ἡ μὲν ἀπὸ τῶν ἐξαρχόντων τὸν διθύραμβον, ἡ δὲ ἀπὸ τῶν τὰ φαλλικὰ ἃ ἔτι καὶ νῦν ἐν πολλαῖς τῶν πόλεων διαμένει νομιζόμενα . . .

Poetics 1449a9–13

Both tragedy and comedy, having started, the former from the leaders of the dithyramb, the latter from those of the phallic processions which are still a custom in many cities . . .

In all likelihood, the phallic processions mentioned by Aristotle were in the nature of carnival. It seems quite fit for Dionysos, the god portrayed in myth as a great master of disguise, inversion, and festival, to be honored with performative rituals encompassing all of those elements.[67] But what was the process of development from these early rituals to the ripe tradition which, as Aristophanes represents it in the fifth century, presupposes that of tragedy, since it incorporates tragedy as part of the existing polis structure that it challenges? Paradoxically, comic performances are likely to have begun as early as tragedy or even earlier. It has been argued that satyric drama was introduced at the City Dionysia "in order to compensate for the loss of Dionysiac elements in the development of tragedy" (Chamaeleon F 38 Wehrli, *On Thespis*; Zenobius 5.40).[68] The paths of tradition are always hard to trace. Until more clarity is reached—if that ever happens— concerning early comedy, it is prudent to assume that in the form of Aristophanic comedy converge multiple and diverse popular, "carnivalistic" traditions. Skirting then once more the issue of an absolute origin of drama, I prefer to speak of the roots of comedy. Because the structure of Old Comedy has seemed to some scholars chaotic and inartistic, especially in that it broke the continuous unity assumed to be a primordial requisite of any drama, it has often been argued that Aristophanes juxtaposed traditions of several foreign origins. That is a gratuitous assumption.

The subject matter of Old Comedy includes public and private affairs, traditions and institutions, myth and cult, tragic characters and language, real and fictitious men and women, animals that are meta-

67. Many variants of these processions are attested; see Burkert 1985.103–105, 151, 290.
68. Nagy 1990b.384, citing Seaford 1984.10–16. See now also Halperin, Winkler, and Zeitlin 1990.

phors for men, and totally fantastic beings. The pace of these plays is quick, abounding in surprises. Nothing in them is stable, neither the language, nor the plot, nor the characters. Semantic shifting is, of course, at the core of the constant verbal equivocation. Unexpected turns of the dramatic action as well as changes of style and meter must have contributed to arouse a tension that was often released (though not completely resolved) in laughter. Aristophanic comedy was antagonistic. And the challenges that Old Comedy thrust at institutions, customs, men, and ideas, we must remember, were part of a practice entertained by the polis in the theater, on the occasion of an important festival in honor of Dionysos. Comedy twisted but did not break hierarchies and traditions, inverted but did not pervert family relationships and allegiances. Violent acts of varying intensity were represented on stage, but in those scenes violence was quickly transmuted into its opposites. The ceremonial aspects of the festival, the highly articulated structure of the plays themselves, provided a frame of containment for comedy's challenge.[69]

I argued earlier that there had been in tragedy a limited desacralization of ritual. How far along this process of desacralization should we place Old Comedy? Comic enactment appears further removed than tragedy from the sacred, and yet humor was present not only in cultic, or semicultic, early performances but also quite remarkably in myths allied with such rituals.[70] However, the strongest argument for a religious significance of Old Comedy is the presence of Dionysos. Aristophanic comedy was an overt celebration of the god that culminated in a theatrical manifestation of the Dionysiac temper. Dionysos was only occasionally a character in tragedy or comedy; the choral odes, however, mention and invoke him frequently. In the body of Greek drama that has been preserved, one tragedy of Euripides, *Bacchae*, a play that enacts a mythic origin of drama, and one comedy of Aristophanes, *Frogs*, not only have the god as a character but define the dramatic essence of Dionysos and of the theater.[71] Yet comedy seems to have found the formula and the proportion that might allow a polis to adopt and "naturalize" Dionysos.

69. It has been observed that comedy is a "solidarising medium." See Segal 1983, Versnel in Bremmer 1986.139, and Eco in Sebeok and Erickson 1984.1–9.

70. Examples abound. One need only think of the *Homeric Hymn to Hermes*, the Iambe episode in the *Hymn to Demeter* 192–204, and the consummate use of comic irony in Euripides' *Bacchae*.

71. For such an interpretation of *Bacchae*, see Seaford 1981, Segal 1982, and Foley 1985; for the *Frogs*, see Segal 1961.

Several of the preserved comedies of Aristophanes end in an explosion
of abundance and release, a quasi-epiphany of Dionysos. In true
Dionysiac spirit but within boundaries, comedy offered the polis the
truth of a distorting mirror.

Aristophanes' *Birds*

The *Birds* is an illuminating example of comedy's critique of the
polis. Among the preserved plays of Aristophanes, this one stands out in
two respects: its extensive use of myth (limited elsewhere mostly to allusions[72]) and the straightforward, linear qualities of its plot. Peisthetairos'
fantastic adventure, begun with Euelpides as a journey away from the
malaise of the city, becomes a quest after an utopian *Nephelokokkugia*
'Cuckoo City in the Clouds' that will force the gods to yield their power
to the birds, and it culminates triumphantly in the comic hero's
apotheosis.[73] Birds and their wings provide a sustained metaphor, to
which Hans-Joachim Newiger first called attention.[74] William Arrowsmith
explored this metaphor's multiple symbolic values. One is metaphysical:
it represents the insatiable desire for something impossible. Another is
political: it stands for the *pleonexia* 'greed' "that made the Athenian man
and the imperial city the new giants of a contemporary Gigantomachy."
And Arrowsmith argues, considering especially visual evidence, that
pteros Erōs 'winged Eros' and the birds serve as a "unifying pattern of
Dionysiac design," a symbol of the erect phallus. Cuckoo City in the
Clouds is thus the "objective bastion of what can only be called an erotic
politics of practical fantasy."[75] Following these clues, then, the critique of
Athens that sets the two men on a quest for non-Athens would actually
lead to the foundation of a replica of Athens in the sky, a city afflicted
with equal or graver ills but immensely powerful. The imperialistic

72. The other exception is, of course, the use of the myths and cult of Dionysos in the
Frogs.

73. The manuscript spelling "Peisthetairos" has been termed impossible (see Marzullo
1970). We would have to choose between *Pithetairos*, which suggests "One who obeys his
companions," and *Peisetairos*, suggesting "One who persuades his companions." Yet it is
proper to preserve and transliterate "Peisthetairos," since the comic hero traverses the
whole range of *peithein* 'persuading': he starts as the victim of persuasion (on a par with
Euelpides: πειθόμενον, ll. 5 and 7) and becomes a deft and successful persuader. Euelpides, in turn, is a man "of good hope," a (gullible) optimist. They represent complementary Athenian traits.

74. See Newiger 1957.

75. Arrowsmith 1973.130.

message (or its opposite, conveyed ironically) would be sealed—appropriately for a comedy—in the joy and celebration of the final scene.

Yet once again we see the subtext of a play belying its text. No doubt that the theme of power has a central role in this play; equally important, however, is another theme—an ideal representation of an idyllic paradise, a theme belonging to the poetic mode known as "pastoral."[76] Descriptions of a utopia, a blissful state remote in space or in time, or a lost garden of delights, wishfully imagined as present in the realm of nature, are common motifs of pastoral. I argue here that what merits to be called a pastoral or idyllic theme should be recognized in the *Birds*, and that it is developed over against the theme of power.[77] I suggest that the spectators whom the play addressed may have perceived its message in the dialectic of these two themes. The idyllic, or pastoral, ideal is conveyed in the play primarily by two motifs associated with the myth of Tereus and Prokne: the thicket where the metamorphosed couple spend a perpetual honeymoon and the song of the nightingale. I examine first these motifs, pointing out how the pastoral motifs are interwoven with the fantasy of power so that the final triumph of Peisthetairos affirms the idyllic utopia they represent, rather than the bellicose Cuckoo City of Peisthetairos' initial masterplan. Finally, I turn to the ambivalent function of the chorus.

In the tradition prior to Aristophanes the myth of Tereus and Prokne had been invested with various meanings.[78] A constant in the

76. See Halperin 1983.33–34, 75–84, and 249–257.

77. The term "pastoral" has been applied to Aristophanic comedy in general and to the *Birds* in particular. Whitman 1964.167, 176–178 calls attention to pastoral motifs in the serenade the hoopoe sings for the nightingale but reads the entire play as an intellectual and linguistic fantasy of "nothingness." Turato 1971–1972 points to what he calls the motif of a return to nature, associated with "a joyful liberation of *eros*," as an "Edenic dimension" in this play. In his view this motif is conveyed by the lyrics of both parabases, and it belongs to the world of the birds. Yet he recognizes in the birds "several dialectic levels." Moulton reclaims the term "pastoral" for Aristophanic comedy. He refers to the pastoral tendency in the *Peace* and in the *Birds*, believing, however, that "the pastoral fantasy is swiftly transformed into Peisethairos' ambiguous utopia" (Moulton 1981.101). Arrowsmith 1973 refers to "the nostalgic vision of a golden age, innocent and unaggressive φύσις, ἀπραγμο-σύνη and ἡσυχία," in the world of the birds that represent the Athenians. In his view they became estranged from that manner of life and those values when they were corrupted by λόγος and πειθώ 'persuasion'—incarnate in the person of Peisthetairos. It is impossible to cite the many passages in which Reckford 1987 develops his insights on the "pastoral world" in Aristophanes, but see esp. 331–333. Discussing the clash between two antithetical themes in the *Birds*, he uses Leo Marx's metaphor, "the disruption of the Garden by the Machine" (333).

78. For other sources of the myth, see Thompson 1936.95–100 and Pollard 1977. For a

multiforms is the transformation of Prokne into a nightingale, whose mourning song for Itys became in tragedy a symbol of eternal lamentation.[79] The comic style gives Aristophanes maximal latitude in handling mythical themes. He is not constrained to reiterate either the myth's large-scale symbolism or the reorganization of that symbolism in the tragic tradition that may be the target of his parody;[80] rather, he makes the myth a part of the play's total fantasy (the movement away from Athens toward an ideal place). As a function of this fantasy, the myth of Tereus and its associations are developed in new symbolic directions. In the *Birds* the myth of Tereus and Prokne is tightly compressed into a setting, the *lokhmē* 'thicket', where Tereus, as a speaking character, and Prokne, a silent one, dwell in a permanent metamorphosis.[81] As birds they enjoy a perpetual honeymoon made sweet by the abundance of natural food and by the music of the nightingale.

We must take a closer look at the abode of Tereus and Prokne, the first station in the two Athenians' journey. Being the scene of the blissful honeymoon of the two birds, the nest is rich in opportunities for sexual double entendre. Furthermore, the vocabulary connected with it has sexual symbolic connotations.[82] The foods of the thicket (and those the birds eat in the gardens) are symbolic of fertility and growth. At 159–160 the hoopoe lists, among the foods birds enjoy, *sēsama* 'sesame seeds' and *murta* 'myrtle berries' associated with Aphrodite, with fertility, and with the nuptial rites. Euelpides exclaims (161): "You live the life of a bridegroom." At 121–122 he describes the thicket in terms of a personal paradise, with features suggesting a maternal fantasy: "soft as a thick rug, to curl up in."[83] It is in the thicket too that is kept the magic

---

study of this myth and parallel stories ending also in bird-metamorphoses, see Fontenrose 1948. For a survey of the occurrences of the myth of Tereus in ancient literature, see Zaganiaris 1973.

79. See Hoffman 1976.72–78.

80. Probably the lost play of Sophocles, *Tereus* (*TGF* 523–528). Tereus was seen sometimes as the embodiment of *hubris*.

81. Prokne's role is essential, *pace* Newiger 1957.84 ("Die Nachtigall . . . gibt mehr nur Atmosphäre"). In the myth Tereus is transformed into a hoopoe, a stunning and unusual bird (*Upupa epops*) with bold cream-white bars over black wings, black tail, pink plumage, and an impressive black-tipped erectile crest. See Cramp 1985 IV.786–795 and Pollard 1977 *s. v.* Epops and Hoopoe).

82. For instance, the names of some plants that birds eat (such as *murton* 'myrtle', 82, and *sisumbrion* 'mint', 160) appear in comedy as obscene references to the female sexual organ. Similar associations are latent in words meaning "nest" (*neottia*), 642, and even in the words for "nightingale" (*aēdōn*) and "thicket" (*lokhmē*). See Taillardat 1965 *s. v.* and Henderson 1975.

83. See Manuel and Manuel 1972.

root that Peisthetairos and Euelpides eat to grow wings (654–655). The symbolic foods as well as the sweetness of the enduring honeymoon pertain to the pastoral mode. The thicket expresses it exemplarily: it is a nook of nature, a secluded place in which a paradigmatic couple enjoys perpetual bliss, a garden of delights abounding in foods that foster growth and fertility, a paradise.

The pastoral image of a recess includes in the *Birds*, paradoxically, that of the open world of nature. Tereus' command, as he is about to exit from his nest, ἄνοιγε τὴν ὕλην "open the woods" 92), points to this inside/outside polarity.[84] The place that Peisthetairos and Euelpides seek is defined both as the opposite of Athens (*topos apragmōn* 'trouble-free place', 44) and as a mirror of the thicket of Tereus and Prokne. At 110, Euelpides says that he and his companion are "antidicastic . . . a seed that can be found in the country." The fertility symbolized by the thicket will reappear in the fully formulated plan of empire (see below). Their description of the utopian city presents a topsy-turvy world, typical of this kind of fantasy.[85] The two men's journey away from Athens is a quest for an ideal locus that resembles the thicket.

Thus far in our analysis, the thicket has appeared as a member of the following polarities. When first found, it cancels the disorientation of the search; then, as we have seen, Aristophanes exploits the paradox of two visions of utopia (garden of delights and benign nature), antithetical and complementary. The thicket and the bucolic image of pure nature stand together and across from the image of the evil city, offering the "escape" component that is proper of pastoral.

The second motif (the song of the nightingale) enhances and diversifies the symbolism of the thicket. The actor representing the nightingale in the *Birds* never actually sings, but the bird's singing is first symbolized by the accompaniment of the double pipes, during the hoopoe's serenade that evokes her song at 209–222, then evoked again by the lyrics of the chorus at 676–684, and finally impersonated by the chorus singing in the first person in the lyrics of 737–751 and 769–784. Let us examine the first of these passages:

84. *Birds* 180–184 offers a pun, best explained by Arrowsmith in a note to his free translation ("The heavens, you see, revolve upon a kind of pole or axis"): "The Greek for 'the vault of the heavens' is *polos*, which leads naturally to *poleitai* (revolves), which resembles *politai* (citizens), which in turn yields polis (city)" (Arrowsmith 1961.319). See also Whitman 1964.177. This pun, playing on the ambiguity of the spaces, actually anticipates the conclusion of the plot.

85. See Turato 1971–1972.

ἄγε σύννομέ μοι παῦσαι μὲν ὕπνου,
λῦσον δὲ νόμους ἱερῶν ὕμνων,
οὓς διὰ θείου στόματος θρηνεῖς
τὸν ἐμὸν καὶ σὸν πολύδακρυν Ἴτυν·
ἐλελιζομένης δ' ἱεροῖς μέλεσιν
     γένυος ξουθῆς
καθαρὰ χωρεῖ διὰ φυλλοκόμου
μίλακος ἠχὼ πρὸς Διὸς ἕδρας,
ἵν' ὁ χρυσοκόμας Φοῖβος ἀκούων
τοῖς σοῖς ἐλέγοις ἀντιψάλλων
ἐλεφαντόδετον φόρμιγγα θεῶν
ἵστησι χορούς· διὰ δ' ἀθανάτων
στομάτων χωρεῖ ξύμφονος ὁμοῦ
     θεία μακάρων ὀλολυγή.

Birds 209–222

Come, melodious companion of my abode [*sunnomos*], waken
and let loose the melody [*nomoí*] of sacred songs
with which your divine voice laments
Itys, our—mine and yours—much-wept Itys.
     From your throat
swiftly modulating holy tunes, the pure strain [*ēkhō*] reaches,
through the thick foliage of the honeysuckle
the seat of Zeus, and there, when golden-tressed Phoibos
hears it, playing on his ivory lyre
in response to your song of lamentation,
he leads song and dance among the gods,
and from immortal throats is heard
the divine cry of grief [*ololugē*] of the blessed ones,
     in harmony with [*sumphōnos*] your own.

Here Tereus serenades Prokne to arouse her and ask her to deliver her song for Itys. Dazzled by Peisthetairos' clever plan, Tereus has agreed to serve as an intermediary between the two men and the birds. Upon arriving among them he had taught the birds the Greek language, and yet to summon them now he needs the song of the nightingale. He calls Prokne *sunnomos* (209), a word in which the polysemy of *nómos* / *nomós* 'law', 'musical measure or mode' / 'pasture' is apparent.[86] Tereus invokes Prokne as his *sunnomos*, his companion, one who shares his food.[87] His plea to her to release the *nomoi humnōn hierōn* 'the melodies

86. See Arrowsmith 1973.157–164 (on *nómos* / *phusis*). For *nómos* / *nomós*, see Whitman 1964.176–178 and Nagy 1990b, chap. 3.
87. See Rogers 1906.

of sacred hymns' (210) refers *sunnomos* also to her music. As the serenade continues, the melody emanating from the thicket transcends the natural landscape. From the honeysuckle (*milax*, 216) the sound rises, says Tereus, to the very throne of Zeus. Apollo, responding with his lyre, leads the dancing of the immortals and their song: the *theia makarōn ololugē* 'divine cry of the Blessed,' *sumphōnos* 'echoing' Prokne's song of mourning. The magic melody spreads, evoking the harmonious choir of the Olympians in response, and thus the pastoral image expands and the locus of the thicket merges with the space of the universe.

This serenade is remarkable from both a dramatic and a thematic point of view. Its dramatic effect consists in opening the enclosure where Prokne sleeps, paralleling the stories of the hoopoe opening magically the nest where his mate or his young have been imprisoned (see Aelian *De Natura Animalium* 3.26 and Servius on *Aeneid* 10.76). In those stories the liberation is the result of applying a magic herb; Aristophanes substitutes song. Thus pairing the motif of music (endowed with magic effect) and that of the thicket, he fashions a suggestive dramatic theme. This piece is important also thematically. The expanded image of the heavenly music in the antistrophe suggests that the mode of the nightingale's song is sacred: *hieroi humnoi* 'sacred hymns' (210), *theion stoma* 'divine throat' (211), and *kathara ēkhō* 'pure echo' (215–216).[88] What it is that these sacred hymns celebrate is something that further lyrics will reveal.

In the second of the lyric passages mentioned above (676–684), the arrival of the nightingale, heralding the spring and the occasion of the Dionysiac festival, is celebrated by the chorus.[89]

ὦ φίλη, ὦ ξουθή,
ὦ φίλτατον ὀρνέων
πάντων, ξύννομε τῶν ἐμῶν
ὕμνων, ξύντροφ' ἀηδοῖ,
ἦλθες ἦλθες ὤφθης,
ἡδὺν φθόγγον ἐμοὶ φέρουσ'·
ἀλλ' ὦ καλλιβόαν κρέκουσ'

---

88. ἐλελιζομένη 'trilling' (213) perhaps alludes to the ποικιλία which is an attribute of lyric song (see Pindar *Nemean* 4.14, 5.25; *Olympian* 9.13).

89. Compare the βρομία χάρις of *Clouds* 311. See Segal 1969.143–161.

αὐλὸν φθέγμασιν ἠρινοῖς,
    ἄρχου τῶν ἀναπαίστων.

Birds 676–684

O dear, trilling tawny bird,
of all the best beloved, companion,
intoning with me the measures of my hymns,
nightingale, sharer of my nurture.
You came! You came! You are here,
you bring sweet sounds to me.
Now, weaving the delightful sounds of your reed,
bring in the spring,
    be the leader of the anapaests.

The parabasis (685–722) proclaims that the time has come for the birds to reign again, as they did in the beginning. Now the nightingale is called upon to strike the tempo for the anapaests. First the chorus invokes her as *sunnomos*, then with the word *suntrophos*. Clearly *sunnomos* means here, in the first place, one who sings the same music, the *hēdus phthongos* 'sweet voice' of 681. The other meanings of *nómos*/*nomós* are evoked too: one who belongs to the birds' realm, a society ruled by *thesmoi arkhaioi* 'ancient decrees' (331), and one who shares their pasture, rich with the bounties of nature (*suntrophos* underscores this association). The call is a fit prelude to the triumphal ornithogony of 685–722.

The lyrics of the ode at 737–751 recapture these themes:

μοῦσα λοχμαία,
τιὸ τιὸ τιὸ τιὸ τιὸ τιοτίγξ,
    ποικίλη, μεθ' ἧς ἐγὼ
νάπαισι <καὶ> κορυφαῖς ἐν ὀρείαις,
    τιὸ τιὸ τιὸ τιοτίγξ,
ἱζόμενος μελίας ἐπὶ φυλλοκόμου,
    τιὸ τιὸ τιὸ τιοτίγξ,
δι' ἐμῆς γένυος ξουθῆς μελέων
Πανὶ νόμους ἱεροὺς ἀναφαίνω
σεμνά τε μητρὶ χορεύματ' ὀρεία,
τιὸτιὸτιὸτιὸτιὸτιὸτιὸτιοτίγξ,
ἔνθεν ὡσπερεῖ μέλιττα
Φρύνιχος ἀμβροσίων μελέων ἀπεβόσκετο καρπὸν ἀεὶ
    φέρων γλυκεῖαν ᾠδάν.
    τιὸ τιὸ τιὸ τιοτίγξ.

Birds 737–751

Muse of the thicket,
tio-tio-tio-tio-tio-tio-tinx,
        modulating [*poikilē*] Muse,
with you, in vales and mountain tops,
        tio-tio-tio-tio-tinx,
perching in ash-trees of rich foliage,
        tio-tio-tio-tio-tinx,
I send forth, from my trilling throat,
the tunes consecrated to Pan
and the Mountain Mother's holy hymns.
Tiotiotiotiotiotiotiotiotiotinx.
Thence did Phrynichus, like a bee,
feeding on the fruit of immortal tunes,
        bring the strain of sweet song.
        Tio-tio-tio-tinx.

The chorus takes the voice of the nightingale; Aristophanes, the chorus' voice, to invoke the "muse of the thicket" (*mousa lokhmaia*), not merely capable of a heroic monotone but *poikilē* (*aux accents variés*, in Hilaire Van Daele's translation). Inspiration comes to the chorus, impersonating the nightingale as it perches in an ash tree (*melia*).[90] A bucolic landscape follows in which places tucked away and high atop the mountains are mentioned. The accumulated symbols, reinforced by the pastoral Pan and by Kybele, the mountain Mother of the Gods (see μητρὶ ὀρείᾳ 746), symbolize the abundance of nature. Pan and Kybele are often associated with Dionysos.[91]

The cosmic echoes of the song are developed once again at 769–784. The ascent of the swans of Apollo conjures up the total calm in the realm of nature, a calm preceding the enchanting sound of the Olympian response in which Muses and Graces partake. From such sources Phrynichus drew, like a bee, his sweet song.[92] Aristophanes refers here to his own art, not in the customary parabatic plea for victory or in an ironic disclaimer, but programmatically, by naming a playwright he

90. In Hesiod the *meliai* 'ash trees' or 'ash nymphs' are born from Gaia, the Earth (see West 1966.187 and 1978.233); bees nest in hollow trees; so do the hoopoe and the woodpecker / Polytekhnos in a myth compared to that of Tereus by Fontenrose 1948 and Detienne 1971.

91. Duchemin 1957 compares the journeys of Dionysos in *Frogs* and Peisthetairos in *Birds*.

92. Bee and honey are familiar metaphors for the poet and poetry before and after Aristophanes (Pindar *Olympian* 6 and *Pythian* 10; also Plato *Ion*). Aristophanes uses them for comic effect in the scene with the bad poet (908).

respects. And the lyrics we have just examined point to one of the fountains of his art: a varied (lyric), nonheroic inspiration, a celebration of life in nature. Apollo and his music symbolize that manner of life and song in this play.[93]

I discuss the wedding song of 1731–1742 further on. Now we must ask how the pastoral theme relates to the plot. One should beware of simply identifying the pastoral ideal in this play with a nostalgic, Hesiodic myth of the Golden Age, or with a description of the hoped-for advent of such an age.[94] It is not nostalgia but irrepressible *erōs* 'desire' for power that propels the plot in the *Birds*.[95] The pastoral-lyric utopia will be established paradoxically, by virtue of the very plan whereby harmony and good order are endangered, and by which they would indeed be destroyed if Aristophanic comedy were rational and realistic.

The powers of the nightingale's song are contrasted pointedly to the powers of cunning reason and persuasive language in the plot of the *Birds*. Peisthetairos' plan is a scheme of power (*dunamis* 'power' 163 and *dunamis meizōn* 'greater power' 455). It is a "contrivance" (*bouleuma* 162) that can be made to succeed by *peithō* 'persuasion', the exercise of *logos*. The word *logos* occurs in this play several times in the contexts of language, discourse, and message (e.g., 313, 381, 434, 1447). No doubt that it also evoked the meanings 'reason, cunning', and the like. These concepts and the vocabulary that conveyed them yet imperfectly were being probed intensely at the time, by the playwrights no less than by the sophists. What is more important for my purpose here is that it is not *logos*, but the song of the nightingale, that at 209–222 opens the enclosure and reaches the immortals with its echoes.

The clever plan of Peisthetairos entails a subversion of hierarchies and even contemplates what is—at least from the birds' standpoint—cannibalism. The theme of violence comes to the fore repeatedly in this play, for example, in the comic eating and cooking of birds (1579–1586). The *agōn* 'debate' beginning at 460 offers an excellent illustration of this opposition of *logos* (as cunning and deceptive speech) and song. It begins very aptly with a parody of *Antigone* 332–383, where

---

93. In Euripides' *Ion*, as I argued earlier, the music of Apollo serves as a symbol of just the opposite mood; in that play the antithesis Apollo / Dionysos is very forceful. In the *Birds* of Aristophanes, Apollo represents the lyric aspect of the pastoral ideal which the Dionysiac end of the play will, I propose, legitimize.

94. Auger 1979 reads the *Birds* exclusively as a Hesiodic myth.

95. See Arrowsmith 1973.

Sophocles inquires into cunning and wisdom, for the *agōn* will pursue the deceitful scheme of Peisthetairos to its utmost consequences.

Amid these multiple oppositions, where do the birds stand? They serve several purposes in this play named after their chorus. Thanks to their ability to fly they are the natural mediators between this world and a higher one from which men and gods may be overpowered. On the one hand, the chorus of birds serves to punctuate the successive stages in the fulfillment of Peisthetairos' plan and its "blending" with the pastoral ideal. The birds (including Tereus) are ambivalent: they offer a benign as well as a hostile aspect. The birds that Tereus summons at 227–262 live in fertile and delightful habitats or in the remote wilderness, and their mild nature is reflected in the gentle sounds they utter. The whole chorus, however, once gathered, is hostile. Their aggressiveness gives Aristophanes an occasion for parody of the heroic. (The martial language in the strophe and antistrophe is worth noting.) That the battle is actually fought with kitchen utensils and that references to food and cooking follow signals the abatement of violence, its festive transmutation. The bucolic aspect of the birds is displayed in the antistrophe of the second parabasis (1088–1100): they favor growth, and they live in blooming meadows. In the final call to all the birds to share in the reign of Peisthetairos and Basileia they are summoned as "all races of *sunnomoi*." This word recalls, of course, the vocatives addressed to Prokne, and it has now been firmly established as a cue to the pastoral ideal. Peisthetairos had stated (616) that the cult of birds would be celebrated in nature, with the olive tree as a shrine. These motifs recur in the strophe of 1058–1070 and its antistrophe (1088–1100, mentioned earlier).

On a larger scale too a festive transmutation takes place when the final triumph of the comic hero enacts a synthesis between his master plan and the pastoral-lyric ideal. Such a synthesis has been intimated at various stages; we have seen above the function of the birds of the chorus in this respect. The thematic crossover is manifest in the scene beginning at 451. The *logos*, the speech of Peisthetairos that will expound his plan is, as he puts it, rising in him like leavened dough that has fermented (462–463). The birds of the chorus, their hostility deposed, promise to support his *gnōmē* 'purpose' with their *rhōmē* 'strength' (637–638). Tereus says it is time to act. The names of the two men are revealed (643). The hoopoe offers the magic root (654–655). The usual accomplishment of purpose preceding the parabasis? Not yet; the music must be evoked too. Now the chorus beseeches Tereus to bring out the nightingale (663), for they wish to partake in the music—and the sexual byplay. We may imagine here that the *ekkuklēma* 'rolling machine' brings the thicket out and an actor emerges in a nightingale costume to provide a visual accompaniment to the double entendre.

That song introduces the ornithogony parabasis, to which I referred earlier (685–722), delivered by the chorus in character. Even though this tirade of the coryphaeus is an arrogant speech of power, the chorus of birds is now imbued with the pastoral-lyric spirit. The scene concludes with the song of 723–751. Here the honey-sweet voice of the Muse of the thicket (*mousa lokhmaia*, 737) is offered to all who wish to be inspired by it. The Muses join in the universal symphony. The birds undertake the prophetic function of Apollo. The chorus, as we saw earlier, impersonates the nightingale. The bounties they promise to men are, as it were, goods "of the thicket," of comedy, that is, of Dionysos: for generation after generation, *eudaimonia* 'happiness', *bios* 'long life', *eirēnē* 'peace', *neotēs* 'youth', *gelōs* 'laughter', *khoroi* 'dance', *thaliai* 'festivities', even the proverbial birds' milk, which would abolish the boundaries between the species.

At this point, paramount from the point of view of dramatic structure, plot, and theme, Aristophanes engages the audience in the fantasy by a clever use of spatial ambiguity. References to real and imaginary spaces are polyvalent, so that the thicket and the theater, on the one hand, and Athens and the fantastic city of birds, on the other, merge in the spectators' imaginations. ἐνθάδε 'there' means "in Athens" at 755 and 757, but at 763, in an invitation addressed to the spectators to join in Cuckoo City, ἐνθάδε means "here, among us, the birds."[96]

Hierarchies are, however, restored in the grand finale. Like other comic heroes—especially like Trygaios in the *Peace*—Peisthetairos is rejuvenated in his final triumph. He has gone from subversive to sovereign, from the role of an intruding outsider to that of legitimate husband of Basileia and successor of mighty Zeus.[97] Peisthetairos

96. I read ἐνθάδε at 763 with the mss, the OCT edition, and Rogers, rather than Coulon's emendation οὗτος. See Rogers 1906.

97. There is no consensus on the interpretation of Basileia. The meter necessitates Βασίλεια 'rule, government' while the scholia imply Βασιλεία 'queen' (at 1537 and 1753). Basileia has been thought by some to be a personification of "government"—whether of the people or of the whole world—while others consider her a persona, a character and a real goddess, identified occasionally with Athena. Newiger 1957.92–103 demonstrates that Basileia is a genuine goddess and a character of the comic play, not a personification, yet he argues that she should not be thought to stand for Athena, referring to Basileia as she appears in the Hellenistic apotheosis and epiphany.

receives the scepter, symbol of the supreme rule, and marries the goddess who once sat by Zeus and will hence be his own *paredros* 'counselor' (1754), thus becoming a god himself. Basileia is the ultimate mediator in the ascent of Peisthetairos. Now the whole universe appears as the realm that Peisthetairos has found in his quest for non-Athens. When he marries Basileia, *euboulia* 'good counsel', *eunomia* 'good order', and *sōphrosunē* 'moderation, prudence' are established. Their union is celebrated with the wedding-song of Zeus and Hera (1731–1742), for the order of the universe has been consolidated. The sacred marriage parallels that of Dionysos in the Anthesteria, and it evokes the married bliss of Tereus and Prokne.[98]

Aristophanes uses marriage as a metaphor for the triumphal establishment of a new order, one in which the natural blessings of life will not have been perverted. The harmonious exchange that would have been abruptly interrupted by the clever plot of power is now resumed. Sacrifice will be offered henceforth to the gods above, as is proper, and so its nature will not degenerate into that of cannibalistic food. The stream of sweet fragrances from sacrifices will flow again from men to gods; from the gods to men will come blessed fortune in return.

The triumph of Peisthetairos does not herald the success of the cunning plan to acquire power, the vision of empire with which he enticed the birds. Only he (Euelpides has faded now from the dramatic point of view) rises to Olympos, while the Athenians willing to participate in the building of the new city and those who wanted to be fitted with wings are beaten, chased, and ridiculed. The Athenian dream of power has been shattered. But Peisthetairos' wings have grown from the thicket, and in the end he rises as the champion of the thicket and of the order of the universe. "A keen old man with new counsel" (δριμὺς πρέσβυς καινὸς γνώμην, 255), Peisthetairos triumphs paradoxically, affirming neither *phusis* 'nature' nor *nómos* 'law, convention', or perhaps both, mutually tempered from a new perspective.[99]

98. See Henrichs 1979.5, n. 18. Newiger 1957 compares the marriage of Peisthetairos to the *Hieros Gamos* 'Holy Marriage' of Dionysos and the Basilinna in the Anthesteria. Duchemin 1957 relates the holy marriage of *Birds* to ancient beliefs and rituals. She detects "shamanistic traces" both in *Frogs* and in *Birds*. Epstein 1981 emphasizes the overthrowing of the Olympians by Peisthetairos as a champion of individualism who fled with Euelpides the "corporate life" of Athens; however, when he comes into possession of Basileia, "who has in her the sovereignty of the natural world and Athenian life . . . the institutions of the city are vindicated."

99. I do not attempt to examine here the complicated polysemy of these two terms and their opposition, for that would require a lengthier study of the entire play. In the thematic synthesis that I am suggesting, *phusis* would represent the benign aspects of the natural world rather than the "wild" aspects of man's nature and behavior.

The pastoral-lyric motifs provided by the myth of Tereus and Prokne are of prime importance in this play because they serve to resolve the ambiguity of the overarching bird-metaphor. The birds' ambitions that Peisthetairos fosters involve the disruption of civilized order, with the transgression of basic rules of communal life. The implications of such crimes were obvious for any Greek who had ever been to the theater. Aristophanes' hero does not carry this hubristic scheme to its conclusion but becomes, by marrying Basileia, the stalwart of good order. In this play Aristophanes brings into question the underpinnings of the Athenian imperialistic dream by transmuting the quality of the fantasy that serves as foundation of the plot.

The Polis in Crisis

The *Birds* was presented at the Great Dionysia of 414 B.C. In the winter of 416–415, Athens had demonstrated, through the ruthless actions taken against Melos, its determination to force all of Greece into submission. In the spring of 415, the assembly refused to listen to Nikias' moderate advice and, embracing with passion the prospect of conquering Sicily, voted to send an expedition in support of Segesta, oppressed by Syracuse.[100] Thus the Athenians, still reeling from the humiliation resulting from the peace they had to negotiate in 421, revived in fact their dream of empire. Had the Sicilian expedition been successful, it might have extended Athenian hegemony in the distant West. Ignoring objections, the Assembly undertook the expedition, yet clearly opinions were divided. The desecration of the Herms that delayed the sailing, the suspicion that Alcibiades had some responsibility in that outrage, and the further charges of sacrilege and conspiracy brought against him (he was one of the *stratēgoi* 'generals' chosen to command the expedition) reflect the uneasiness and concern of those who, perceiving its risks, were not committed to Athens' imperial project.[101] The fantastic and ironic plot of the *Birds* will have spoken to their discontent. The relief of comedy, the play's idyllic and pacifist resolution, allowed them to experience in the theater what was denied to them in reality. The Sicilian adventure would indeed be catastrophic.[102]

100. Thucydides 6.6, 6.8–26.
101. Thucydides 6.27–32.
102. See Hammond 1986.387–399. Alcibiades, recalled to stand trial, deserted to the Peloponnesian league. Under the hesitant comand of Nikias and Lamakhos, Athens failed

Although we know the date of the performance of the *Birds* and the historical circumstances surrounding it, the dating of *Ion* can at best be the object of educated guessing.[103] Yet accurate historical correspondences matter little to my purpose here. Both plays were performed in Athens in the latter part of the fifth century. Both reflect the ideological armature of the Athenian polis which drove it to the abuses of imperialism and eventually to self-destruction. Both offer an alternative.

Euripides, in the lighter and playful style that makes some of his tragedies undeserving of the name (in a modern sense), enacts the advent of Dionysos to conclude a plot that appeared to be aiming only at the consolidation of a tradition of autochthonous kingship sanctioned by the Apollonian order. The transit of Ion, and the movement for which the *Ion* of Euripides is pleading, is one from closure to openness, from an exclusive affirmation of the principle of order to a balanced integration of all the sources of patriotic zeal. For that the Athenians must open their city to the Dionysiac temper.

Aristophanes mocks and challenges the underpinnings of the Athenian imperialistic dream in a brilliant comic fantasy that concludes with the unexpected triumph of a counterideal (the image of life in untainted nature), the permanence of which is guaranteed by a Dionysiac *hieros gamos* 'holy marriage'.

It is not coincidental that both dramatists evoked Dionysos. Dionysos took many shapes in myth and in Greek history; his cultural significance has not yet been sufficiently explained.[104] In the fifth century he certainly already possessed the aspects that would prevail in Hellenistic times. Then Dionysos would appear predominantly as a civilizing deity, a giver of wine just as Demeter was the giver of grain. In the cult of the god in Classical times the violence and disorder symbolically present in his myths are exorcised. The Orgia were merely ritual enactments; the double movement of Maenads or Thyiades to the mountain and then back to the city, in excited dance and song, symbolizes an

---

to achieve a decisive victory in the winter of 414. In the months that followed, the Athenians were not able to sustain the renewed hostilities on land and sea. In the spring of 413 a grievous defeat at Syracuse in which the greater part of the Athenian fleet was destroyed, many Athenians were killed, and many taken prisoner "dealt a shattering blow to the power and the prestige of Athens. All hope of expansion was at an end" (Hammond 1986.400). Thucydides calls the Sicilian campaign "the greatest action that we know of in Hellenic history—to the victors the most brilliant of successes, to the vanquished the most calamitous of defeats" (Thucydides 7.87.5–6, Warner's translation).

103. See Walsh 1978.313–315.
104. See Henrichs 1979 and Detienne 1989.

expulsion, an expurgation of excess and violence. Thus the opposite aspects of Dionysos are revealed. Numerous pictorial depictions suggest that Dionysos was primarily a benign god, the giver of *sophrosunē*.[105] The Anthesteria offers an apt symbol of this function of Dionysos in fifth-century Athens, for his gift of wine is tempered with water for men to drink during the festival.

The institution of the theater of Dionysos created a center for the codification of myth, cult, and ideology. The organization of the festival could have made of the dramatic performances an unmitigated instrument of Athenian cultural and political hegemony. Yet in the latter years of the fifth century, drama echoed the deep politicocultural conflicts of the polis; for the polis, in this time of crisis, turned upon itself *critically* in the theater. Whether a resolution was negotiated successfully, and how the historical transition to a new constellation of values occurred, are matters that lay beyond the responsibility of the theater and its god.

105. See Segal 1982, esp. 339–347.

CHAPTER 8

Alexander the Great:
Myth, the Polis, and Afterward

Martha Payne

The rise to power of Philip II of Macedon in the fourth century B.C. forcefully eliminated most of the rivalry between poleis by uniting them under the domination of one ruler. That his son Alexander's charismatic personality held this imposed political unity together becomes clear in view of the dissolution of his empire under his successors, the Diadochoi. Alexander's charisma, however, endured much longer than his empire. A historico-mythical account of his life, Βίος Ἀλεξάνδρου τοῦ Μακεδόνος καὶ πράξεις, "The Life and Deeds of Alexander the Macedonian," otherwise known as the *Alexander Romance* of "Callisthenes," is a valuable witness of this afterlife of Alexander.[1] It offers interest also because it reflects earlier traditions associated with the foundation of Alexandria in Egypt.[2] Located on the periphery of the Classical Greek world, at a time when the Greek autonomous poleis had succumbed on the mainland, this city was destined to become the center of the Hellenistic world dominated by powerful rulers. Furthermore, the

---

1. Van Thiel 1983. The term "romance" is actually a misnomer for this particular work. A romance is a narrative concerning private persons, their interests and emotions, designed to entertain or give spiritual benefit (Perry 1967.45). Although this can be said of the *Alexander Romance*, it does not have a love story as the main focal point, which is another element of the definition of romances (Perry p. 35). It combines aspects of older genres—epic, fantastic travel tales, biography, and historiography—and is hence one of the forerunners of the modern novel (see Hägg 1983.109).

2. Because of the exotic adventures presented in the work, historians do not regard the *Romance* as a primary source of information for Alexander's life. Fraser 1972.I.4, however, considers the description of the founding of Alexandria in the *Romance* valuable for its information on the topography of the ancient city, since it is likely that the earliest Greek version was authored by an Alexandrian.

Alexander Romance illustrates the range and interest of the fabulous adventures attributed to Alexander in Hellenistic times, to which the later folk tradition also attests.

The *Alexander Romance* is a quasihistorical account of Alexander's life and exploits compiled from several sources: a Hellenistic history of his life, a series of letters supposedly written by Alexander, and Greek and Egyptian folk elements.[3] Alexander's conquest of the giant Persian Empire and his travels beyond the fringes of civilization known to the Greeks had captured the imagination of the Hellenistic population and easily stimulated the attribution to him of other, more miraculous feats. These wonders are presented in the *Romance* along with historical events. Examples of Alexander's amazing adventures are the following: he attempts to explore the depths of the sea (Book II.38.7–11); he goes into the heavens in a basket carried by large birds (II.41.8–13); he searches to find the End of the Earth (II.37.5). The ambition that drove the restless historical Alexander to expand the boundaries of his empire readily translated him into a folk figure striving to venture beyond human limitations.[4]

Although the original works from which the *Romance* was compiled belong to the Hellenistic period,[5] the earliest manuscript of the work as we now have it should be dated to the third century A.D.[6] Despite our lack of information about the author's name, evidence within the work, such as the extensive descriptions of the founding of Alexandria in Egypt and its cults, suggests that the author was an Alexandrian with a Ptolemaic bias. Recensions in Greek and in other languages (such as Latin, Armenian, and Syriac) are extant.[7] The manuscript used as the basis for this study is Manuscript L (*Leidensis Vulcanianus* 93), which dates to the

3. On the historical sources of the *Alexander Romance*, see Merkelbach and Trumpf 1977.20–47, 80, 108–155 for a detailed analysis of the *Romance* including indications of where it overlaps with history.

4. See Merkelbach and Trumpf 1977.63.

5. Welles 1962.272; Fraser 1972.I.4.

6. Wolohojian 1969.1; Fraser 1972.I.4, 677; Dawkins 1937.173–174. Callisthenes, a relative of Aristotle who took part in the journey, wrote one of the earliest reports about it. The author of the *Romance* took his *nom-de-plume* and part of his story from the genuine Callisthenes. Much of his narrative, however, comes from many other sources as well (see Pearson 1960.22).

7. See Merkelbach and Trumpf 1977.93–108, 201–210 for a discussion of textual transmission and manuscript tradition and p. 211 for the manuscript stemma.

fifteenth century.[8] Certain information, as we see below, is lacking in L, but these gaps may be supplemented from the Armenian recension.[9]

Alexander as Hero and Founder in Hellenistic Tradition

Although Alexander's tomb provided a tangible center for his cult as a hero, the mythic tradition that developed around the figure of Alexander the Great was longlasting and widespread. The numerous times that the prose version of the *Alexander Romance* was copied, and the number of poetic versions it originated, attest to Alexander's popularity.[10] On the other hand, the *Romance*—in particular, the episode of Alexander and the Water of Life—became the basis for a living folk tradition including tales and incantations. Aside from these traditions stemming from the *Romance*, Alexander was a popular figure in other ways. He is also a stock character in the Greek shadow theater plays that feature Karagheozis, the popular folk antihero.[11] Alexander was even said to be responsible for the design of a particular type of traditional headdress.[12] Alexander's conquest of the traditional enemy of the ancient Greeks, the Persians, may well have been a model which encouraged Greek resistance in the fight for freedom against the Turks.[13]

The *Alexander Romance* comprises three books. The first concerns Alexander's birth and upbringing, his conquest of Greece, the foundation of Alexandria, and his first moves against Darius. The second book relates the defeat of Darius and the fantastic adventures of the so-called *Wunderbriefe*, Letters of Wonders. Here Alexander encounters strange new worlds and their inhabitants and marches into the Land of the Blessed. The third book concerns the conquest of India and Alexander's return march during which he meets Queen Kandake of

8. Van Thiel 1983. This is the most readily available text and translation of the manuscripts which contain the episode of Alexander and the Water of Life. See also Merkelbach and Trumpf 1977.96, 203–204.

9. Wolohojian 1969.

10. Veloudis 1968, chaps. 1–3. See also Merkelbach and Trumpf 1977.212–214.

11. Veloudis 1968, chap. 8.

12. Dragoumis 1919.298 (from Karagouni, Thessaly; the headdress was tied in the shape of a helmet); Ninou 1980.92 (wedding dress from Gidas, Roumlouki, Emathia = watercolor from the Benaki Museum in Athens: *Album of Greek National Costume* no. 49).

13. Veloudis 1968.194–214; Ninou 1980.83 (broadsheet of Rhigas Velestinlis 1797. Athens, National Historical Museum Inv. no. 2133).

Ethiopia and the Amazons. It also depicts Alexander's visit to the home of the gods and the last part of his life. Of special interest to a consideration of political myth are the sections in Books I and III which not only establish divine parentage for Alexander but also discuss his founding of Alexandria and his burial within that city.

At the time of the compilation of the *Alexander Romance,* the Ptolemies ruled Egypt, having been more successful than the other Macedonian monarchs in maintaining the integrity of their territory. This may have been partly due to the (real or fictitious) continuity of traditions proper to the two main nationalities under their rule: the Macedonians and Greeks Ptolemy I brought with him, and the native Egyptians. By adopting certain Egyptian institutions and by creating others more in accordance with Greek customs, Ptolemy, the son of Lagos, was able to form a temporary compromise satisfying both populations to some extent.[14] Like the pharaohs, Ptolemy became an autocratic ruler and adopted the bureaucratic system by which they had run the country. The primarily Greek cities of Alexandria, Naukratis, and Ptolemaîs, however, were organized along the lines of the Greek polis. In Alexandria, for example, only the Greeks were known as "citizens," just as only native born Athenians were known as "citizens" of Periclean Athens. The population of Alexandria was divided into four "tribes" (*phulai*), and in each magistrates were appointed to care for building, public health, and the courts of law.[15] The whole population of Alexandria was, however, under the charge of a governor appointed by Ptolemy.[16]

Ptolemy I was equally pragmatic in religious affairs, since he permitted Egyptians and Greeks to worship their traditional gods. Ptolemy also took on the pharaonic role of Son of the Sun God in order to give his rule the appearance of legitimacy in the eyes of his Egyptian subjects.[17] Yet, recognizing the need for some form of common ground for Egyp-

14. Dawkins 1937.173–174. For a thorough examination of Ptolemaic ruler-ideology and comments concerning the success of the policy, see Koenen 1983.143–190.

15. These groups were arbitrarily set; that the designation is the same as that which identified the *phulai* in earlier Greece shows the desire to enhance them with the dignity of the old kinship groups.

16. For a thorough discussion of Alexandria's population, organization, and government, see Fraser 1972.I.38–92, 93–131. Tarn 1930.161 states that the population of Alexandria was divided into four "tribes"; Fraser (p. 40) notes five and suggests that the "tribes" may have corresponded to the five districts of the city lettered A–E and possibly named after them. Later I refer to the five letters Alexander had inscribed on the foundations of one of the city's buildings. Van Thiel 1983.176, in the commentary to I.32.4, notes that the inscription provides one of the usual aetiologies for the districts of Alexandria.

17. Tarn 1930.174.

tians and Greeks, Ptolemy fostered the worship of a syncretic all-powerful god as a religious base for both populations. This god was Sarapis, an underworld deity of the Egyptians established in the ancient Egyptian capital of Memphis by the pharaoh Sesonkhosis.[18] The Greeks of Egypt readily accepted this Egyptian god just as mainland Greeks had previously accepted other deities, such as Isis and Bendis, or even Dionysos, who in his myths was said to come from distant lands.[19] In addition, Ptolemy established a cult of Alexander the Great and built a temple to him in Alexandria, possibly at the site of Alexander's tomb.[20] The *Alexander Romance* represents this attempt at syncretism, for it mentions Sesonkhosis, Sarapis, and the tomb of Alexander.

The romanticized figure of Alexander himself, of course, ensured maximum continuity for the Greek tradition in Hellenistic Egypt, and the *Romance* furnishes Alexander with a native Egyptian pharaoh for a father, the sorcerer Nektanebos, who fled to Pella when the Persians attacked Egypt.[21] Furthermore, an oracle predicts Alexander's advent into Egypt, announcing that the Egyptians' king will return not as an old man but as a young one and will defeat their Persian enemy. Through various machinations at Pella, in the disguise of the Libyan god Ammon, Nektanebos lies with Queen Olympias and Alexander is conceived (I.1–14). Alexander thus becomes the son of both man and god, as well as the son of a "Greek."[22] As the son of Ammon and the pharaoh, Alexander was the heir to Egyptian rule, continuing the Egyptian tradition whereby the ruling pharaoh was considered the human incarnation of

18. Merkelbach and Trumpf 1977.39, n. 98, 42. For a discussion of Sarapis as an Egyptian and Ptolemaic deity, see Fraser 1972.I.246–247, 276; see also Helck 1959 and Koenen 1985.187–188. The popularity of Sarapis among Greeks in general is shown by the fact that temples to Sarapis were erected outside of Egypt (e.g., two temples to Sarapis in Corinth, Pausanias 2.4.6). However, despite Ptolemy's attempt to unite the two cultures through Sarapis, active religious life in Alexandria was almost entirely a pursuit of the Greeks rather than of the native population.

19. See Davison in Chap. 3 for deities or founders whose authority was enhanced in the myths that made them "foreign."

20. Plaumann 1920.78.

21. Merkelbach and Trumpf 1977.79 and n. 13 comment that there are analogues for the episode in which a subject people attempts to console itself for its condition by making the present foreign ruler a son of a native parent. An example is the Mede mother of the Persian king Cyrus (Herodotus 1.107). Fraser 1972.I.680 notes that the Nektanebos story was added to the "historical" tradition that Alexander was the son of Ammon. See Fraser pp. 681–687 for a discussion of Nektanebos in Greco-Egyptian tradition.

22. Olympias actually came from Epiros and became queen of Macedon by her marriage to Philip. Veloudis 1968.266 compares Alexander's mixed parentage with the mixed parentage of the Byzantine hero Digenis Akritis.

the chief god. The Egyptian parentage of Alexander thus justified his rule of Egypt, as is made clear in a later passage in which Alexander is crowned king of Egypt at Memphis and recognized as the son of Nektanebos (I.34). But in sections of the *Romance* that have little to do with Egypt, Alexander's patronymic is "son of Philip."[23] Ptolemy's rule in Egypt is validated in the tale in an equally fictional manner. He is marked as Alexander's representative and future successor in a later episode of the *Romance* (III.19.2–4) wherein Alexander dresses Ptolemy in his own clothing and has Ptolemy take his place temporarily.

The title *Kosmokratōr* 'Ruler of the World' is given to Alexander twice in the first book (I.7.3; I.17.4). The Egyptian pharaoh Sesonkhosis also uses this title, first on an obelisk which Alexander encounters at the temple of Sarapis near the site of the future Alexandria (Armenian 90).[24] Second, Sesonkhosis refers to himself by that title when Alexander meets him at the "Home of the gods" (III.24.2). Hence, by adopting the title used by two former pharaohs in Egypt, Alexander is considered both as the new Nektanebos and the new Sesonkhosis, and as a "ruler of the world."[25] Although the title is not one that appears in other accounts of Alexander's career, we see later that variations of it exist in Greek folk tradition.

The *Romance* relates several events that take place while Alexandria is being built. These stem from Greek traditions, but in some cases they are modified to fit Egyptian circumstances. After conquering Greece and earning the respect of Rome as "the king of the Romans and of the whole world" (βασιλεὺς Ῥωμαίων καὶ πάσης γῆς, I.29.2),[26] Alexander marches from Sicily to Africa and seeks out the sanctuary of Ammon in Libya to verify that his father was the god Ammon, as Nektanebos had told him (I.30.1–5). His paternity by Ammon verified, Alexander next asks where to found a city that will bear his name. The god then appears

23. Book II.15.4: οὗτός ἐστιν ὁ Φιλίππου παῖς . . .; II.15.5: αὐτός ἐστιν Ἀλέξανδρος ὁ Μακεδόνων βασιλεὺς ὁ πάλαι Φιλίππου γεγονώς . . .; II.21.2: Βασιλεὺς Ἀλέξανδρος υἱὸς Φιλίππου βασιλέως καὶ βασιλίσσης Ὀλυμπιάδος.

24. Merkelbach and Trumpf 1977.40 note that an Egyptian king was normally considered a "world ruler" (*kosmokratōr*).

25. See Pfister 1964.60–63 for a discussion of *kosmokratōr* and its Egyptian origin. See Koenen 1985.192–193, suggesting that the Ptolemaic work "The Dream of Nektanebos" may also have predicted the rule of Alexander.

26. The encounter with Rome is drawn from second-century B.C. historians whose works seek to console the successors of Alexander who were then feeling the pressure of growing Roman imperialism. See Van Thiel 1983.xviii–xix.

to him in the form of an old man wearing ram's horns, who gives him the following oracle:[27]

ὦ βασιλεῦ ['Αλέξανδρε], σοὶ Φοῖβος <ὁ> μηλόκερως ἀγορεύει·
εἴγε θέλεις αἰῶσιν ἀκηράτοισ<ι> νεάζειν,
κτίζε πόλιν περίφημον ὑπὲρ Πρωτηΐδα νῆσον,
ἧς προκάθητ' Αἰὼν Πλουτώνιος αὐτὸς ἀνάσσων
πενταλόφοις κορυφαῖσιν ἀτέρμονα κόσμον ἑλίσσων.

Alexander Romance I.33.2[28]

O King [Alexander], ram-horned Phoibos announces to you:
if you want to be young in undefiled eternity,
found a high-famed city across from the Proteus island,
which lord Aion Ploutonios himself protects,
as, from the five-peaked mountain, he turns the unending world.

Having chosen a site for his city near the village of Rhakotis, Alexander notices an island across from it, which he learns is the island of the hero Proteus, who has lived there and is buried there (I.31.1). This fact reinforces his belief that he has chosen the location prophesied by the god. The boundaries of the city are then marked with flour, and as soon as the flour is put down, birds eat it (I.32.2). This is interpreted to mean that the new city, Alexandria, will nourish the whole world and that the men born in the city will spread out over the entire earth (I.32.3).

Alexander was worshipped as *ktistēs* 'founder' in Alexandria.[29] It had been customary to honor the mythical founder of a city by naming after him the entire city or a part thereof; thus the citadel of Thebes, Kadmeia, was named after Kadmos. Such an honor, however, was not granted traditionally to historical founders. The first to break the taboo was Alexander's father, Philip, who founded two cities and named them after himself: Philippi (in 358 B.C.) and Philippopolis (in 342 B.C.). Following his father's model, Alexander names the newly founded Egyptian

27. According to Plutarch *Alexander* 26.3, Ammon appeared to Alexander in his sleep (just as Sarapis does in the *Romance*, Armenian 92). Plutarch says that an elderly white-haired gentleman appeared and spoke the following words: νῆσος ἔπειτά τις ἔστι πολυκλύστῳ ἐνὶ πόντῳ / Αἰγύπτου προπάροιθε· Φάρον δέ ἑ κικλήσκουσιν "Then there is an island in the high-surging sea / in front of Egypt; they call it Pharos" (*Odyssey* iv 354–355).

28. The same text is found at 1.30.6 with slight variants.

29. Founders of colonies were accorded the cult status of *ktistēs* and were eligible for certain special religious rites after death. See Burkert 1985.206; Alexiou 1974.18; also Pfister 1964.64–66.

city after himself. The oracle given in the *Alexander Romance* stresses
that Alexander will live on because of the city (I.30.6).

Not content with the city's name as a reminder to posterity, Alexander takes measures to ensure that, should the city be destroyed, the
very foundations will indicate the founder's identity. On the largest
parts of the stone foundations Alexander has masons inscribe five letters:
Α Β Γ Δ Ε, meaning τὸ μὲν Α Ἀλέξανδρος, τὸ δὲ βῆτα βασιλεύς, τὸ δὲ Γ
γένος, τὸ δὲ δέλτα Διός, τὸ δὲ Ε ἔκτισεν πόλιν ἀμίμητον "King Alexander,
of the Race of Zeus, founded the inimitable city" (I.32.4).

Having discovered that his city is in the right place, Alexander
immediately sacrifices to Proteus and reerects a grave monument to him
to ensure the hero's blessing (I.32.1). While a sanctuary is being built,
signs are given to Alexander showing which local spirits to propitiate. In
the course of building the gate to the sanctuary, an old inscribed slab
falls down and snakes that have been hiding behind it, slither out and
glide into nearby houses. The guardians at the gate recognize the
snakes as *agathoi daimones* 'good spirits' and worship them (I.32.5–6),
and they put garlands on the work animals and give them a rest (I.32.6).
Since then, the Alexandrians began celebrating that day, the 25th of
Tybi, as "Founder's Day" (I.32.7). The Armenian version (section 87)
adds that on that day Alexander gives grain to the guards, who then
make bread, which is given to the inhabitants. The later celebration of
the city's foundation included garlanding the work beasts, making
sacrifices to the god in honor of the serpents, who were thought to protect the homes, and handing out bread.[30]

After these propitious signs, Alexander wants to find out the identity
of the god Aion Ploutonios, mentioned by Ammon in the oracle. On
hills nearby Alexander finds columns called Helonian (*hēlōnes stuloi*)
and a cult statue (I.33.1). Opposite the *hērōion* 'shrine of a hero', Alexander builds an altar and makes a sacrifice to the god (I.33.3). Unexpectedly, an eagle swoops down and takes the sacrificial entrails; then it
rises and lets the entrails fall on another altar (I.33.4). Alexander sees
that the altar is very old. There he sees a temple with an enthroned
wooden cult statue (*xoanon*) whose right hand is patting a multiform
beast; in the left hand is a scepter and next to the statue is a very large
statue (*agalma*) of a girl (I.33.5). Upon inquiring, Alexander learns that

30. Wolohojian 1969.51–52. In Greek tradition the foundation of a city was celebrated
either on the birthday of the patron deity or on the anniversary of the city's religious consecration. The latter method was adopted by the Alexandrians, who honored the *agathoi
daimones* and possibly even Alexander himself as *ktistēs*.

local tradition identifies the sanctuary as one belonging to Zeus and Hera (I.33.6). Appropriately, it was the bird of Zeus which had picked up the entrails and shown Alexander where to look. Thus the Egyptian Sarapis is equated with the Greek Zeus.[31]

Alexander sees obelisks bearing an inscription (I.33.7).[32] They belonged to Alexander's predecessor as *kosmokratōr*, Sesonkhosis, and the dedicatory inscription on the shrine is "I, Sesonkhosis, king of Egypt and conqueror of the world, built and dedicated this to Sarapis, the first god revealed to this land" (Armenian 90; Wolohojian 1969.53). Alexander asks what god ruled the land and Sarapis himself appears to him in his sleep (Armenian 91). Then he asks Sarapis if Alexandria will always bear his name, and the god assures him that it will and that the city will flourish under Sarapis' protection (Armenian 92). Thus both the continuation of the city and Alexander's own survival in the memory of his descendants are assured. By linking Sarapis with Alexandria's founder, the *Alexander Romance* legitimates worship of Sarapis in the Ptolemaic period. Armenian 94 makes the link stronger by having Alexander build an altar and shrine to Sarapis. Nevertheless, Fraser notes that Ptolemy Soter was the actual cult founder and that Alexander had little if any role in establishing the cult.[33] The immortality of Alexander's name through his city is underscored in a later prediction by Sesonkhosis when Alexander encounters him in Ethiopia in the "Home of the Gods":

"χαίροις 'Αλέξανδρε· οἶδάς με τίς εἰμι ἐγώ; ἐγώ εἰμι Σεσόγχωσις κοσμο-
κράτωρ. οὐ τοσοῦτον δὲ εὐτύχησα ὅσον σύ· ἔχεις γὰρ ὄνομα ἀθάνατον
κτίσας τὴν περιπόθητον ἐν Αἰγύπτῳ 'Αλεξάνδρειαν πόλιν.

III.24.2

"Greetings, Alexander. Do you know who I am? I am Sesonkhosis, Ruler of the World. I have not been as fortunate as you; for you have an immor-

---

31. Welles 1962.284. See Helck 1959 on the syncretic nature of Sarapis, which combines Aion / Ploutonios (Hades), Osiris, and Zeus. Sarapis is depicted with the bearded head of Zeus and underworld icons such as a measure of grain and Kerberos. See Tacitus' comments (*Histories* 4.83–84) on the god's arrival in Egypt from the Black Sea and on his varied nature. See Fraser 1972 I.209–211 for a discussion of this episode, the "Oracle of the Potter," the *agathoi daimones*, and their links with Egyptian deities. See also Koenen 1985.187–188.

32. Here the β recension of the *Alexander Romance*—of which L is a contaminated copy—leaves out a section that can be supplied from the Armenian recension.

33. Fraser 1972 I.246, 248–249. See the "Oracle of the Potter," which predicts the foundation of Alexandria and the cult of Sarapis (Koenen 1968.187).

tal name, since you have founded the much-beloved city of Alexandria in Egypt."

According to Sarapis' prophecy, Alexandria will have many temples, greater population than other cities, and a favorable climate: καλλίναος, ὑπερφέρουσα πλήθει ὄχλων πολλῶν, ἀέρων εὐκρασίαις ὑπερβάλλουσα "[a city] rich in temples, soaring over all others in abundant population and a gentle climate" (I.33.8). At his crowning as king of Egypt in Memphis, Alexander actually calls Alexandria the capital of the whole civilized world: μητρόπολιν δὲ οὖσαν ὅλης τῆς οἰκουμένης (I.34.7).

Alexandria, a splendid city especially in the Hellenistic period, with its beauty, luxury, and sophistication, earned the title of "first city of the civilized world" (πρώτην ἀριθμεῖσθαι τῶν κατὰ τὴν οἰκουμένην, Diodorus Siculus 17.52.5),[34] and that of "a world-class city" is attested in a papyrus fragment of the first century B.C.[35] Such praises were so common that in antiquity Alexandria was known as "the City."[36] The prophecies and predictions voiced in the *Alexander Romance* aggrandized the historical city by making it fulfill the promise of a mythical past.

Alexander founded many other Alexandrias, but Alexandria in Egypt was surely the most famous. While Alexandria in Egypt perpetuated Alexander's name through its own and through its glory reflected Alexander's, it was linked to him in yet another way: it became the site of his tomb. In a continuation of his prophecy, Sarapis predicts that Alexander will be honored as a god after his death and will receive gifts from kings: οἰκήσεις δὲ αὐτὴν καὶ θανὼν καὶ μὴ θανών· τάφον γὰρ ἕξεις αὐτὴν ἣν κτίζεις πόλιν "you will inhabit it [sc. the city] dying yet not dying; for you will have as a tomb the city which you founded" (I.33.9). The glory of Alexandria and the location of Alexander's body in it are

34. The praise of Alexandria in the *Alexander Romance* may well have been influenced by literary praises of cities or countries. Isocrates, in his *Busiris*, highlights Egypt's advantages, which include the fertility of the land (224.13–14). Poets also praised cities or countries: see the praise of Athens in Euripides *Medea* 824–845 and Menander *Samia* 98–104. A papyrus fragment with a poem from the second century A.D. seems to praise Alexandria's climate, fertility, and manufactured products: papyrus, glass, flax. See Hendricks, Parsons, and Worp 1981.74 = P. Gron. Inv. no. 66.

35. Koerte 1923.240, no. 634, P. Berlin no. 13045, 1.28–29: αἱ μὲν γὰρ ἄλλαι πόλε[ις] τῆς ὑποκειμέ[νης χώ]ρας πόλεις εἰσίν, Ἀλεξανδρείας δὲ κῶμαι· τῆς γὰρ οἰκουμένης Ἀλ[ε]ξάνδρεια πόλις ἐστίν "The other cities belong to the adjacent country, and they are towns of Alexandria, but Alexandria is a city of the civilized world."

36. Tarn 1930.159. Compare the later designation "the City" given to Constantinople, the cultural and political center of the Byzantine Empire, just as Alexandria had been for the Hellenistic world (Alexiou 1974.224, n. 33).

part also of the prediction Sesonkhosis makes to Alexander in the "Home of the Gods":

τὴν μέντοιγε κτίζεις πόλιν περιφανῆ πᾶσιν ἀνθρώποις, πολλοὶ βασιλεῖς ἐπιβήσονται τοῦ ἐδαφίσαι αὐτήν. οἰκήσεις δὲ αὐτὴν καὶ θανὼν καὶ μὴ θανών· τάφον γὰρ αὐτὴν ἕξεις ἣν κτίζεις πόλιν.

III.24.4

The city you found will have renown among all men. Many kings will advance, wanting to destroy it. But you will dwell there both dying and not dying; for you will have as a tomb [*taphos*] the city that you found.

In a later segment, the predictions concerning Alexander's body are fulfilled. After Alexander conquers the Persian king Darius and the Indian king Poros and reaches the End of the Earth, he dies in Babylon (III.33). Although the Persians want to take Alexander's body to their land, Ptolemy says that they should consult the oracle of Babylonian Zeus (III.34.1). The oracle replies that they must "enthrone" (*enthronizein*) the body in Memphis. Ptolemy has a lead sarcophagus built; in it he puts Alexander's embalmed body and takes it to Memphis (III.34.3). In Memphis, however, the high priest refuses to keep the body and says that it must be sent to the city Alexander has founded in Rhakotis (Alexandria), adding, ὅπου γὰρ ἐὰν ἦ τὸ σῶμα τοῦτο, ἀκαταστατεῖ ἡ πόλις ἐκείνη πολέμοις καὶ μάχαις ταραττομένη "for wherever this body is, that city will be unstable, disturbed by wars and battles" (III.34.4). Ptolemy then takes the body to Alexandria and builds Alexander's tomb (*taphos*) in the sanctuary, which is named the *Sōma Alexandrou* 'Body of Alexander' (III.34.5).[37]

   In Strabo's time the burial site of the Ptolemaic kings and of Alexander in Alexandria was known as the *Sēma* 'tomb, sign', and it was a part of the palace complex. In the same passage (17.1.8 C794), Strabo reports that Ptolemy I had put Alexander's mummy in a sarcophagus of gold but that the mummy was now in a glass sarcophagus. The *Sēma* Strabo mentions may well have been the area called the *Sōma* of Alex-

37. This account reflects historical events, for Alexander's body was taken first to Memphis and then to Alexandria; it is uncertain when that transfer occurred. See Welles 1962.273, n. 8. Strabo 17.1.8 C794 confirms the statement of the *Alexander Romance* that it was Ptolemy I who brought this about. Plaumann 1920.78, however, suggests that the transfer may not have taken place until the reign of Ptolemy II Philadelphos (283–246 B.C.). Fraser 1972.I.16, II.31–33, and n. 79 says that Ptolemy I Soter moved the body and that the body did not remain longer than two to three years in Memphis.

ander reported in the *Alexander Romance* III.34.5,[38] and this area was probably the center of the cult of Alexander as eponym founded by the Ptolemies.[39] In Homeric epic the *sēma* of a dead hero was the physical manifestation of the great deeds he had accomplished in his lifetime.[40] Many centuries later that symbolism was conjured up purposefully to carry out the desire of an ambitious ruler (Ptolemy) and his successors: overcoming death by means of the perpetual memorial of a living city.

The presence of a hero's tomb had played an important political role in the conflict-torn relationships of the Archaic and Classical poleis of Greece. In Alexandria—the facsimile of an Archaic or Classical polis—the Ptolemies erected a magnificent tomb for Alexander and promoted religious rites in his honor. Thus they not only honored Alexander, the city's founder and their predecessor, but enhanced their own prestige and stature. The Ptolemaic propaganda is apparent in the *Alexander Romance*. Just as the Ptolemies attempted to ensure a strong spiritual base for the Egyptian population through the adoption of Ammon and Sarapis, they did the same for the Greeks, by adopting the form of government of a traditional polis and, especially, by establishing traditional Greek rituals associated with the foundation of a city, which were to be carried out in honor of Alexander.

For the minority Greek population in Egypt, a familiar religious link with Greece such as was established by the cult of Alexander at Alexandria was undoubtedly as important a means for communal gatherings as the familiar Greek political institutions Ptolemy established in the new city. Whoever brought the body of Alexander to Alexandria, whether Ptolemy I or Ptolemy II, must have earned considerable esteem from the Greeks of Alexandria for having done so. By that action he was following another Greek tradition, for there had been much political maneuvering in connection with the bones of heroes in the Greek world before Alexander's time.[41]

Traditionally, the tomb of a dead hero brought protection to the city in which it was located,[42] yet, according to the *Alexander Romance*, the

38. See Plato *Cratylus* 400c for the Orphic identification of *sōma* and *sēma*, and see van Thiel 1983.195.

39. See Plaumann 1920.98 and Fraser 1972 I.225.

40. Nagy 1990a. 215–216.

41. Burkert 1985.204, 206. Alexiou 1974.18–19 notes that reforms made by Athenian leaders in the sixth century B.C. which renamed tribes and phratries for the names of state heroes rather than clan heroes were moves designed to take power away from the clans and distribute it democratically.

42. See Burkert 1985.207. See Sophocles *Oedipus at Colonus* 1518–1538, where the dying Oedipus promises Theseus that his hidden tomb will defend Athens against its enemies.

Egyptians predicted that Alexander's tomb would have the opposite effect.[43] Undeterred by the predictions of Egyptian priests, Ptolemy installed the body in Alexandria, where the Greeks preserved the customs of the motherland.

Folk Tradition

The sections of the *Alexander Romance* known as the Letters of Wonders (letters that Alexander supposedly addressed to his mother, Olympias, to his father, and to his teacher), particularly the episode of the Water of Life, offer valuable evidence of the continuity of a tale that has persisted in modern Greek folklore. Alexander decides to march to the End of the World, and in the course of this march he goes into the depths of the sea in a glass diving bell (II.38.7–11), and up in the air in a basket carried by large birds (II.41.8–13). Having ventured into areas beyond the limits of most men, Alexander then continues his search. He arrives in the Land of the Blessed, where the sun does not shine, a mark of a supernatural place (II.39.1–2). With a group of picked men, Alexander marches into the mysterious land and arrives at a place with several springs, one of which glistens like lightning (I.39.11).[44] Alexander orders his cook, Andreas, to prepare a meal, and the cook, obeying, takes a salted fish to the sparkling spring to wash it. To the cook's amazement, when the water touches it, the fish springs to life and slips out of his hands (II.39.12). The cook drinks some of the water and puts

43. Van Thiel 1983.195, note to III.34.4, points out that originally it was predicted that Alexander's place of rest would give power and fortune to the surrounding area, but that the compiler of the *Romance* gave the opposite power to the body, apparently to explain the continuous unrest present in the city in his own day. The prediction of Alexandria's destruction may also have been influenced by Egyptian tradition. Consider the predicted destruction of Alexandria and subsequent arrival of a new king and prosperity in the "Oracle of the Potter" (129 B.C.), which is linked to Egyptian mythology of destruction and refounding of the world. See Koenen 1968.180, 182–186, 1984.9, 1985.189–191, and Fraser 1972 I.683–684.

44. Arrian *Anabasis Alexandri* 3.3, in describing the historical Alexander's march to the Siwah oasis, where he is said to have been addressed by the god Ammon, offers striking parallels with the *Alexander Romance*. Alexander longs to visit the oracle of Ammon (3.3.1; cf. End of the Earth); he loses his bearings when the wind whips up sand (3.3.4; cf. land of darkness where he cannot see a path); serpents with human voices, or crows, act as Alexander's guides (3.3.5–6; cf. the *Romance*'s warning sirens); there is a miraculous spring in the Siwah oasis (3.4.2; cf. the shining springs in the *Romance*). Friedlaender 1910b.197 points out parallels to these events in Babylonian literature.

some of it in a bottle. Alexander and the other men drink from the other springs (II.39.13).

The march to the End of the World continues, and birds with human faces and voices tell Alexander to turn back because he is trespassing on land that belongs to the gods; he cannot enter, they say, the Islands of the Blessed (II.40).[45] Alexander and his men rejoin the rest of their band. The cook tells him of the fantastic event at the spring, but he does not report that he drank some of the miraculous water or that he saved some of it. Angered, Alexander reprimands the cook (II.41.2). The cook then approachs Alexander's daughter *Kalē* 'Beautiful' and seduces her, promising to give her some of the water of the immortal spring. Upon learning of this, Alexander, envying them their immortality (II.41.3), banishes his daughter; having aimed at immortality, she had become a *daimōn* 'divinity' (II.41.4). He continues with these words:

[Καλὴ μὲν τῷ ὀνόματι ἐκλήθης, ἀρτίως δὲ καλέσω σὲ Καλὴν τῶν ὀρέων ὅτι ἐν αὐτοῖς τοῦ λοιποῦ κατοικήσεις.] ἔσῃ δὲ κεκλημένη Νεραΐδα, ὡς ἐκ τοῦ νεροῦ τὸ ἀΐδιον δεξαμένη·

II.41.5

[You were given the name *Kalē* 'Beautiful', but I shall call you more properly *Kalē Oreōn* 'Beautiful of the Mountains,' for there henceforth you will dwell.] You will be called *Neraïda* 'Nereid', since from water [*nero*] you received immortality.

The girl leaves weeping and goes to live among the *daimones* 'spirits' in the mountains. The punishment of the cook is even more severe. Alexander orders him to be thrown into the sea with a millstone hung around his neck. He also becomes a *daimōn,* and the place where he

45. Vermeule 1979.18 points out that the representation of the soul in bird form is found in ancient Greece as well as in ancient Egypt. As an example from Greek literature she cites Sophocles *Oedipus the King* 175–178; her figure 14 illustrates the representation in art in an Attic fifth-century red-figured krater by the Hephaistos Painter (London E477.ARV²): a human-headed bird hovering over the figure of a dying Prokris. Human-headed birds in art are called "sirens" and are found on bronze cauldrons of the Geometric period at Olympia and Athens. Their origins were from the East. See also Hampe and Simon 1981.113 and figures 160–163. Danforth 1982.113 points out that in modern Greek folk tradition birds serve as symbols mediating between life and death. Human beings are characterized as birds in laments and wedding songs. The birds with human faces in the *Alexander Romance* mark the boundary between human and divine worlds, but from the standpoint of Greek ancient tradition and modern folk tradition they may also mark the boundary between life and death.

sank forever is called after his name, Andreas (Adriatic, II.41.6). Scholars connect Andreas' story with the older Greek myth of the Boeotian fisherman Glaukos, who jumped into the sea and became a sea creature after drinking the Water of Life.[46] Other than the folk aetiological explanation for the name of the Adriatic Sea, the Andreas story has not survived as an independent base of folk legend in modern Greece.

The story of a sister of Alexander, also called Kale or Neraïda, has, however, survived. In modern folk stories she has taken on three manifestations, all of which are found in the *Alexander Romance*: a half human, half fish creature of the sea, a Nereid of the mountains, and Kale, the leader of the Nereids. In modern Greek folklore the female figure is linked to Alexander as a daughter (Politis 1904.1194; Lawson 1964.189); as a sister or sisters (Veloudis 1968.236; Politis 1904 nos. 552, 651); as his mother, who is a sea creature called *Phokia* 'Seal' (Politis 1904, no. 554); or as a lover (Politis 1904, no. 652). Three tales render versions resembling the episode in the *Alexander Romance*. The woman or women involved either use up (Politis 1194) or pour out (Politis no. 552 = Dragoumis 1919.298–301) the Water of Life before Alexander gets to drink it. In none of these tales do we find the cook Andreas. The stories offer folk explanations for characteristics of certain plants and birds.[47]

In two versions (Politis 1194 and no. 552) the woman falls or jumps into the sea and turns into a creature half human and half fish which, in Politis no. 551, is called a *Gorgona* 'Gorgon'. In Politis no. 651, the guilty sisters of Alexander are turned into Nereids and live in the valleys and rocks. Clearly, in the case of the woman becoming a sea creature, the traditions of the daughter and the cook of the *Alexander Romance*, both immortal *daimones*, one of the mountains and the other of the sea, have been combined. As the stories in the Politis collection show, however, the *Gorgona* is a folktale creature which may have an identity separate from that of Alexander the Great.[48] Because the sisters of Alex-

46. Friedlaender 1910a.95–96 links the cook to the Chadhir legends. See also 1910b.191–202 and Merkelbach and Trumpf 1977.135.

47. Politis no. 552 notes that the water Alexander's sister poured out fell on wild onions and that is why onions do not dry up. He says (no. 651) that the water fell on a μπότσικας plant [sea squill = *Urginea maritima* (L.) Baker, a member of the lily family; see Kabbadas n.d. 6.2689, 2964]. Like the wild onion, sea squill does not dry up. Politis p. 1194 notes that the water fell on wild garlic and that is why garlic does not grow from seeds but from cloves.

48. See Politis nos. 978–980 for Greek folk tales about the Water of Life but without a Gorgona; also Politis no. 659 (Nereids of the mountains and sea Nereids; the mountain Nereids hate the sea Nereids and they fight on Saturday nights); no. 666 (Nereid of the spring); nos. 671 and 672 (Nereids of the well). In antiquity the Nereids were sea nymphs,

ander become Nereids of valleys and rocks, there seems to be a link with the *Alexander Romance*, wherein Alexander's daughter is named Neraïda and becomes a *daimōn* of the mountains.[49] In the last manifestation, Kale is called the leader of the Nereids and this name may well be derived from the name of Alexander's daughter Kale in the *Alexander Romance*. Margaret Alexiou notes that the name is a continuation of the cult title of Artemis Kalliste, the virgin huntress, goddess of the woods. There is even testimony for a Saint Kale, sometimes called the cousin of the Virgin Mary.[50]

One particular motif links the stories mentioned above with other, shorter tales about Alexander and a woman called Gorgona, Nereid, or Phokia, but not Kale. The metamorphosed woman threatens destruction to those who pass her way. In four of the stories (Politis 1904, nos. 551, 552, 554; Veloudis 1968.235–236) the woman has become a half fish half woman sea creature who communicates with those on passing ships by asking ζῆ ὁ βασιλιᾶς ὁ Ἀλέξαντρος; "Does Alexander live?" If the answer is negative, she makes a storm and sinks the ship, killing all on board. If the sailors answer ζῆ καὶ βασιλεύει "He lives and rules," she lets the ship pass unharmed, sometimes singing songs which the sailors then learn.[51] Other variations of the answer are ζῆ καὶ βασιλεύει καὶ τὸν κόσμον ἐρηνεύει (Politis no. 551) "He lives and rules and pacifies the world"[52] and ζῆ καὶ βασιλεύει καὶ ζωὴ νά 'χετε καὶ σεῖς "He lives and rules and may you also have life." Another common answer is ζῆ καὶ βασιλεύει καὶ τὸ κόσμο κυριεύει "He lives and rules and governs the world," which is a nice variant on Alexander's title of *Kosmokratōr* 'Ruler of the World' in the *Alexander Romance*. The story of Alexander and his sisters (Politis no. 651) begins by saying that the action takes place when Alexander ἐκυρίευσεν οὖλον τὸν κόσμον "ruled the whole world."

the daughters of Nereus. The fact that in modern Greek tales they are sometimes linked with water is reminiscent of their ancient heritage (Schmidt 1871.100, 107).

49. See Politis nos. 550 and 551, and Lawson 1964.184–188 on the nature of the modern Greek Gorgons. Lawson (p. 190) points out that the modern Greek Gorgon is something of a mixture of ancient Greek monsters: Scylla, sirens, and the Gorgons.

50. Alexiou 1974.75. See also Politis 1904, nos. 660 and 661.

51. See Politis nos. 551 and 552. He notes that the Gorgona, usually found in the Black Sea, grasps the prow of the ship before asking the question. In a version from Syros she appears on Saturday night, about midnight. With the correct response she does no harm; with the incorrect one, her wails of lamentation precipitate a storm. See Zora 1960.346–365 for representations of the Gorgona in modern Greek folk art.

52. This phrase is common in current Greek folk tradition. I owe this observation to Vassilis Lambropoulos.

Nereids may manifest themselves in whirlwinds; someone who sees a whirlwind may ward off harm by reciting an incantation similar to those used against the mermaids, ζῆ 'Αλέξανδρος ὁ βασιλιᾶς, ζῆ καὶ βασιλεύει "King Alexander lives, he lives and rules" (Politis no. 651), or ζῆ, ζῆ καὶ βασιλεύει ὁ Μέγας 'Αλέξανδρος (Abbott 1969 [1903]. 251),[53] or one that is slightly different, μέλι καὶ γάλα στὰ φτερά σας "Honey and milk in your feathers" (Politis no. 653). While such liquids could slow down a bird-like causer of whirlwinds by gumming up the feathers, another version states simply μέλι καὶ γάλα στὸν δρόμο σας "Honey and milk in your path" (Abbot 1969 [1903].251; Schmidt 1871.124). In a footnote, Schmidt indicates that the phrase had been heard in the vicinity of the Hill of the Nymphs in Athens and hence is "a dark reminiscence of the former cult of the Nymphs on the top of this hill."[54] The honey and milk are offerings promised in return for a safe passage. Schmidt links the honey and milk offerings promised to the modern Nereids with similar offerings given to their ancient predecessors. Such wineless libations would have been appropriately offered to chthonic deities in ancient Greece.[55] Not only in association with these female figures is the tradition of Alexander "Ruler of the World" continued, but he appears on his own as the ruler of the world in a song that accompanied a folk dance known as Arnaoute. This dance was described to the eighteenth-century French traveler and writer P. A. Guys by Madame Chénier as one performed at Easter by a guild of butchers in Constantinople.[56] The dance seemed to reenact the battles of Alexander the Great, and Madame Chénier's fertile imagination even allowed her to pick out the dancers who portrayed Alexander's generals Hephaistion, Parmenion, Seleukos, and others.[57] The dance music was provided by lyre players who sang, at the beginning of the dance, the following lines: πού ἴν ὁ 'Αλεξάνδρος ὁ Μακέδονις, που ὁρίσεν τὶν ὀκουμένιν ἱλίν "Where is Alexander of

53. Veloudis 1968.241–242 notes that there are other incantations connected with Alexander either to ward off sickness and harmful animals or to bring about the fruitfulness of trees.

54. Schmidt 1871.127. See also p. 125 for a folk poem from Kephalonia used to ward off evil: χαιράμεναις, καλόκαρδαις, / μέλι καὶ γάλα, / σ' τοῦ βασιλέα τὴν τάβλα! / Στὴ ψυχὴ τοῦ βασιλέως τοῦ 'Αλέξανδρου, κακὸ μὴ μοῦ κάμετε! 'To the happy ones, the kindly ones, / honey and milk, / at the table of the king! / By the soul of King Alexander, / don't harm me!"

55. See Burkert 1985.70–73.

56. Guys 1783.192–193. Madame Chenier, born in Constantinople, was the Greek mother of the French Revolutionary poet André Chenier. See Veloudis 1968.241, who notes that most Greek butchers in Constantinople came from Macedonia.

57. Guys 1783.198.

Macedon, who ruled the whole world?"[58] Although the lines are not used for warding off danger as they are in the folk tale tradition, they sound strangely like questions often posed in laments for fallen cities both ancient and Byzantine.[59] Were the Greeks of eighteenth-century Constantinople under Turkish rule lamenting the loss of one who had not only ruled the world but had become a symbol of Greek independence?[60]

While the Greek Archaic and Classical poleis had sought in mythical tradition a divine or heroic founder who would protect them and legitimize their authority and dominion, Alexander himself founded, in the vast territory he had conquered, cities that would perpetuate his name. Alexandria in Egypt eventually became the seat of Ptolemaic rule and gave Alexander the afterlife he sought. Here was his body (*Sōma*), destined to become a tomb and sign (*Sēma*). Alexandria was fated to be "the City," the capital of the civilized world; similarly, Pericles had proclaimed Athens "the school of Greece" (Thucydides 2.41.1–2). The *Romance*, a compilation of earlier historico-fictional accounts of the life of Alexander and the foundation of his city, projects this foundation onto a mythical, prophetic past. The tomb of Alexander, erected by the Ptolemies, who revived ancient ritual customs associated with tombs of heroes, served to buttress their power. Cultic and mythic traditions were evoked after the demise of the political centers in which they had emerged, because the continuity manifested in these traditions was essential for creating and mantaining new centers of power. The episode of the Water of Life illustrates suggestively the popular beliefs associated with the charismatic figure of Alexander, whose vast empire raises him to the ranks of the divine. In later times, folk stories of metamorphoses, formulas of incantation, and popular ritual song accompanied by dance no longer suggest the climactic moment of glory and power Alexander and his city, Alexandria, enjoyed in the past but convey rather a lamentation for their fall.

58. Guys p. 194.
59. Troy, Constantinople, Herakleion; see Alexiou 1974.84–86, 92.
60. See Veloudis 1968.182, 198–211 for references to Alexander used to inspire resistance against the Turks.

CHAPTER 9

The Greeks Are Indeed like the Others: Myth and Society in the West African *Sunjata*

Thomas J. Sienkewicz

The mark Greek mythology has left on Western thought and culture is undeniable and indelible. The use of Greek myths as standard themes and points of reference for Western artists, writers, and poets, and the survival and flourishing of Greek mythology in the modern world, have been interpreted by some as a sign of the universality of Greek mythology, of its unique adaptability to different and changing social and cultural needs.

This view of Greek mythology as both unique and universal among the world's mythologies has been eloquently voiced by George Steiner, who proposes that the Greek language and the Greek myths are inseparably linked and that the syntax of the Greek language and the myths expressed therein reflect basic, universal human experiences and forms of expression.[1] In Steiner's view this basic bond between Greek mythology and the Greek language creates a collection of myths which incorporates all the diverse modes of human language and experience. In short, the Greeks have said it all and little original material has been left by the Greeks for later generations to develop. Hence the special place of Greek mythology and the reason why the Greeks are different from the others.

Marcel Detienne has challenged this Hellenocentric view.[2] Focusing

1. Steiner 1984.135–138. For example, Steiner argues that the myth of Prometheus is connected with the future tense and that of Narcissus with the first-person singular verb.
2. Detienne 1979. The title of this chapter alludes to Detienne's sarcastic title: "The Greeks Are Not like the Others."

on "misunderstandings" between traditional Hellenists and structuralists, Detienne rejects the Hellenists' quest for the so-called original version of a myth in favor of his own structuralist preference for reading mythic multiforms within their ethnographic contexts. It is the variants that show the essence of myth as "recurrence and repetition in variation."[3] Such variation, caused by inevitable reworking of myth to adapt to changing times and different locales, emphasizes a bond between myth and society, long recognized, especially by Malinowski in his well-known theory of charter myths.[4]

As the previous chapters show, *muthos* emerges and develops in the context of a society, a polis. Each polis could and did adapt traditional tales to changing social and political needs. Greek myths reflect the society in which they flourished and reveal a tension between the poleis and pan-Hellenism, between local diversity and pan-cultural unity. Pan-Hellenism necessitated the rejection, revision, and reinterpretation of many local myths.

In this tension between local variants and pan-cultural canonicity the Greeks are not unique. Similar tendencies can be noted in medieval Europe and in the Islamic world. In all three contexts there is a diversity of local multiforms overspread and controlled by a dogmatic religious and cultural center. Just as Delphi and Athens often functioned as processing centers for a pan-Hellenic version of a local myth, so too did medieval Rome serve as the religious and cultural unifier of a disparate and diverse Christian Europe. Indeed, Rome has long maintained the authority to canonize or reject particular beliefs and doctrines. A combination of an *imprimatur* and an *index of forbidden books* in the Roman church aimed at determining the official versions of hagiographic and other texts. In a similar way, Mecca has functioned for the Islamic world, not only as a religious center, but also as a source of many pan-cultural myths. Yet in all three areas particular variants have continued to thrive despite such unifying tendencies. It is through the flexibility of mythic variants that broad cultural groups can maintain their sense of unity without completely sacrificing their sense of local pride.

Interest in the relationship between myth and society has led modern scholars to the living mythologies of the so-called under-developed countries. Such study is often primarily anthropological in nature and, until very recently, it started from an assumption of Western

3. Detienne 1979.6.
4. See Malinowski 1931 or excerpts in Lessa and Vogt 1979.63–72.

cultural superiority which labeled such cultures "primitive." Yet all human cultures are now recognized to be much closer in terms of intellectual development, and "primitive" has come to be seen essentially as an invalid assessment of the myopic West.[5]

In this chapter I first examine the relationship between myth and society in one Third World culture, that of the Manding of West Africa, and then compare this study of Manding poetry in its social context with the Greek experience. A tension between poetry and society, between *muthos* and polis, is revealed in several significant features of Manding oral poetry, in which the dynamics of multiformity versus canonicity operate within the context of the limited literacy given in that society. At the end of this chapter I compare briefly the role of oral poetry in Manding and Greek cultures and consider the relationship between literacy and canonicity in both cultures.[6]

Manding society possesses both a vigorous pan-cultural tradition and a constant pull toward diversity. Crossing several modern political boundaries, including those of Mali, the Gambia, and Ivory Coast, and speaking a number of closely related languages, such as Malinke, Bambara, and Soninke, the Manding are an ancient people with a long and well-established sense of history and a living oral literature.

The Manding oral tradition includes praise songs, creation myths, circumcision songs, hunting songs, and heroic legends.[7] Sufficient material has been collected, especially of Manding heroic legends, to demonstrate the existence of diverse multiforms within this oral literature.[8] These multiforms tend to be localized in origin; that is, each Manding area has its own preferred version of the tradition. The persistence of such multiforms is due to an oral tradition that allows for local diversity and for adaptation over temporal and spatial distance. The Manding peoples believe that their oral stories retell the experiences of their common past, yet the diversity of their multiforms shows the ability of these stories to adapt to changes of time and locality.

Many of the features of oral poetry noted in modern Yugoslavian and ancient Greek epics by Albert Lord can be found also in the Mand-

---

5. The similarities between "civilized" and "primitive" are discussed in Goody 1977.

6. Not the least significant of the parallels between the West African Manding culture and the ancient Greek culture is that the Manding poetic tradition is the primary vehicle of myths of foundational value to the Manding society.

7. On circumcision songs, see Innes 1972; on hunting songs, see Bird 1972; on creation myths, see Dieterlen 1957.

8. On multiforms of Manding heroic legends, see Zemp 1966.

ing tradition.[9] Conservatism and fluidity create a dynamic tension within this oral culture, which simultaneously retains its traditional stories and adapts them to changing performative situations. Oral literature represents both past and present transformations of society. It is a record of the past as perceived in the present. Essentially performative by nature, such oral literature is recreated each time it is presented to an audience. No two oral performances of the same myth are ever identical word for word. Manding singers are aware that multiforms of the same story exist; for example, one singer says:

> You see one griot,[10]
> And he gives you an account of it one way,
> And you will find that that is the way he heard it;
> You see another griot,
> And he gives you an account of it in another way,
> And you will find that what he has heard has determined his version.
>
> Innes 1974.145, ll. 8–13.

Built into the griot's statement is the assumption that there is a common core to this legend, upon which multiforms are built.

Charles S. Bird has noted several distinctive features of the Manding language. One characteristic is a marked cohesiveness within the Manding language group—a "high degree of mutual intelligibility among all the dialects."[11] Manding speakers are able to communicate easily with each other, even while using different dialects. A parallel can be noted here with ancient Greece, where dialects were also mutually understandable. Such linguistic cohesiveness provides a ready means to establish unity within diversity and is thus critical for the creation of a common culture.

Bird accounts for the cohesiveness of the Manding group by a linguistic "wave theory" characterized by both a core of grammatical rules which all the dialects share and a diverse group of overlapping rules shared only by particular areas.[12] This wave theory reflects the

---

9. See Lord 1960.

10. While a singer of songs like the *Sunjata* (the equivalent of a Greek *aoidos* 'bard') is known in some parts of the Manding world as a jeli, "griot" is more common in English. The etymology of "griot" is mysterious. Possibly derived from the Portuguese word *criar* 'to educate, to instruct', "griot" comes into English from the French *griot*, widely used in the 1960s to refer to West African singers. There is an extensive bibliography on the etymology of *griot*. See Labouret 1951, who argues a Portuguese provenance.

11. Bird 1970.148.

12. Bird pp. 150–152.

Manding's simultaneous diversity and unity on the level of language.

Linguistic simplicity, avoidance of redundance, is another important feature of Manding. Bird argues that such simplicity made Manding an important trade language and fostered extensive communication both within and beyond the Manding-speaking region.[13] This linguistic feature provides further structural support for a unified Manding society.

Communication in the Manding area has been encouraged, too, by a relatively stable political situation lasting for several centuries. Bird points out that the Manding peoples have always been associated with great empires that facilitated trade in the area and provided protection from some of the violent vicissitudes of war.[14] The Manding empire also fostered a common political bond, creating a great source of pride, identity, and unity for its diverse population.

All of these characteristics of the Manding, which Bird notes in the context of extralinguistic factors affecting linguistic change, also illustrate a significant tension between diversity and unity on linguistic, political, and cultural levels. The Manding are a group of many peoples speaking separate dialects, but with a common language and history. While the Manding peoples see themselves as sharing a mutual heritage and genealogy, their common culture, retaining distinctly local elements, maintains, from tribe to tribe and place to place, differing versions of this heritage.

The primary vehicle for the transmission of this common culture is Manding oral literature, the centerpiece of which is an epic about the hero Sunjata (1230–1255), founder of the Manding empire and its greatest chief.[15] Remembered in West Africa through oral tradition for seven centuries, Sunjata's life receives some independent evidence in the chronicle of Ibn-Khaldūn, a fourteenth-century Arabic writer.[16] Although the historical basis of the hero myth, that is, Sunjata's actual existence, is not questioned by modern historians, the legend itself has been handed down orally with noteworthy variation according to locality. The entire oral tradition, filled with contradictory details, cannot be accepted as fact; it is simply too fluid, too marked by local variants. Sunjata the hero has become more important than Sunjata the man. He has become the tradition's unifying element and the genealogical center to

13. Bird p. 154.
14. Bird p. 153.
15. English spellings of Manding words, including proper names, vary greatly. Thus *Sunjata* also appears as *Sundiata, Sun-Jata,* and *Son-Jara.*
16. Ibn-Khaldūn 1868.

whose life and history all the various ruling families have traced their ancestry. Sunjata's legend has become the cultural linchpin that unites diverse traditions, genealogies, and histories.

Multiforms of the *Sunjata* contain several thematic parts: the miraculous conception, birth, and childhood of the hero, his exile, and his defeat of the Susu king Sumanguru to become ruler of the Manding. These sections may be expanded or contracted, but usually they appear in every version. To this narrative core, several subtales are sometimes added, including, at the beginning, the story of Sunjata's mother and the source of her special powers, and at the end, a narration of various battles and events following the defeat of Sumanguru. Some discretion is thus allowed in the presentation of the tale.

The length of the *Sunjata* varies considerably from version to version. Bird notes that one version may be told in a single evening whereas another may take up to thirty hours to recite.[17] Such variation in length is a general characteristic of oral epic poetry notable too in Greece and in Yugoslavia. Shorter and longer versions, both equally valid depending upon context, can exist for the same episode. Lord says of a Yugoslavian singer that "the length of his songs and the degree to which he will ornament them will depend on the demands of the audience."[18] Lord also notes that Parry's interest in Petar Vidić's song resulted in a second version almost twice as long as the first.[19] An example of a Greek tale told in both longer and shorter versions can be found by comparing *Odyssey* ix–xii with *Odyssey* xxiii 300–343.

The epic nature of the *Sunjata* has been the object of much discussion as a result of Ruth Finnegan's controversial "Note on Epic."[20] Although Finnegan argues in this brief treatment of the subject that no "relatively long narrative poems" have been composed in Africa, there is no question that both the *Sunjata* and other African poems have many affinities with such primary, oral epics as the *Iliad* and *Odyssey* or those in the Yugoslavian tradition.[21] Finnegan's negative statement concerning African epic is based upon texts that are not reliably transmitted. A good example of such poor transmission is Niane's edition of the *Sunjata*

17. Bird 1970.156–157.
18. Lord 1960.25.
19. Lord p. 113.
20. Finnegan 1970.108–110.
21. On the epic form in Africa, see Biebuyck 1968, Biebuyck and Mateene 1978, Okpewho 1979, Johnson 1980 and 1986, and Seydou 1983.

(1965), which offers a reworked prose form very different from the performed poetic version. On the other hand, multiforms of the *Sunjata* such as those recorded by Innes (1974) and by Johnson (1979, 1986) exhibit, in fact, the poetic language that Finnegan thinks African epics lack.

Like the Homeric epics, the Manding epic uses a special poetic language that separates it from everyday speech. Bird has noted the restricted nature of Manding epic diction, which is both archaic and dialectal.[22] The language of the epic is thus simultaneously conservative and local in nature. Like the Manding language itself, the diction of the *Sunjata* is both unifying, as the language of a national epic, and diverse, in its preference for dialectal forms.

Several aspects of the *Sunjata* particularly illustrate the tension between diversity and unity in Manding society: the effect of the audience upon the variant, the relationship between the past and the present within the epic, and the conflict between Islam and animism. In each of these areas can be noted a balance between variants, an acceptance of multiforms recognizing the coexistence of diversity and unity within the same epic. The *Sunjata* thus becomes a primary vehicle for expressing both local individuality and national conformity in a single context.

The relationship between audience and variants in the Manding epic is especially revealing. Perhaps in no other oral epic tradition is there such significant evidence for the way a particular audience can affect the performance of the singer and the multiform that is created. Thanks to the care with which field researchers such as Gordon Innes and J. W. Johnson have recorded the circumstances of particular performances of the epic, it is now possible to illustrate how the composition of the audience can determine the multiform. I examine such variation of song in several different versions.

The first is Bamba Suso's version, recorded by Innes (1974) as it was performed at a school in Brikama in the Gambia.[23] This multiform has a notable emphasis on genealogies, aetiologies of surnames and the foundation legends of towns near Brikama, whereas all of this information is notably lacking in other variants. These features may be due to the fact that the griot was asked to tell the pupils "something of the history of their people" and "to give as full an account as possible."[24] Brikama itself receives special notice, although it is not mentioned in other variants.

---

22. Bird 1970.157.
23. See Innes 1974.37–38 for a description of the circumstances of Bamba's performance.
24. Innes p. 370.

Most notably, in Bamba's multiform, Brikama is settled by Sankareng Madibe Konte, Sunjata's maternal grandfather and one of his generals.[25] The present chief of Brikama claims descent from Sankareng.[26] In this context it is significant that the special arrow that causes Sumanguru's defeat is shot by Sankareng in Bamba's song and not elsewhere.[27]

The second version I refer to is that of Dembo Kanute, also recorded by Innes. This is the only published variant not gained from contrived circumstances, that is, not sung for and before a fieldworker with recording equipment. No outsider was present at the performance of Dembo's song, sung at the griot's own suggestion. The host himself, Seni Darbo, taped the performance.[28] In Dembo's version, it is a Darbo who shoots the arrow that defeats Sumanguru.[29]

A third example of the relationship between the site of the performance and the song can be seen in the version of Magan Sisòkò recorded by Johnson (1979). Sisòkò, singing at Kita in Mali, interrupts the narrative in order to sing the praises of this town:

This is Kita.
Mount Kita and Budòfò.
O city of Magan, the Tall!
O city of holy men!
Tayakun and Tayaba.
This is Kita!
Kita's ancient name was Mount Geni.
Let us turn to Kita now.

Johnson 1979.127–128, ll. 2130–2137[30]

A foundation legend of Kita follows these lines.

Clearly the real pressures of local interests and individual listeners have determined the forms of Bamba's, Dembo's, and Sisòkò's songs. The singers must balance the tendency toward a unified tale of Sunjata with the demands of local pride and relevance.

Integration of more recent historical events into the traditional epic is another feature of the *Sunjata*. Allusion to nineteenth-century jihads

25. See Innes p. 85, l. 958 for Sankareng's settlement of Brikama.
26. Innes pp. 128–129, note to l. 957.
27. Innes p. 79, ll. 836–840.
28. See Innes pp. 264–265 for a fuller description of the circumstances of this performance.
29. Innes p. 309, ll. 956–972.
30. See also Johnson 1979.162, l. 2889.

or Moslem religious wars, and to leaders such as the insurrectionist Musa Molo is sometimes woven into the narrative of Bamba Suso's song.[31] Fode Kaba, archenemy of both Molo and the French colonials, is mentioned in the songs of both Bamba Suso and Banna Kanute.[32] These references provide historical and thematic links between the distant epic past of Sunjata and the twentieth-century audience. Just as in Homer, anachronisms easily slip into the narrative: for example, the use of guns in Sunjata's battles, which took place before the introduction of gunpowder.[33]

A striking illustration in the *Sunjata* of the tension between diversity and unity is the integration of Islam into the originally animistic epic. Here one can see the traditional religion of the Manding coming to terms with the increasing presence of Islam within its society. Islamic influence seems to have appeared in the area as early as the century following that of Sunjata, when one of his successors, Mansa Musa (1373/4–1387/8), made a pilgrimage to Mecca, the rumor of which reached even European ears. Despite the Islamic faith of Musa, Sunjata himself was probably not a Moslem and Manding rulers and peoples may have retained their animistic faith for several centuries. Only in the early nineteenth century did Islam begin to make larger inroads in the area, mostly due to population upheavals and traumatic jihads in the 1840s.[34] We can therefore assume that the largest integration of Islamic themes into the *Sunjata* occurred after this period.

Animistic themes are prominent in the *Sunjata*. Both Sunjata's mother and Sumanguru possess special magical powers conceived animistically. In several multiforms, a significant portion of the epic traces the animistic powers of Sunjata's mother back to the *jinn* of a buffalo woman.[35] The animistic powers of Sumanguru, who can be conquered only by a counterspell, are also a constant of the epic. Islamic influence emerges in other parts of the multiforms. In Magan Sisòkò's song, Sunjata's genealogy shows Islamic elements and Sunjata becomes a descendant of the Prophet.[36] In Banna Kanute's song, the first four Mand-

31. Innes 1974.97–99, ll. 1223, 1240, 1242, 1248, 1297.

32. For Bamba's references to Fode Kaba, see Innes 1974.97–99, ll. 1240, 1242, 1249, 1280. For Banna's, see Innes 1974.185, ll. 895, 896, 901.

33. See Innes p. 231, ll. 1918–1921.

34. For more detailed discussion of these nineteenth-century events, see Quinn 1972 and also Schaffer and Cooper 1980.

35. *Jinn*, an Arabic word borrowed by the Manding, refers to powerful animistic spirits. *Jinn* is also the source of the English word "genie." Versions of the *Sunjata* with the buffalo woman episode are recorded by Johnson 1979 and 1986 and Niane 1965.

36. See Johnson 1979.34–37, ll. 1–72. The fluidity of Sunjata's genealogy within the oral

ing tribes to convert to Islam become major sources of support to Sumanguru in his conflict with Sunjata.[37]

The tension between animism and Islam remains essentially unresolved both in the epic and in Manding society. Islam has not yet succeeded, if it ever will, in displacing all the animistic elements of the epic. The appearance of Islamic themes in the traditional *Sunjata* epic illustrates the way the historical process reflects social pressure within the epic. Because of changes in Manding society since the nineteenth century, Sunjata himself has developed Islamic tics, despite the historical improbability of such links.[38]

The Manding singer shows himself aware of and affected by modern political pressures. Praise of current political leaders is not uncommon,[39] and fieldworkers have mentioned that modern politicians often patronize griots in the expectation that the singers will interweave references to them into their songs.[40]

Traditionally the jeli was a member of a hereditary caste of singers who were linked, family by family, with specific tribal rulers. Thus a Kuyate has always been the jeli of a Keita ruler of Mali.[41] The jeli was considered to be, not merely an entertainer, but also the preserver of tribal heritage through his song and the primary source of praise for his ruler. Furthermore, the traditional jeli served as the chief's spokesman or herald and advisor. Bala Faasigi Kuyate, Sunjata's griot, frequently has in the epic the role of the hero's spokesman; for example, it is Bala who calls Sunjata's troops together for him in Bamba's version of the *Sunjata*.[42] In return for his services, the jeli looked to his chief as a patron who supported him financially. The dependence of the griot

tradition can be compared with the changing genealogies of the Tiv people, noted by Goody and Watt 1968.31–34.

37. These families are the Siises, the Jaanes, the Kommas, and the Tures. See Innes 1974.157–181. Innes discusses the prominence of Islam in this version on p. 241, note to l. 83.

38. Conrad 1985 offers a detailed discussion of the integration of Islam into Manding oral tradition.

39. Dembo refers to Fili Daabo, a Malian politician and Dembo's patron. See Innes 1974.267, l. 4 and 313n.

40. See Innes 1974.10–11.

41. The relationship between the Kuyates and the Keitas is illustrated in Bamba Suso's song (Innes 1974) and in Niane's 1965 version of the epic. Bamba especially emphasizes these ties with the following statement: "There is a special relationship / Between the members of the Keita family and the members of the Kuyate family. / Even today, if a member of the Kuyate family deceives a member of the Keita family, / Things will go badly for him" (Innes 1974.61, ll. 470–473).

42. Innes 1974.61–71.

upon his chief is illustrated by a destitute Sunjata's efforts to support the griots in Bamba's version, where it is said that

> They went and begged from him.
> When they went and begged from him,
> He did not have anything.
> He went and got honey in the bush,
> And brought it back for the griots.
> Whatever he gave them, they did not scorn it.
>
> Innes 1974.47, ll. 142–147

Religious ceremonies, such as the reroofing of the sacred hut in Kaaba (Kangaba) in southern Mali, have been important in the training of griots by providing opportunities for the sharing of songs among griots from different regions. Bird suggests that such occasions "exert a normalizing force on the society's linguistic behavior."[43] These events may have also served as a normalizing force in the development of the *Sunjata* epic, as a means of national control over local multiforms. In this sense, Kaaba may, like Delphi, Rome, and Mecca, be an example of a center for pan-cultural assimilation of regional myths.

The advent of colonial rule and the deterioration of the power and wealth of tribal chiefs have meant a parallel decrease in the modern griot's duties and social status. Traditional occasions for performance of the griot's song have become more and more rare, and, without wealthy chiefs to support them, the singers have found it difficult to retain their position in society. The following lament, voiced by Banna Kanute, reveals the singer's frustration with the current situation:

> In Sunjata's day a griot did not have to fetch water,
> To say nothing of farming and collecting firewood.
> Father World had changed, changed.
>
> Innes 1974.159, ll. 320–322

The griots have lost not only their financial support but also several of the functions upon which their status was founded. No longer are they advisors and spokesmen to kings and chiefs. As noted above, the modern political situation has only marginal use for a jeli who is sometimes employed by aspiring politicians to sing their praises. To support themselves some griots have tried to adapt their song to different media, such as radio, in their own countries. Indeed the very survival of the

---

43. See Bird 1970.156.

singers and their oral tradition is currently in jeopardy. The pressures of the modern world may yet force the *Sunjata* into a static, uniform version, and the epic may take on pan-Manding features by losing its fluidity and variety. Changes in society and the influence of modern media may create what several centuries of oral tradition never did: a canonical, national form of the *Sunjata*.

The traditional role of the griot frequently emerges from the epic itself. The modern singer often reminds his audience of the once-important status of the jeli; for example, in Bamba's song, the only part of his father's property that Sunjata wants are the griots.[44] The prominence of the jeli is built into the very structure of the epic, in which the hero develops a close bond with his singer. In Bamba's version Sunjata even serves his unsuspecting singer flesh from his own thigh when both are starving on the savannah.[45] Frequently in the variants Sunjata is unable to accomplish his tasks without the assistance of the singer. Usually the singer's aid consists of verbal encouragement.[46] At the least, Sunjata needs his singer to voice his praises.[47] The jeli can also use his song to exhort an unwilling or incapacitated hero to action, or even to transform the hero's uninspiring or disreputable actions into praise. When Sunjata runs away in battle, the griots are able to save the hero's reputation by making the incident part of Sunjata's praise name.[48]

The contrast between the griot's role in the epic and his place in the modern world thus illustrates the tension between a tolerant tradition that accepted diversity and a modern world that strives for homogeneity.

The hero's ties with other characters in the epic and with other members of his society reveal a great deal of variety and interchangeability of roles from multiform to multiform. In one version Sunjata performs a deed that is done by another character in another multiform. The most striking example of this interchangeability occurs in the balafon scene. In this episode, the first balafon, a type of xylophone, is discovered and played.[49] In Banna's version, it is Sunjata who obtains the balafon and plays it.[50] In Dembo's version, it is Sumanguru who per-

---

44. Innes 1974.45, ll. 125–127.
45. Innes pp. 59–61, ll. 437–475.
46. In Banna's song, Bala Faasigi sings Sunjata's praises as a song of encouragement as the hero prepares for his final encounter with Sumanguru. See Innes 227, ll. 1844–1863.
47. E.g., see Innes p. 155, ll. 244–246.
48. Innes p. 71, ll. 684–691.
49. On the importation of the xylophone to West Africa, see Jones 1971.
50. Innes 1974.209–213, ll. 1465–1526.

forms the same deed.[51] In several multiforms, the griot then comes upon the instrument, plays it without permission, and is hamstrung by the owner, whether Sunjata or Sumanguru.[52] The parallels between these versions suggest a very close link between the hero and his enemy in the epic.[53]

Another episode of the epic showing role interchangeability is the firing of a special arrow to defeat Sumanguru. In Banna's version it is Sunjata who makes the shot.[54] But in Bamba's song it is Sunjata's maternal grandfather, Sankareng.[55] Dembo sings that yet another man, the Darbo ancestor of his host, is the slayer of Sumanguru.[56]

The *Sunjata* is an epic that praises the community as a whole, and its hero is someone with whom everyone in his society is closely associated. Not only is Sunjata, as the victor over Sumanguru, the savior of his society, but, as the representative of his society, Sunjata also becomes, through his victory, the means to the heroic apotheosis of his whole society. His epic becomes the Manding national epic and the source of unity out of diversity.

Through its hero the *Sunjata* epic becomes a communal experience that unites all members of society, not only in the epic past but also in the performative present.[57] The epic is more than the tale of its characters; it is at the same time about its audience. The bond between the *Sunjata* and the audience is created by various literary features of the Manding epic. Sometimes the audience is integrated into the epic in direct address by the griot. Such references to the live audience are not uncommon in the Manding epic, in the form of an address. During Bamba's performance the musical accompanist asks the griot questions

51. Innes pp. 273–275, ll. 133–203.

52. E.g., Innes pp. 213–215, ll. 1548–1564, and Niane 1965.38–40.

53. A similar relationship exists between Hermes and his antagonist, Apollo, in the *Homeric Hymn to Hermes*. The newborn Hermes, who had invented the lyre, stole the sacred cows of Apollo but returned them at the command of Zeus. Apollo was charmed by the instrument, which Hermes played and sang to, and thus the two gods exchanged privileges. Apollo, receiving the lyre from Hermes, bestowed upon him the staff that would mark him as cowherd and poet.

54. Innes 1974.231, ll. 1937–1939.

55. Innes p. 79, ll. 835–842.

56. Innes pp. 309–311, ll. 956–980.

57. Even so did ancient Greek performative poetry create *kharis* 'mirth', a bond between poet and audience and a communal act of the society to which they belonged. This can be illustrated with examples in epic (*Odyssey* ix 3–11) and, especially, in epinician poetry, such as Pindar *Olympian* 7.93–94, 14.13–16. For further illustrations of this phenomenon in oral cultures, see Edwards and Sienkewicz 1990.

and receives responses.[58] In several versions the singer directly addresses his host several times. Banna addresses his host and wishes him long life.[59] Dembo and Sisòkò end their songs by singing directly to their hosts.[60] These references can be at times exhortations to do something in life worthy of memory, such as the following plea by Dembo to his host:

> Seni Daabo, do something, sir;
> Life consists of doing something,
> Not of doing everything,
> For there is no end to that, and failure wins no support.
>
> Innes 1974.269, ll. 67–70

These references can also be critical, such as the following rebuke by Banna:

> But the griots have a complaint, Demba:
> Don't you know
> That an ordinary narrator and an expert singer are not the same?
>
> Innes 1974.201, ll. 1264–1266

Direct address in the *Sunjata* is often linked with the use of praise songs. Sung in a style different from the narrative sections of the epic,[61] these passages of praise are usually directed toward characters in the epic. For instance, a standard praise song of Sunjata, based upon the names of the hero's father and mother, is

> Sukulung Kutuma,
> And Sukulung Yammaru,
> Naareng Makhang Konnate,
> Cats on the shoulder,
> Simbong and Jata are at Naarena.
>
> Innes 1974.149, ll. 116–120

Members of the audience can also be included in such praise songs. Banna sings the following praise of his host, Bakari Sidibe:

58. Innes 1974.67, ll. 594–596; 69, ll. 614–625; 71, ll. 661–664, and 77, ll. 794–797.
59. Innes p. 171, ll. 574–579.
60. Innes p. 311, ll. 1016–1020, and Johnson 1979.194, ll. 3628–3631.
61. See Innes 1974.17–20 for a discussion of the different modes of song in the *Sunjata*.

Praise be to God, Master of the worlds.
Kibili Demba, thank you.
Salimata Dembo,
Husband of a Jebate woman, Demba, thank you.
If you take it from here,
You must join it to Karata.
You come from
Jallo and Jagite,
Great Sidibe and Sankare.
Dembo, who used to live with the people of the Island,
Dembo, son of a Sanyang woman, thank you.

Innes 1974.201, ll. 1253–1263

This passage combines praise of Sidibe with references to his ancestors and his place of origin and thus makes the performance of personal interest to the singer's audience. The *Sunjata* serves as a mechanism of praise simultaneously for past and present members of Manding society.

Past and present are also united in the epic by association of various towns, regions, and family names with episodes in the hero's life. Thus, in Bamba Suso's song, the foundations of many towns in the Gambia are traced back to deeds of Sunjata and his generals.[62] Particularly common are the aetiologies of surnames, which are sometimes even traced to actual phrases spoken by Sunjata. Bamba tells the following story to explain the origin of the family name Noomo:

When Sunjata had been told what had happened,
He sent Tira Makhang,
With orders to proceed against that king.
Tira Makhang captured the king,
Destroyed his residence,
Bound him,
And took him to Sunjata.
When Sunjata saw him,
He said to him, "*Noomo*" 'Defeated'.
Even today the surname Noomo is in existence.

Innes 1974.83, ll. 932–941

For the listener with the surname Noomo, this passage makes the epic

62. For example, Innes p. 85, l. 958, the settlement of Brikama, where Bamba's performance takes place, is traced to Sankareng, Sunjata's general and grandfather.

real and personal; thus the modern Manding listener becomes a part of the *Sunjata*.

References to several Manding social customs within the epic create further points of identity for the audience. The ceremony surrounding the circumcision of young boys is an important tradition among the Manding and becomes, in several versions of the *Sunjata*, the occasion when the crippled hero learns to walk.[63] In Bamba's song the circumcision ceremony is linked not only with the walking episode but with another test based upon magic trousers.[64] In Banna's version the references to the circumcision rite itself are lengthier and more detailed and include several attempts by the antagonist to dispose of his enemy.[65] Plot and social custom are combined in these passages to create for the Manding audience a further link between the hero and themselves.

Manding family and clan structure are integrated into the epic. Polygamy sometimes dominates the story through a bitter rivalry of Sunjata's mother and another wife of his father.[66] Maternal ties are particularly important in Manding culture and are emphasized in the epic by Sunjata's ties with his mother.[67] In Niane 1965 and Johnson 1979 the hero's special powers are derived explicitly from his mother's animistic associations with the *jinn* of a buffalo woman. The exiled hero's return home and victory over Sumanguru are also frequently linked with the impending death of his mother. The most elaborate use of this theme appears in versions where the hero demands and receives two supernatural signs joining his mother's death with Sunjata's victory over Sumanguru.[68]

Ties between brother and sister are likewise strong in Manding society and are reflected in the close relationship between Sunjata and his sister Sugulun, another necessary adjunct to Sunjata's heroic power. One of the standard and most memorable episodes of the epic is the seduction of Sumanguru by Sugulun, who thus obtains for her brother the knowledge necessary to defeat the Susu king.[69]

63. On the importance of this ceremony, see Schaffer and Cooper 1980, and Innes 1972.
64. Innes 1974.43–45, ll. 85–121.
65. Innes pp. 181–207, ll. 845–1405. The circumcision episode covers about one-third of this version.
66. See Niane 1965 and Johnson 1979 and 1986 (version of Fa-Digi Sisòkò).
67. See Schaffer and Cooper 1980.87–90.
68. See Innes 1974.287, ll. 447–477, Niane 1965.45–47, Johnson 1979.165–172, ll. 2980–3147, and Johnson 1986.164–165, ll. 2410–2450.
69. See Innes 1974.73–79, ll. 693–842; 215–219, ll. 1565–1689; 303–307, ll. 829–913; Johnson 1979.182–183, ll. 3381–3415; also Johnson 1986.171–173, ll. 2668–2741.

Relationships between modern clans and tribes are explained and reinforced in multiforms of the *Sunjata*; for example, a strongly Islamic version gives great prominence to the four Manding families that first converted to Islam.[70] Traditional ties between certain ruling families and certain griot families such as the relationship between the Kuyates and the Keitas,[71] appear in other variants.

All of these features of the *Sunjata* show how the West African epic operates as a social unifier joining diverse peoples in the present by creating communal unity with the past. The living epic is a dynamic link between past and present, between hero and audience, between local diversity and "national" unity.

The Manding culture shares with the Greek culture a dynamic blend of local and national trends. Tension between diversity and unity is especially strong in the Manding region, which encompasses an area larger than France and includes over four million speakers. The Manding language serves as a principal medium of communication in a significant part of West Africa, and the large number of speakers and their broad geographic spread are considered unusual in an African context. So also the Greek language became widespread in the Mediterranean world beginning at least as early as the age of colonization in the eighth century B.C., and it became the *lingua franca* there in the Hellenistic Age. Manding is thus a special case in Africa, just as Greece was special in the ancient Mediterranean world.

This social and cultural dynamic within the oral Manding tradition parallels the relationship between Greek *muthos* and polis, especially in the early stages of pan-Hellenism before local multiforms were displaced by more generic, pan-Hellenic versions. A good example of this process in Greece is the canonization of the tale of the conflict between Achilles and Agamemnon over such variants as the conflict between Achilles and Odysseus at Troy.[72] The multiformity of these quarrel scenes in the Greek tradition calls to mind a similar multiformity in the *Sunjata* epic, where particular deeds are attributed to different characters in different variants. The Greek tradition thus reflects a process of selection and canonization which the Manding tradition lacks.

70. See Innes 1974.157–181, ll. 265–844.
71. See Niane 1965.1 and Innes 1974.61, ll. 471–475.
72. Nagy 1979.42–58 has shown that the Homeric texts contain evidence for a multiform that focused on the Achilles-Odysseus conflict. Creation of a pan-Hellenic version necessitated the suppression of such a variant in favor of the Achilles-Agamemnon conflict upon which the *Iliad* is based.

The Manding epic differs from the Greek epic tradition in its exten-sive use of direct address. Homer's audience hardly ever intrudes into the *Iliad* or the *Odyssey*, whereas the membership of a particular Mand-ing audience can even determine the specific multiform used by the singer. The exclusion of the audience from the Greek epic may be the result of canonization, which is inevitably a process of universalizing the audience. It is possible that earlier multiforms of the Greek tradition prior to canonization contained references to a specific audience, as do Odysseus' tales to the Phaiakians and Eumaios.[73] Pan-Hellenism, how-ever, brought the need to remove localized features of the epic, and the audience lost its diversity as the epic itself was made more universal.

In one significant respect the Manding epic tradition is different from its Greek counterpart: it lacks a fixed text. Despite the inroads of literacy and mass media in the twentieth century, the tradition has remained oral and there is as yet no discernible tendency toward canoni-zation of versions. Local variants are very strong.

Particularly noteworthy in the West African context is the coex-istence of oral literature and limited literacy. There is a long tradition of literacy in the Manding area, restricted to particular strata of society in an Islamic context. Universal literacy was never the goal of Manding society, where only the *marabout*, or Islamic teacher, needed to know how to read in order to study the Koran. The function of literacy in Manding society has thus been primarily religious, not secular.[74] In a similar way, literacy was generally restricted to the religious classes of medieval Europe, where not even the ruling nobility were necessarily literate. In the Manding area, oral tradition, not writing, has been the vehicle for preserving and remembering past events. Thus, in this part of West Africa, castes of unlettered poets—those generally known to us as griots—transmitted oral history to a largely illiterate society that received Islamic teaching from a literate religious class (the *marabouts*).

The existence of an oral literature in Manding culture with its lim-ited literacy raises important questions about the relationship between the introduction of writing in Greece and the establishment of the Homeric texts. It is often thought that the appearance of the Greek alphabet caused immediate transcription of oral literature such as the Homeric epics and that there was a clear-cut transition in Greece from

73. See, e.g., *Odyssey* ix 2–18 and xiv 462.
74. On the association of literacy and Islam in West African countries, see Goody 1987.125–138.

an illiterate or oral society to a literate one. Goody assumes an unusually rapid increase in literacy in Greece between the eighth and fifth centuries B.C. and an unusually high literacy rate in fifth-century Greece. Yet there is no firm evidence for this. Certainly literacy was common in fifth-century Athens, especially among citizens and metic merchants, but what percentage of the population did this represent?[75] Athenian society had a very restricted citizenship that excluded all women and slaves. Pre-inscribed *ostraka* 'shards' discovered in the Athenian *agora* 'place of assembly' suggest that literacy was not all that common among citizens, even in the fifth century,[76] and it is not insignificant that Greek literature until the end of the fifth century was primarily performative in nature, meant to be presented orally even if not so composed. Such performative literature includes epic, lyric, tragedy, and comedy. In this context, it is also noteworthy that one of Athens' greatest philosophers, Socrates, wrote no philosophical treatises, but taught orally, and is known only through the writings of his pupils Plato and Xenophon and the burlesque comedy of Aristophanes. Even some of the treatises of Aristotle, a century later, survive only via a semi-oral medium in the form of lecture or student notes, not in Aristotle's own published text. In the case of the Greek mythic corpus, it is not unlikely that Hesiod and Homer existed in fixed, oral versions decades before these works were written down. Rhapsodes, reciters of fixed Homeric texts, were probably active in Greece long before the first known Homeric recension by the Peisistratids.[77] Clearly literacy did not displace oral composition and presentation in Greece overnight.[78] The transition from an orally oriented society to a literate one is a slow, subtle, and not necessarily inevitable process, as can be demonstrated in the case of the Manding.

Ruth Finnegan especially questions whether narrative form is a prominent feature in such African epics as the *Sunjata*, which is, to a large extent, interspersed with praise songs. Yet the frequently panegyric nature of the *Sunjata* does not detract from its narrative focus on the life of Sunjata; rather, as Johnson has noted, the combination of narrative with praise song emphasizes the multigeneric nature of African epic.[79] Nagy has pointed out the relationship of *epos* 'poetic utterance'

75. See Harvey 1966.
76. See Harvey pp. 590–593 and Hands 1959.76–79.
77. For a detailed ancient illustration of a fourth-century rhapsode in action, see Plato's *Ion*. On performance of oral poetry in ancient Greece, see Nagy 1990b, chaps. 1 and 2.
78. See Havelock 1986.
79. See Johnson 1980.321.

and *ainos* 'praise' in the Homeric tradition.[80] Mixing of genres is thus a structural expression of diversity and unity within both the Manding and Greek epics.

Johnson also emphasizes the multifunctional features of the *Sunjata*, which offers a model for Manding social relations, especially among clan families.[81] The epic reinforces, too, certain social and religious institutions and practices, such as circumcision, and serves as a medium of national unity among the Manding. Yet even this characteristic is not restricted to Africa, for the Greek epic served similar multifunctional purposes, especially in its pan-Hellenic stage as the Greek national poem.[82]

The *Sunjata* centers around a single character in much the same way that events in the *Iliad* turn around Achilles, who sulks in the background for much of the first half of the epic while other characters, such as Menelaos, Diomedes, and Ajax, occupy the limelight. However, unlike the heroes described in Sir Maurice Bowra's heroic world, which is isolated from the real world, Sunjata's actions do not set him apart from his contemporary society and from the modern Manding world.[83] He is not a hero who is different and solitary. He is a Manding hero because he is an active member of his society and because other members of his society help him. West African epic emphasizes, rather than the isolated individual as a hero, the heroic individual as a member of a community of equals. Sunjata cannot defeat Sumanguru without the direct assistance of his sister, his mother, his griot, and the community itself. Sunjata's success is their success, too.[84] Unlike the Greeks, for whom there was an unbridgeable gap between the present and the Heroic Age, the Manding have a sense of communality with their past. Sunjata is as much a hero of the present as he is of the past.

Sunjata's ability to unify Manding people across temporal boundaries has been noted by Massa M. Diabaté, a prominent Malian scholar and poet, who has said that the *Sunjata* epic "attributes the entire cultural experience of a society to one character who has made a mark on his time . . . and deriving all past and present values of that society from this character, thus rendering the epic a source of identity serving to

80. Nagy 1979.222–242.
81. Johnson 1980.319–320.
82. On multifunctionalism in Greek myths, see Kirk 1974.
83. Bowra 1964.
84. See Bird 1976.

distinguish that group from others."[85] Analysis of the *Sunjata* epic in terms of Manding society thus illustrates important features of an oral tradition in its social context. The tension between diversity and unity which exists in the Manding tradition provides significant perspective for the Hellenist and demonstrates that the bond between *muthos* and polis is not unique to the Greek experience. Every oral society creates its own peculiar relationship between its myths and its sociocultural contexts. The Greeks are indeed like the others.

85. From Diabaté's unpublished doctoral thesis at the University of Paris. Translated by Seydou 1983.49–50.

Glossary of Greek Words

adelphos, *adelphoi* (pl.): brother

aglōssos (m., f.), *aglōsson* (n.): tongueless, dumb

agōn, *agōnes* (pl.): contest, debate

agora: place of assembly, marketplace

agos: pollution, religious crime and the ensuing malediction

aidōs: shame to be thought dishonorable, respect for god or superior

ainos: praise, poetry of praise

aiskhros (m.), *aiskhra* (f.), *aiskhron* (n.): shameful, dishonorable, disgraceful;
  to aiskhron: disgrace

anomiē (*anomia*): transgression of *nómos*, lawlessness

aretē: striving toward and achievement of a noble goal, excellence

arkhē: power, imperial rule

astunomoi orgai: impulses governing political life

atimos (m., f.), *atimon* (n.): dishonored

autadelphos, *autadelphoi* (pl.): one's own brother or sister, one from the same
  womb

biē: strength, physical force, violence

daimōn: divinity or hero; *agathoi daimones*: good spirits

delphus: womb

dēmokratia: democracy

dēmos: district, its population (excluding its leaders); community

didaskein: teach, train a chorus; *didaskalos*: teacher, poet / producer who trains a
  chorus

dikē: justice; *Dikē*: goddess of justice

diploun sēma: a double-meaning sign

dolos: trick; *dolios* (m.), *dolia* (f.), *dolion* (n.): crafty or cunning
doxa: opinion, fame
draō: do, accomplish, offer a sacrifice, perform mystical rites
dunamis: power, empire
enkōmion: praise, song of praise
ekkuklēma: rolling machine of the theater
ekphora: procession
enthronizein: enthrone
ephēbos, epheboi (pl.): male adolescent
epos: utterance, poetic utterance, epic poetry
Erinus: Fury, goddess of vengeance
eris: strife, discord, competitive impulse
erōs: love, desire
es meson: at the center
eukleia: honorable fame
eunomia: observance of laws (*nómoi*), good government
Gaia: Earth
genos: extended family, patriliny, lineage; territorial subdivision of *phulē*
gnōmē: sententious saying, proverb, opinion
goaō: to mourn; *goēs*: enchanter
gunē: woman
haima: blood
hērōion: hero shrine
hestia: hearth of a house, altar of the goddess Hestia
hetairos, hetairoi (pl.): companion; *hetairoi philtatoi*: most near and dear companions
hieron: sacred place, temple
Hieros Gamos: Holy Marriage
homosplankhnoi: those sharing inner parts
hubris: wanton violence, outrage; exuberance in plants
humēnaion: wedding song
iambos, iamboi (pl.): iambic poetry, mock abuse conveyed by iambic poetry; *iambizō*: to lampoon
ideia: craft
Kalē: Beautiful (f. of *kalōs*)
kalos (m.), *kalē* (f.), *kalon* (n.): fine, beautiful, noble
kēdos: care, concern
keleustēs: boatswain
kleos: glory, glory conferred by poetry
kōmos: a celebrating group of men or boys, revel
kosmokratōr: ruler of the world
kosmos: arrangement, order, law and order, the social order, the universal order; *to kosmion*: decorum, order
kreōn (m.): he who rules, king (cf. Kreon); *kreousa* (f.): she who rules, princess (cf. Kreousa)
ktistēs: civic founder

logos: speech, argument, reason, language, cunning
makhē: battle; *makhomai*: to fight
megas Telamōnios Aias: great Telamonian Ajax
megethos: greatness, stature
melia, meliai (pl.): ash tree, ash nymph
mētis: cunning, skill
mimēsis: imitation
mousa lokhmaia: muse of the thicket
neikos: quarrel, blame
nomima: established customs, traditions
nómos, nómoi (pl.): custom, norm, law; *nomós, nomoí* (pl.): habitation, melody,
    strain
noos: perceptive intelligence; *noein*: possess or exercise *noos*
nosos: disease, derangement of mind
oduromai: lament
Odusseus polumētis: Odysseus of many wiles
oikos, oikoi (pl.): house, home, household goods, a reigning house
ololugē: loud ritual cry, wailing cry
ōmophagos (m.), *ōmophagoi* (pl.): devourer of raw meat
orgia: secret rites
ostrakon, ostraka (pl.): shard; *ostrakismos*: banishment (voted upon with *ostraka*)
pais: child
paratragōidia: mock tragedy
partheneion: maidens' song
parthenos, parthenoi (pl.): virgin, maiden
paskhō: to experience, to suffer
patēr: father
peithō: persuasion; *peithein*: persuade
penthos: grief
peplos: robe
pharmakos: scapegoat; *pharmakon*: purificatory sacrifice
philos, philoi (pl.): near and dear; *philotēs*: state of being *philos*, amity
phratria, phratriai (pl.): phratry, kin group larger than *genos* and territorial subdi-
    vision of *phulē*
phrazomai: tell, give counsel, devise
phthonos: envy, greed; *to phthonein*: malicious envying
phulē, phulai (pl.): usually translated as "tribe," mythic and historical subdivision
    of a people
phusis: nature
pinutē: understanding, wisdom
polis, poleis (pl.): city, city-state; *politēs, politai* (pl.): citizen
prothesis: vigil or wake
psogos, psogoi (pl.): blame, poetry of blame, invective
psukhē: realm of consciousness, mind, heart, spirit, life
rhapsōdos: singer of traditional lays, singer
rhōmē: strength

rhothos : rumor of protest
sebein : to honor, worship
sēma : grave mound, tomb; sign
sōma : body
sōphrosunē : temperance
sparagmos : dismemberment
stratarkhēs : army commander
sumphilein : to share in *philotēs*
sumphōnos : in harmony with
sunaimos : blood sharer
sunekhthein : to share in hatred
taphos : tomb
therapōn : attendant squire, ritual substitute
thrēnos, thrēnoi (pl.): dirge
Thuiades : Women in a ritual hurry
tolmē, tolmai (pl.): daring action; *tolmēeis* (m.), *tolmēessa* (f.), *tolmēen* (n.):
    strong-hearted, enduring
turannos : tyrant
xoanon, xoana (pl.): wooden cult-statue

Bibliography

Abbot, G. F. 1903. *Macedonian Folklore.* Institute for Balkan Studies no. 110. Reprinted 1969, Chicago.

Adams, S. M. 1955. "The *Ajax* of Sophocles." *Phoenix* 9:93–110.

Albini, U. 1975. "Funzione di Io nel Prometeo." *Parola del Passato* 30:278–284.

Album of Greek National Costume. n.d. Benaki Museum, Athens.

Alexiou, M. 1974. *The Ritual Lament in Greek Tradition.* Cambridge.

Andrewes, A. 1971. *Greek Society.* Harmondsworth, U.K.

Arrowsmith, W. 1973. "Aristophanes' *Birds*: The Fantasy Politics of Eros." *Arion* n.s. 1.1:119–167.

———, trans. 1961. *The Birds.* Reprinted 1984, in *Four Plays by Aristophanes,* New York.

Auger, D. 1979. "Le théâtre d'Aristophane: Le mythe, l'utopie et les femmes." In Rosellini, Said, and Auger, 1979.71–101.

Bachofen, J. J. 1967. *Myth, Religion, and Mother Right.* Princeton, N.J.

Bakhtin, M. 1984. *Rabelais and His World.* Trans. H. Iswolsky of *Tvorchestvo Fransua Rable,* Moscow, 1965.

Ballabriga, A. 1986. *Le soleil et le Tartare: L'image mythique du monde en Grèce archaïque.* Recherches d'histoire et de sciences sociales 20. Paris.

Barthes, R. 1972. *Mythologies.* Trans. A. Lavers. New York.

Benveniste, E. 1969. *Le vocabulaire des institutions indo-européenes.* I. *Économie, parenté, société.* II. *Pouvoir, droit, religion.* Paris = *Indo-European Language and Society.* Trans. E. Palmer. London, 1973.

Bergman, J. 1968. "Ich bin Isis: Studien zum memphitischen Hintergrund der griechischen Isisaretalogien." *Acta Universitatis Upsaliensis* (= *Historia Religionum* 3). Uppsala.

207

Bernal, M. 1987. *Black Athena*. vol. 1: *The Fabrication of Ancient Greece 1785–1985*. New Brunswick, N.J.

Bernand, A. 1955. "Influence de l'Égypte et innovation d'Eschyle dans la représentation d'Io." *Annals of the Faculty of Arts, Ain Shams University* 3:77–103.

———. 1985. *La carte du tragique: La géographie dans la tragédie grecque*. Paris.

Bianchetti, S. 1988. "Il confine Europa-Asia in Eschilo." *Sileno* 14.1/2:205–214.

Bickerman, E. 1952. "Origines Gentium." *Classical Philology* 47:65–81.

Biebuyck, D. 1968. *The Mwindo Epic*. London.

Biebuyck, D., and K. Mateene. 1978. *Hero and Chief: Epic Literature from the Banyanga, Zaïre Republic*. Berkeley.

Bird, C. S. 1970. "Development of Mandekan (Manding): A Study of the Role of Extra-linguistic Factors in Linguistic Change." In *Languages and History of Africa*, ed. D. Dalby, 146–159. New York.

———. 1972. "Heroic Songs of the Mande Hunters." In *African Folklore*, ed. R. Dorson, 275–293. New York.

———. 1976. "Poetry in the Mande: Its Form and Meaning." *Poetics* 5:89–100.

Boardman, J. 1980. *The Greeks Overseas: Their Early Colonies and Trade*. 2d ed. London.

Boedeker, D. 1974. *Aphrodite's Entry into Greek Epic*. Leiden.

Bohringer, F. 1980. "Mégare: Traditions mythiques, espace sacré et naissance de la cité." *L'Antiquité Classique* 49:5–22.

Bolton, J. D. P. 1962. *Aristeas of Proconnesus*. Oxford.

Bourriot, F. 1976. *Recherches sur la nature du génos: Études d'histoire sociale athénienne* I/II. Lille.

Bowra, M. 1964. "The Meaning of the Heroic Age." In *The Language and Background of Homer*, ed. G. S. Kirk, 3–28. Cambridge.

Braun, T. F. R. G. 1982. "The Greeks in the Near East." In *The Cambridge Ancient History*. 2d ed., vol. 3.3, ed. C. J. Gadd, I. E. S. Edwards, and N. G. L. Hammond, 1–31. Cambridge.

Brelich, A. 1958. *Gli eroi greci*. Rome.

Bremmer, J. 1983. "Scapegoat Rituals in Ancient Greece." *Harvard Studies in Classical Philology* 87:299–320.

———, ed. 1986. *Interpretations of Greek Mythology*. Totowa, N.J.

Brown, N. O. 1951. "Pindar, Sophocles and the Thirty Years' War." *Transactions of the American Philological Association* 82:1–25.

Bühler, W. 1968. *Europa: Ein Überblick über die Zeugnisse des Mythos in der antiken Literatur und Kunst*. Munich.

Burian, P. 1972. "Supplication and Hero Cult in Sophocles' *Ajax*." *Greek, Roman, and Byzantine Studies* 13:151–156.

Burkert, W. 1962a. "Caesar und Romulus-Quirinus." *Historia* 11:356–376.

———. 1962b. "Γόης: Zum Griechischen 'Schamanismus'." *Rheinisches Museum* 105.36–55.

———. 1966a. "Greek Tragedy and Sacrificial Ritual." *Greek, Roman, and Byzantine Studies* 7:87–121.

———. 1966b. "Kekropidensage und Arrhephoria." *Hermes* 94:1–25.

———. 1972. *Lore and Science in Ancient Pythagoreanism.* Cambridge, Mass. Trans. E. L. Minar of *Weisheit und Wissenschaft: Studien zu Pythagoras, Philolaos und Platon*, Nürnberg, 1962.

———. 1975. "Apellai und Apollon." *Rheinisches Museum* 118.1–21.

———. 1979. *Structure and History in Greek Mythology and Ritual.* Berkeley.

———. 1983. *Homo Necans: The Anthropology of Ancient Greek Sacrificial Ritual and Myth.* Berkeley. Trans. P. Bing of *Homo Necans: Interpretationen altgriechischer Opferriten und Mythen*, Berlin, 1972.

———. 1985. *Greek Religion.* Cambridge, Mass. Trans. J. Raffan of *Griechische Religion der archaischen und klassischen Epoche*, Stuttgart, 1977.

Burnett, A. P. 1970. *'Ion' by Euripides.* Englewood Cliffs, N.J.

———. 1971. *Catastrophe Survived.* Oxford.

Bury, J. B., S. A. Cook, and F. E. Adcock, eds. 1927. *The Cambridge Ancient History.* vol. 5. Cambridge.

Calame, C. 1977. *Les choeurs de jeunes filles dans la Grèce archaïque.* 2 vols. Rome.

Callen King, K. 1985. "The Politics of Imitation: Euripides *Hekabe* and the Homeric Achilles." *Arethusa* 18:47–66.

Campbell, J. 1964. *The Masks of God: Occidental Mythology.* New York.

Casanova, G. 1966–1971. *History of My Life.* 12 vols. in 6. New York.

Cerri, G. 1969. "*Isos dasmos* come equivalente di *isonomia* nella silloge teognidea." *Quaderni Urbinati di Cultura Classica* 8:97–104.

Clifford, J. 1982. *Person and Myth: Maurice Leenhardt in the Melanesian World.* Berkeley.

Conrad, D. C. 1985. "Islam in the Oral Traditions of Mali: Bilali and Surakata." *Journal of African History* 26:33–49.

Cramp, S., ed. 1985. *Handbook of the Birds of Europe, the Middle East, and North Africa.* 4 vols. Oxford.

Crowley, A. 1970. *The Confessions of Aleister Crowley: An Autohagiography.* New York.

Danforth, L. M. 1982. *The Death Rituals of Rural Greece.* Princeton, N.J.

Dawe, R. D. 1984. *Sophocles: Tragoediae.* vol. 1, 2d ed. Leipzig.

Dawkins, R. M. 1937. "Alexander and the Water of Life." *Medium Aevum* 6:173–192.

DELG = Chantraine, P. 1968–1980. *Dictionnaire étymologique de la langue grecque.* I, II, III, IV–1, IV–2. Paris.

Detienne, M. 1971. "Orphée au miel." *Quaderni Urbinati di Cultura Classica* 12:7–23. In Gordon 1981. Cambridge.

———. 1977. *The Gardens of Adonis.* Hassocks, Sussex. Trans. J. Lloyd of *Les jardins d'Adonis: La mythologie des aromates en Grèce*, Paris, 1972.

———. 1979. *Dionysos Slain.* Baltimore. Trans. M. Muellner and L. Muellner of *Dionysos mis à mort*, Paris, 1977.

———. 1986. *The Creation of Mythology.* Chicago. Trans. M. Cook of *L'invention de la mythologie*, 1981, Paris.

———. 1989. *Dionysos at Large.* Cambridge, Mass. Trans. A. Goldhammer of *Dionysos à ciel ouvert*, Paris, 1986.

————, and J.-P. Vernant. 1978. *Cunning Intelligence in Greek Culture and Society.* Hassocks, Sussex. Trans. J. Lloyd of *Les ruses de l'intélligence: La métis des grecs,* Paris, 1974.

Dieterlen, G. 1957. "The Mande Creation Myth." *Africa* 27:124–38.

DK = Diels, H., and W. Kranz, eds. 1952. *Die Fragmente der Vorsokratiker.* 3 vols., 6th ed. Berlin.

Dodds, E. R. 1951. *The Greeks and the Irrational.* Berkeley.

Douglas, M. 1966. *Purity and Danger: An Analysis of the Concepts of Pollution and Taboo.* London.

Dover, K. J. 1964. "The Poetry of Archilochus." *Archiloque: Entretiens Hardt* 10:183–222.

Dragoumis, J. 1919. "Old Greek Tales and Legends." *Balkan Review* I.4:297–301

Duchemin, J. 1957. "Recherche sur un thème aristophanien et ses sources religieuses: Les voyages dans l'autre monde." *Les Études Classiques* 25:273–95.

————. 1979. "La justice de Zeus et le destin d'Io: Regard sur les sources procheorientales d'un mythe eschyléen (1)." *Revue des Études Grecques* 92:1–54.

Dumézil, G. 1982. *Apollon sonore et autres essais.* Paris.

Easterling, P. E. 1985. "Sophocles." In Easterling and Kenney 1985, 295–316.

Easterling, P. E., and E. J. Kenney, eds. 1985. *The Cambridge History of Classical Literature.* Cambridge.

Eco, U. 1984. "The Semiotic Theory of Carnival as the Inversion of Bipolar Opposites." In Sebeok and Erickson 1984. 1–9.

Edmunds, L. 1975. "Thucydides' Ethics as Reflected in the Description of Stasis (3.82–83)." *Harvard Studies in Classical Philology* 79:73–92.

————, ed. 1990. *Approaches to Greek Myth.* Baltimore.

Edwards, R. B. 1979. *Kadmos the Phoenician: A Study in Greek Legends and the Mycenaean Age.* Amsterdam.

Edwards, V., and T. J. Sienkewicz. 1990. *Oral Cultures Past and Present: Rappin' and Homer.* Oxford.

Eliade, M. 1964. *Shamanism: Archaic Techniques of Ecstasy.* Princeton, N.J.

Epstein, P. D. 1981. "The Marriage of Peisthetairos to *Basileia* in the *Birds* of Aristophanes." *Dionysus* 5:5–28.

Euben, J. P., ed. 1986. *Greek Tragedy and Political Theory.* Berkeley.

Fagles, R., and W. B. Stanford. 1975. "A Reading of the *Oresteia*: The Serpent and the Eagle." In Aeschylus *The Oresteia,* trans. R. Fagles. New York.

Farnell, L. R. 1921. *Greek Hero-Cults and the Idea of Immortality.* Oxford.

FGH = Jacoby, F., ed. 1923–. *Die Fragmente der griechischen Historiker.* Berlin.

Figueira, T. J. 1985a. "The Theognidea and Megarian Society." In Figueira and Nagy 1985, 113–159.

————. 1985b. "Chronological Table: Archaic Megara, 800–500 B.C." In Figueira and Nagy 1985, 264–307.

Figueira, T. J., and G. Nagy, eds. 1985. *Theognis of Megara: Poetry and the Polis.* Baltimore.

Finnegan, R. 1970. *Oral Literature in Africa.* Oxford.

Foley, H. P. 1985. *Ritual Irony: Poetry and Sacrifice in Euripides.* Ithaca, N.Y.

Fontenrose, J. E. 1948. "The Sorrows of Ino and of Procne." *Transactions of the*

American Philological Association 79:125–67.

Ford, A. L. 1985. "The Seal of Theognis: The Politics of Authorship in Ancient Greece." In Figueira and Nagy 1985, 82–95.

Fortes, M. 1969. *Kinship and the Social Order*. Chicago.

Foucault, M. 1978. *The History of Sexuality*. New York. Trans. R. Hurley of *Histoire de la sexualité*, Paris, 1976.

Frame, D. 1980. *The Myth of Return in Early Greek Epic*. New Haven, Conn.

Franz, M.-L., von. 1970. *An Introduction to the Psychology of Fairy Tales*. New York.

——. 1981. *Puer Aeternus*. 2d ed. Santa Monica, Calif.

Fraser, P. M. 1972. *Ptolemaic Alexandria*. I. Text, II. Notes. Oxford.

Frazer, J. G. 1922. *The Golden Bough*. Abridgment in 1 vol. London.

Freud, S. 1969. *An Outline of Psycho-Analysis*. New York.

Friedlaender, I. 1910a. "Zur Geschichte der Chadhirlegende." *Archiv für Religionswissenschaft* 13:92–110.

——. 1910b. "Alexanders Zug nach dem Lebensquell und die Chadhirlegende." *Archiv für Religionswissenschaft* 13:161–246.

Friis Johansen, H., and E. W. Whittle, eds. 1980. Aeschylus, *The Suppliants*. 3 vols. Aarhus.

Fritz, K., von. 1943. "*Noos* and *noein* in the Homeric Poems." *Classical Philology* 38:79–93.

Fromm, E. 1949. "The Oedipus Myth." *Scientific American* 180.1:22–27.

Geertz, C. 1983. "Notions of Primitive Thought." In *States of Mind*, ed. J. Miller, 192–210. New York.

Gennep, A. van. 1960. *The Rites of Passage*. Chicago. Trans. M. B. Vizedan and G. L. Caffe of *Les rites de passage*, Paris, 1909.

Gentili, B., and C. Prato, eds. 1979. *Poetarum Elegiacorum Testimonia et Fragmenta*, Part I. Leipzig.

Gernet, L. 1968. *Anthropologie de la Grèce antique*. Paris = *The Anthropology of Ancient Greece*, trans. J. Hamilton and B. Nagy, Baltimore, 1981.

Gnoli, G., and J. P. Vernant, eds. 1982. *La mort, les morts dans les sociétés anciennes*. Cambridge.

Goldman, A. 1981. *Elvis*. New York.

Goody, J. R. 1977. *Domestication of the Savage Mind*. Cambridge.

——. 1987. *The Interface between the Written and the Oral*. Cambridge.

Goody, J. R., and I. Watt. 1968. "The Consequences of Literacy." In *Literacy in Traditional Societies*, 27–68. Cambridge.

Gordon, R. L., ed. 1981. *Myth, Religion and Society*. Cambridge.

Gourevitch, D., and M. Gourevitch. 1979. "Histoire d'Io." *L'évolution psychiatrique* 2:263–279.

Graf, Fritz. 1986. "Orpheus: A Poet among Men." In Bremmer 1986.80–106.

Green, P. 1985. "After the Successors." *Times Literary Supplement*, August 16, 1985: 891–893.

Grote, G. 1846–1862. *A History of Greece*. 8 vols. London.

Guthrie, W. K. C. 1952. *Orpheus and Greek Religion*. 2d ed. London.

Guys, P. A. 1783. *Voyage littéraire de la Grèce*. vol. 1. 3d ed. Paris.

Hägg, T. 1983. *The Novel in Antiquity*. Oxford.

Hallo, W. W. 1964. "The Road to Emar." *Journal of Cuneiform Studies* 18:57–88.

Halperin, D. M. 1983. *Before Pastoral: Theocritus and the Ancient Tradition of Bucolic Poetry*. New Haven, Conn.

Hammond, N. G. L. 1986. *A History of Greece to 322 B.C.* 3d ed. Oxford.

Hampe, R., and E. Simon. 1981. *The Birth of Greek Art: From the Mycenaean to the Archaic Period*. New York.

Hands, A. R. 1959. "Ostraka and the Law of Ostracism: Some Possibilities and Assumptions." *Journal of Hellenic Studies* 79:69–79.

Harding, M. E. 1947. *Psychic Energy*. New York.

———. 1965. *The 'I' and the 'Not-I'*. Princeton, N.J.

Harrison, J. E. 1890. *Mythology and Monuments of Ancient Athens*. London.

Hartog, F. 1980. *Le miroir d'Hérodote: Essai sur la représentation de l'autre*. Paris.

Harvey, A. E. 1955. "The Classification of Greek Lyric Poetry." *Classical Quarterly* 5:157–175.

Harvey, F. D. 1966. "Literacy in the Athenian Democracy." *Révue des Études Grecques* 79:585–635.

Havelock, E. 1986. *The Muse Learns to Write: Reflections on Orality and Literacy from Antiquity to the Present*. New Haven, Conn.

Helck, H. W. 1959. "Sarapis." In *Der kleine Pauly* vol 4.1549. Munich.

Henderson, J. 1975. *The Maculate Muse: Obscene Language in Attic Comedy*. New Haven, Conn.

Hendricks, I. H. M., P. J. Parsons, and K. A. Worp. 1981. "Papyri from the Groningen Collection I: Encomium Alexandriae." *Zeitschrift für Papyrologie und Epigraphik* 41:71–83.

Henrichs, A. 1978. "Greek Maenadism from Olympias to Messalina." *Harvard Studies in Classical Philology* 82:121–160.

———. 1979. "Greek and Roman Glimpses of Dionysos." In *Dionysos and His Circle: Ancient through Modern*, ed. C. Houser, 1–11. Cambridge, Mass.

Herington, J. 1985. *Poetry into Drama: Early Tragedy and the Greek Poetic Tradition*. Berkeley.

Hicks, R. I. 1962. "Egyptian Elements in Greek Mythology." *Transactions of the American Philological Association* 93:90–108.

Hoffman, H. 1976. *Mythos und Komödie: Untersuchungen zu den Vögeln des Aristophanes = Hypomnemata* 68. Hildesheim.

Ibn Khaldūn, Walī al-Dīn 'Abd al-Rahmān b. Muhammad. 1868. *Kitāb al-'Ibār wa-diwan al-mubtada wa'l-Khabar*. Bulak. = *Histoire des Berbères et des dynasties musulmanes de l'Afrique septentrionale*. Trans. Commission internationale pour la traduction des chefs d'oeuvre. Beirut, 1956–1959.

Innes, G. 1972. "Mandinka Circumcision Songs." *African Language Studies* 13:88–112.

———. 1974. *Sunjata: Three Mandinka Versions*. London.

Jacobi, J. 1967a. *Complex/Archetype/Symbol in the Psychology of C. G. Jung*. Princeton, N.J.

———. 1967b. *The Way of Individuation*. New York.

———. 1968. *The Psychology of C. G. Jung*. 8th ed. New Haven, Conn.

Jacoby, F. 1944. "*Genesia*: A Forgotten Festival of the Dead." *Classical Quarterly* 38:65–75. Reprinted in *Abhandlungen zur Griechischen Geschichtsschreibung*. Leiden, 1966.

Jebb, R. C., ed. 1896. *Sophocles: The Plays and Fragments*. With introduction and commentary. Cambridge.

Johnson, J. W. 1979. *The Epic of Sun-Jata according to Magan Sisòkò*. Bloomington, Ind.

———. 1980. "Yes, Virginia, There Is an Epic in Africa." *Research in African Literatures* 11:308–26.

———. 1986. *The Epic of Son-Jara: A West African Tradition*. Bloomington, Ind.

Jones, A. M. 1971. *Africa and Indonesia: The Evidence of the Xylophone*. 2d ed. Leiden.

Jones, N. F. 1980. "The Order of the Dorian Phylai." *Classical Philology* 75.197–215.

Jung, C. G. 1958. *Psychology and Religion: West and East*. New York.

———. 1966. *Two Essays on Analytical Psychology*. 2d ed. Princeton, N.J.

———. 1967. *Symbols of Transformation*. 2d ed. Princeton, N.J.

———. 1968a. *The Archetypes and the Collective Unconscious*. 2d ed. Princeton, N.J.

———. 1968b. *Psychology and Alchemy*. 2d ed. Princeton, N.J.

———. 1969. *The Structure and Dynamics of the Psyche*. 2d ed. Princeton, N.J.

———. 1970a. *Analytical Psychology*. New York.

———. 1970b. *Civilization in Transition*. 2d ed. Princeton, N.J.

———. 1970c. *Mysterium Coniunctionis*. 2d ed. Princeton, N.J.

———. 1973. *Letters*. 2 vols. Princeton, N.J.

Jung, C. G., M.-L. von Franz, J.-L. Henderson, J. Jacobi, and A. Jaffé. 1968. *Man and His Symbols*. New York.

Kabbadas, D. n.d. *Eikonographēmenon Botanikon-Phytologikon Lexikon*. vol. 6. Athens.

Kahn, C. H. 1985. *Anaximander and the Origins of Greek Cosmology*. 2d ed. Philadelphia.

Kakridis, J. T. 1949. *Homeric Researches*. Lund.

Kirk, G. S. 1974. *The Nature of Greek Myths*. New York.

Kirk, G. S., J. E. Raven, and M. Schofield. 1983. *The Presocratic Philosophers: A Critical History with a Selection of Texts*. 2d ed. Cambridge.

Kirkwood, G. M. 1965. "Homer and Sophocles' *Ajax*." In *Classical Drama and Its Influence: Studies Presented to H. D. F. Kitto*, ed. M. J. Anderson, 51–70. London.

Knox, B. M. W. 1961. "The *Ajax* of Sophocles." *Harvard Studies in Classical Philology* 65:1–37.

———. 1964. *The Heroic Temper: Studies in Sophoclean Tragedy*. Sather Classical Lectures 35. Berkeley.

———. 1983. "Greece à la Française." *New York Review of Books*, March 3, 1983:26–30.

Koenen, L. 1968. "Die Prophezeiungen des 'Töpfers'." *Zeitschrift für Papyrologie und Epigraphik* 2:178–209.

——. 1983. "Die Adaptation ägyptischer Königsideologie am Ptolemäerhof." *Egypt and the Hellenistic World: Proceedings of the International Colloquium, Leuven 1982*:143–150 (= *Studia Hellenistica*, ed. W. Peremans).

——. 1984. "A Supplementary Note on the Date of the *Oracle of the Potter*." *Zeitschrift für Papyrologie und Epigraphik* 54:9–13.

——. 1985. "The Dream of Nektanebos." In *Classical Studies Presented to William Hailey Willis. Bulletin of the American Society of Papyrologists* 22:171–194.

Koerte, A. 1923. "Literarische Texte mit Ausschluss der christlichen." *Archiv für Papyrusforschung* 7:225–258.

Kretschmer, P. 1894. *Die griechischen Vaseninschriften ihrer Sprache nach untersucht*. Gütersloh.

Labouret, H. 1951. "À propos du mot 'griot'." *Notes Africaines* 50:56–57.

Lacroix, L. 1974. "Héraclès, héros voyageur et civilisateur." *Bulletin de la Classe des Lettres de l'Académie Royale de Belgique* 60:34–59.

Lattimore, R., trans. 1951. *The Iliad of Homer*. Chicago.

Lawson, J. C. 1964. *Modern Greek Folklore and Ancient Greek Religion: A Study in Survivals*. New Hyde Park, N.Y., reprint of Cambridge, 1910.

Lefkowitz, M. R. 1981. *The Lives of the Greek Poets*. Baltimore.

——. 1989. " 'Impiety' and 'Atheism' in Euripides' Dramas." *Classical Quarterly* 39:70–82.

Legon, R. P. 1981. *Megara: The Political History of a Greek City-State to 336 B.C.* Ithaca, N.Y.

Lessa, W. A., and E. Z. Vogt. 1979. *Reader in Comparative Religion: An Anthropological Approach*. 4th ed. New York.

Lévi-Strauss, C. 1972. "The Structural Study of Myth." In *Myth: A Symposium.*, ed. T. A. Sebeok, 81–106. Bloomington, Ind.

Levy, R. 1948. *The Gate of Horn*. London.

Lévy-Bruhl, L. 1966. *How Natives Think*. New York.

Lincoln, B. 1986. *Myth, Cosmos, and Society: Indo-European Themes of Creation and Destruction*. Cambridge, Mass.

Linforth, I. M. 1910. "Epaphos and the Egyptian Apis." *University of California Publications in Classical Philology* 2.5:81–92.

——. 1941. *The Arts of Orpheus*. Berkeley. Reprinted 1973.

Lloyd, A. B. 1975. *Herodotus: Book II, Introduction*. Leiden.

——. 1976. *Herodotus, Book II: Commentary 1–98*. Leiden.

——. 1988. *Herodotus, Book II: Commentary 99–182*. Leiden.

Loraux, N. 1977. "La 'belle mort' spartiate." *Ktema* 2:105–120.

——. 1979. "L'autochthonie, une topique athénienne: Le mythe dans l'espace civique." *Annales: Économies Sociétés Civilisations* 34.1:13–26.

——. 1981. *L'invention d' Athènes. Histoire de l' oraison funèbre dans la cité classique*. Paris. Trans. A. Sheridan as *The Invention of Athens: the Funeral Oration in the Classical City*. Cambridge, Mass., 1986.

Lord, A. 1960. *The Singer of Tales*. New York. Reprinted 1976. Cambridge, Mass.

LP = Lobel, E., and D. L. Page, eds. 1955. *Poetarum Lesbiorum Fragmenta*. Oxford.

LSJ = Liddell, H. J., P. Scott, and H. Jones, eds. 1940. *Greek-English Lexicon.* 9th ed. Oxford.

Luce, T. J., ed. 1982. *Ancient Writers: Greece and Rome.* 2 vols. New York.

Luck, G. 1985. *Arcana Mundi.* Baltimore.

McGuire, W., and R. F. C. Hull, eds. 1977. *C. G. Jung Speaking.* Princeton, N.J.

Malinowski, B. 1931. "Culture." In *Encyclopedia of the Social Sciences,* ed. E. Seligman and A. Johnson. vol. 4. New York.

Manuel, F. E., and F. P. Manuel. 1972. "Sketch for a Natural History of Paradise." *Daedalus* 101:83–128.

Markle, M. M., III. 1976. "Support of Athenian Intellectuals for Philip: A Study of Isocrates' *Philippus* and Speusippus' *Letter to Philip.*" *Journal of Hellenic Studies* 96:80–99.

Martin, R. P. 1989. *The Language of Heroes: Speech and Performance in the* Iliad. Ithaca, N.Y.

Marzullo, M. 1970. "L'interlocuzione negli 'Ucceli' d'Aristofane." *Philologus* 114:181–94.

Masaracchia, A. 1958. *Solone.* Florence.

Mattoon, M. A. 1981. *Jungian Psychology in Perspective.* New York.

Merkelbach, R., and J. Trumpf. 1977. *Die Quellen des griechischen Alexanderromans.* = *Zetemata* 9. 2d ed. Munich.

Merkelbach, R., and M. L. West, eds. 1983. "Fragmenta Selecta." In *Hesiodi Theogonia, Opera et Dies, Scutum,* ed. F. Solmsen, 109–232. Oxford.

Michelini, A. N. 1987. *Euripides and the Tragic Tradition.* Madison, Wis.

Moulton, C. 1981. *Aristophanic Poetry.* = *Hypomnemata* 68. Göttingen.

Mourelatos, A. P. D. 1970. *The Route of Parmenides: A Study of Word, Image and Argument in the Fragments.* New Haven, Conn.

MSG = Jan, K., ed. 1895. *Musici Scriptores Graeci.* Leipzig.

Müller, G. 1975. "Beschreibung von Kunstwerken im Ion des Euripides." *Hermes* 103:25–44

Murray, O. 1983. *Early Greece.* Stanford.

Murray, R. D. 1958. *The Motif of Io in Aeschylus'* Suppliants. Princeton, N.J.

MW = Merkelbach, R., and M. L. West, eds. 1967. *Fragmenta Hesiodea.* Oxford.

Mylonas, G. E. 1976. "Eleusis." In *PECS,* 296–298.

Nagy, G. 1979. *The Best of the Achaeans: Concepts of the Hero in Archaic Greek Poetry.* Baltimore.

———. 1982a. "Hesiod." In Luce 1982.I.43–72. Rewritten as part of Nagy 1990a chap. 1.

———. 1982b. Review of Detienne 1981 (trans. 1986). *Annales: Économies Sociétés Civilisations* 37:778–780.

———. 1983a. "On the Death of Sarpedon." In *Approaches to Homer,* ed. C. A. Rubino and C. W. Shelmerdine, 189–217. Austin, Tex. Rewritten as part of Nagy 1990a chap. 5.

———. 1983b. "*Sēma* and *Noēsis*: Some Illustrations." *Arethusa* 16:35–55. Rewritten as Nagy 1990a chap. 8.

———. 1985. "Theognis and Megara: A Poet's Vision of His City." In Figueira and Nagy 1985, 22–81.

——. 1986a. "Pindar's *Olympian* 1 and the Aetiology of the Olympic Games." *Transactions of the American Philological Association* 116:71–88.

——. 1986b. "Ancient Greek Praise and Epic Poetry." In *Oral Tradition in Literature: Interpretation in Context,* ed. J. M. Foley, 89–102. Columbia, Mo.

——. 1987a. "Herodotus the *Logios.*" *Arethusa* 20:175–184, 209–210.

——. 1987b. "The Indo-European Heritage of Tribal Organization: Evidence from the Greek *Polis.*" In *Proto-Indo-European: The Archaeology of a Linguistic Problem. Studies in Honor of Marija Gimbutas,* ed. S. N. Skomal and E. C. Polomé, 245–266. Washington, D.C. Rewritten as Nagy 1990a chap. 12.

——. 1988. "Mythe et prose en Grèce archaïque: l' *ainos.*" In *Métamorphoses du mythe en Grèce ancienne,* ed. C. Calame, 229–242. Geneva.

——. 1989. "Early Greek Views of Poets and Poetry." In *Cambridge History of Literary Criticism,* ed. G. Kennedy, I.1–77.

——. 1990a. *Greek Mythology and Poetics.* Ithaca, N.Y.

——. 1990b. *Pindar's Homer: The Lyric Possession of an Epic Past.* Baltimore.

Nagy, J. F. 1985. *The Wisdom of the Outlaw: The Boyhood Deeds of Finn in Gaelic Narrative Tradition.* Berkeley.

——. 1990. "Indo-European and Greek Mythology." In Edmunds 1990, 199–238.

Nettl, B. 1956. *Music in Primitive Culture.* Cambridge, Mass.

Neumann, E. 1970. *The Origins and History of Consciousness.* Princeton, N.J.

——. 1972. *The Great Mother: An Analysis of the Archetype.* 2d ed. Princeton, N.J.

Newiger, H.-J. 1957. *Metapher und Allegorie: Studien zu Aristophanes* = Zetemata 16: 80–103. Munich.

——. 1980. "War and Peace in the Comedy of Aristophanes." *Yale Classical Studies* 26:219–37.

Niane, D. T. 1965. *Sundiata: An Epic of Old Mali.* London.

Nilsson, M. P. 1951. *Cults, Myths, Oracles, and Politics in Ancient Greece.* Lund. Reprinted 1972, New York.

——. 1957. *The Dionysiac Mysteries of the Hellenistic and Roman Age.* Lund.

Ninou, K., ed. 1980. *Alexander the Great: History and Legend in Art.* Trans. J. Binder and D. Hardy. Thessalonike.

Odajnyk, V. W. 1976. *Jung and Politics.* New York.

OF = Kern, O., ed. 1922. *Orphicorum Fragmenta.* Berlin.

Okin, L. A. 1985. "Theognis and the Sources for the History of Archaic Megara." In Figueira and Nagy 1985, 9–21.

Okpewho, I. 1979. *Epic in Africa.* New York.

Onians, R. B. 1954. *The Origins of European Thought: About the Body, the Mind, the Soul, the World, Time and Fate.* Cambridge.

Ostwald, M. 1969. *Nomos and the Beginnings of the Athenian Democracy.* Oxford.

Owen, A. S., ed. 1939. *Euripides: Ion.* With introduction and commentary. Oxford.

Pallottino, M. 1975. *The Etruscans.* Bloomington, Ind.

Palmer, L. R. 1980. *The Greek Language.* London.

Parke, H. W. 1977. *Festivals of the Athenians.* Ithaca, N.Y.

Parke, H. W., and D. E. W. Wormell. 1956. *The Delphic Oracle*. 2 vols. Oxford.

Parker, R. 1986. "Myths of Early Athens." In Bremmer 1986.187–214.

Pearson, L. 1960. *The Lost Histories of Alexander the Great*. Philadelphia.

PECS = *Princeton Encyclopedia of Classical Sites*. 1976. Ed. R. Stillwell, W. MacDonald and M. McAllister. Princeton, N.J.

Perry, B. E. 1967. *The Ancient Romances: A Literary-Historical Account*. Berkeley.

Pfister, F. 1909–1912. *Der Reliquienkult im Altertum*. I–II. Giessen.

———. 1964. "Alexander der Grosse: Die Geschichte seines Ruhms im Lichte seiner Beinamen." *Historia* 13:37–79.

Picard, C. 1927. "Sur la patrie et les pérégrinations de Démeter." *Revue des Études Grecques* 40:320–369.

Pickard-Cambridge, A. 1968. *Dithyramb, Tragedy and Comedy*. 2d ed. rev. T. B. L. Webster. Oxford.

Plaumann, G. 1920. "Probleme des alexandrinischen Alexanderkultes." *Archiv für Papyrusforschung* 6:70–99.

PMG = Page, D. L., ed. 1962. *Poetae Melici Graeci*. Oxford.

Polignac, F. de. 1984. *La naissance de la cité grecque*. Paris.

Politis, N. G. 1878. "Νεοελληνικὴ μυθολογία· ἐνιάλιοι δαίμονες· Γοργόνα (Modern Greek Mythology. Sea Demons: The Gorgona)." Παρνασσός (*Parnassos*) 3.259–275. Athens.

———. 1904. Μελέται περὶ τοῦ βίου καὶ τῆς γλώσσης τοῦ Ἑλληνικοῦ λαοῦ· Παραδόσεις (*Studies concerning the Life and Language of the Greek People: Traditions*). 2 vols. Athens.

Pollard, J. K. T. 1977. *Birds in Greek Life and Myth*. London.

Pozzi, D. C. 1986. "The Pastoral Ideal in *The Birds* of Aristophanes." *Classical Journal* 82.3:119–129.

———. 1989. "The Metaphor of Sacrifice in Sophocles' *Antigone* 853–56." *Hermes* 117.4:500–505.

Privitera, G. A. 1970. *Dioniso in Omero e nella poesia greca arcaica*. Rome.

———. 1977. "Il ditirambo: Da canto cultuale a spettacolo musicale." In *Rito e poesia corale in Grecia; Guida storica e critica*, ed. C. Calame, 27–37. Rome.

Puhvel, J. 1987. *Comparative Mythology*. Baltimore.

Quinn, C. A. 1972. *Mandingo Kingdoms of the Senegambia*. Evanston, Ill.

Ramin, J. 1979. *Mythologie et géographie*. Paris.

Reckford, K. 1987. *Aristophanes' Old-and-New-Comedy*. Chapel Hill, N.C.

Redfield, J. M. 1975. *Nature and Culture in the Iliad: The Tragedy of Hektor*. Chicago.

Regardie, I. 1982. *The Eye in the Triangle: An Interpretation of Aleister Crowley*. Phoenix, Ariz.

Robertson, N. 1983. "The Riddle of the Arrhephoria at Athens." *Harvard Studies in Classical Philology* 87:241–88.

Rogers, B. B. 1906. *Aristophanes* ΟΡΝΙΘΕΣ. London.

Rosellini, M., S. Said, and D. Auger. 1979. *Aristophane: Les femmes et la cité*. Fontenay aux Roses.

Rosenmeyer, T. G. 1963. *The Masks of Tragedy: Essays on Six Greek Dramas*. Austin, Tex.

Ross, D. J. A. 1985. *Studies in the Alexander Romance*. London.

Rossi, L. E. 1971. "I genere letterari e le loro leggi scritte e non scritti nelle letterature classiche." *Bulletin of the Institute of Classical Studies* 18:69–94.

Roussel, D. 1976. *Tribu et cité*. Annales Littéraires de l'Université de Besançon. 193. Paris.

Rusten, J. 1985. "Interim Notes on the Papyrus from Derveni." *Harvard Studies in Classical Philology* 89:121–140.

Ste. Croix, G. E. M. de. 1972. *The Origins of the Peloponnesian War*. London.

Samuels, A. 1985. *Jung and the Post-Jungians*. Boston.

Saxonhouse, A. W. 1986. "Myths and the Origins of Cities: Reflections on the Autochthony Theme in Euripides' *Ion*." In Euben 1986, 252–273.

Schaefer, H. 1955. "Das Problem der griechischen Nationalität." In *Probleme der alten Geschichte*, 269–306. Göttingen.

Schaffer, M., and C. Cooper. 1980. *Mandinko: The Ethnography of a West African Holy Land*. New York.

Schmidt, B. 1871. *Das Volksleben der Neugriechen und das hellenische Alterthum*. Part 1. Leipzig.

Schneider, M. 1957. "Primitive Music." In *New Oxford History of Music* I, ed. E. Wellesz, 1–82. London.

Schwartz, E. 1984. "Aspects of Orpheus in Classical Literature and Myth." Ph.D. diss., Harvard University.

Schwartz, M. 1982. "The Indo-European Vocabulary of Exchange, Hospitality, and Intimacy." *Proceedings of the Berkeley Linguistic Society* 8:188–204.

Seaford, R. 1976. "On the Origins of Satyric Drama." *Maia* 28:209–221.

——. 1977–1978. "The 'Hyporchema' of Pratinas." *Maia* 29:81–94.

——. 1981. "Dionysiac Drama and the Dionysiac Mysteries." *Classical Quarterly* 31:252–275.

——, ed. 1984. *Euripides: Cyclops*. With introduction and commentary. Oxford.

Sebeok, T. A. and M. E. Erickson, eds. 1984. *Carnival!* Berlin.

Segal, C. P. 1961. "The Character and Cults of Dionysus and the Unity of the *Frogs*." *Harvard Studies in Classical Philology* 65:207–242.

——. 1969. "Aristophanes' Cloud-Chorus." *Arethusa* 2:143–161.

——. 1981. *Tragedy and Civilization: An Interpretation of Sophocles*. Cambridge, Mass.

——. 1982. *Dionysiac Poetics and Euripides' 'Bacchae'*. Princeton, N.J.

——. 1983. "Greek Myth as a Semiotic and Structural System and the Problem of Tragedy." *Arethusa* 16.173–98.

——. 1989. *Orpheus: The Myth of the Poet*. Baltimore.

Segal, R. A. 1990. *Joseph Campbell: An Introduction*. 2d ed. New York.

Severyns, A. 1926. "Le cycle épique et l'épisode d'Io." *Musée Belge* 30:119–130.

Seydou, C. 1983. "The African Epic: A Means for Defining the Genre." *Folklore Forum* 16.47–68.

Shelmerdine, S. C. 1985. "Hermes and the Tortoise: A Prelude to Cult." *Greek, Roman, and Byzantine Studies* 26:201–208.

Sifakis, G. M. 1971. *Parabasis and Animal Choruses: A Contribution to the History of Attic Comedy.* London.

SIG = Dittenberger, W., ed. 1960. *Sylloge Inscriptionum Graecarum.* 3d ed., Leipzig, 1915–1924. Hildesheim.

Simpson, M. 1969. "Sophocles' *Ajax*: His Madness and Transformation." *Arethusa* 2:88–103.

Singer, J. 1973. *Boundaries of the Soul.* Garden City, N.Y.

Snodgrass, A. M. 1980. *Archaic Greece: The Age of Experiment.* Berkeley.

Sourvinou-Inwood, C. 1983. "A Trauma in Flux: Death in the 8th Century and After." In *The Greek Renaissance of the 8th Century B.C.: Tradition and Innovation,* 33–49. Symposium of the Swedish Institute in Athens, Stockholm.

Stanford, W. B., ed. 1963. *Sophocles: Ajax.* Bristol.

Steiner, G. 1972. *Language and Silence: Essays on Language, Literature and the Inhuman.* New York.

——. 1984. *Antigones.* New York.

Svenbro, J. 1984. "La découpe du poème: Notes sur les origines sacrificielles de la poétique grecque." *Poétique* 58:215–229.

Taillardat, J. 1965. *Les images d'Aristophane: Études de langue et de stile.* Paris.

Tarn, W. W. 1930. *Hellenistic Civilization.* 2d ed. London.

TGF = Nauck, A., ed. 1889. *Tragicorum Graecorum Fragmenta.* Leipzig. Reprinted 1964, with *Supplementum* by B. Snell, Hildesheim.

Thalmann, W. G. 1978. *Dramatic Art in Aeschylus's* Seven against Thebes. New Haven, Conn.

Thiel, H., van, ed. and trans. 1983. *Leben und Taten Alexanders von Makedonien: Der griechische Alexanderroman nach der Handschrift L.* 2d ed. Darmstadt.

Thompson, D. W. 1936. *Glossary of Greek Birds.* Oxford. Reprint 1966.

TrGF = Radt, S., ed. 1985, 1977. *Tragicorum Graecorum Fragmenta.* vol. 3, Aeschylus. vol. 4 (with R. Kannicht), Sophocles. Göttingen.

Trump, D. H. 1980. *The Prehistory of the Mediterranean.* New Haven, Conn.

Turato, F. 1971–1972. "Le leggi non scritte negli 'Ucelli' di Aristofane." *Atti e Memorie dell'Academia Pataviana di Scienze, Lettere et Arti* 84/3:113–143.

Turner, V. 1967. *The Forest of Symbols: Aspects of Ndembu Ritual.* Ithaca, N.Y.

Tyrrell, W. B. 1984. *Amazons: A Study in Athenian Mythmaking.* Baltimore.

Van Brock, N. 1959. "Substitution rituelle." *Revue Hittite et Asianique* 65:117–146.

Veloudis, G. 1968. *Der neugriechische Alexander: Tradition in Bewahrung und Wandel.* Munich.

Vermeule, E. 1979. *Aspects of Death in Early Greek Art and Poetry.* Berkeley.

Vernant, J.-P. 1982. *The Origins of Greek Thought.* Ithaca, N.Y. Trans. of *Les origines de la pensée grecque,* Paris, 1962.

——. 1983. *Myth and Thought among the Greeks.* Trans. of *Mythe et pensée chez les Grecs,* Paris, 1965.

Vernant, J.-P., and P. Vidal-Naquet. 1988. *Myth and Tragedy in Ancient Greece.* New York. Trans. J. Lloyd of *Mythe et tragédie en Grèce ancienne,* Paris, 1972, and *Mythe et tragédie en Grèce ancienne* II, Paris, 1986.

Verrall, A. W. 1895. *Euripides the Rationalist: A Study in the History of Art and Religion.* Cambridge.

Versnel, H. S. 1986. "Greek Myth and Ritual: The Case of Kronos." In Bremmer 1986.121–152.

Veyne, P. 1983. *Les Grecs ont-ils cru à leurs mythes?* Paris.

Vian, F. 1952. *La guerre des géants.* Paris.

Vidal-Naquet, P. 1981. "The Black Hunter and the Origin of the Athenian Ephebeia." In Gordon 1981, 147–162.

——. 1986a. "Land and Sacrifice in the *Odyssey*: A Study of Religious and Mythical Meanings." In Vidal-Naquet 1986b, 1–38.

——. 1986b. *The Black Hunter: Forms of Thought and Forms of Society in the Greek World.* Baltimore. Trans. A. Szegedy-Mazak of *Le chasseur noir: Formes de pensée et formes de société dans le monde grec*, Paris, 1981.

Villanueva Puig, M.-C. 1986. "A propos des Thyiades de Delphes." In *L'association dionysiaque dans les sociétés anciennes*, 31–51. Rome.

Walsh, G. 1978. "The Rhetoric of Birthright and Race in Euripides' *Ion.*" *Hermes* 106:301–315.

Wehrli, F. 1967. "Io, Dichtung und Kultlegende." *Antike Kunst* 4:196–199.

Welles, C. B. 1962. "The Discovery of Sarapis and the Foundation of Alexandria." *Historia* 11:271–298.

West, M. L., ed. 1966. *Hesiod: Theogony.* With introduction and commentary. Oxford.

——. 1974. *Studies in Greek Elegy and Iambus.* Berlin.

——, ed. 1978. *Hesiod: Works and Days.* With introduction and commentary. Oxford.

——, ed. 1983. *The Orphic Poems.* With introduction and commentary. Oxford.

——. 1985. *The Hesiodic Catalogue of Women: Its Nature, Structure and Origins.* Oxford.

Whitman, C. H. 1951. *Sophocles: A Study of Heroic Humanism.* Cambridge, Mass.

——. 1958. *Homer and the Heroic Tradition.* Cambridge, Mass.

——. 1964. *Aristophanes and the Comic Hero.* Cambridge, Mass.

——. 1974. *Euripides and the Full Circle of Myth.* Cambridge, Mass.

Whitmont, E. 1969. *The Symbolic Quest.* New York.

Wickersham, J. M. 1986. "The Corpse Who Calls Theognis." *Transactions of the American Philological Association* 116:65–70.

Willcock, M. 1976. *A Companion to the* Iliad. Chicago.

Winkler, J. J. 1990. "The Ephebes' Song: *Tragōidia* and *Polis.*" In *Nothing to Do with Dionysos? Athenian Drama in Its Social Context*, ed. J. J. Winkler and F. I. Zeitlin, Princeton, N.J., 20–62.

Wolff, C. 1965. "The Design and Myth in Euripides' *Ion.*" *Harvard Studies in Classical Philology* 69:169–194.

Wolohojian, A. M., trans. 1969. *The Romance of Alexander the Great by Pseudo-Kallisthenes: Translated from the Armenian Version.* New York.

Yalouris, Nikolaos. 1986. "Le mythe d'Io: Les transformations d'Io dans l'iconographie et la littérature grecques." In *Iconographie classique et identités régionales. Paris 26 et 27 mai 1983*, ed. L. de Kahl et al., Paris = *Bulletin de Correspondance Hellénique* Suppl. XIV:3–23 and fgs. 1–16.

Yunis, H. 1988. *A New Creed: Fundamental Religious Beliefs in the Athenian Polis and Euripidean Drama* = *Hypomnemata* 91. Göttingen.

Zaganiaris, N. J. 1973. "Le mythe de Terée dans la littérature grecque et latine." *Platon* 25:208–232.

Zeitlin, F. 1978. "The Dynamics of Misogyny: Myth and Mythmaking in the *Oresteia.*" *Arethusa* 11.1–2:149–184.

———. 1982. *Under the Sign of the Shield: Semiotics and Aeschylus'* Seven against Thebes. Rome.

———. 1986. "Thebes: Theater of Self and Society in Athenian Drama." In Euben 1986.101–41.

———. 1989. "Mysteries of Identity and Designs of the Self in Euripides' *Ion.*" *Proceedings of the Cambridge Philological Society*, vol. 215.144–197.

Zemp, H. 1966. "La légende des griots malinké." *Cahiers d' Études Africaines* 6:611–42.

Zora, P. 1960. "Ἡ Γοργόνα εἰς τὴν Ἑλληνικὴν λαϊκὴν τέχνην (The Gorgona in Greek Folk Art)." Παρνασσός (*Parnassos*) 331–365.

Contributors

David J. Bradshaw chairs the English Department at Warren Wilson College, where he teaches English and Classics. He also serves as scholar in residence for the North Carolina Shakespeare Festival and is editor of the *Warren Wilson Review.* He is currently completing a book concerned with Milton's response to Virgilian themes and influence.

Jean M. Davison is Roberts Professor of Classical Languages and Literature and Professor of Ancient History at the University of Vermont. She has participated in several archaeological excavations and has published books on Attic Geometric pottery and Italic tomb groups, and articles on Near Eastern and Greek cultural history. Her current research concerns Egyptian influence on the Greek myth of Io.

William K. Freiert, Professor of Classics at Gustavus Adolphus College, was the 1986 recipient of the Edgar M. Carlson Award for Distinguished Teaching. He also received a 1990 award for excellence in teaching from the American Philological Association. He has lectured and delivered numerous papers on the *Odyssey* and on the classical tradition in the arts and literature. Most of his publications deal with the influence of mythology on American fiction.

John Hamilton is Associate Professor of Classics at the College of the Holy Cross. He has published in the areas of Greek literature, religion, and myth and is especially interested in the use of social anthropology to aid in the understanding of Archaic Greek society.

222

Martha Payne is Assistant Professor of Classics at Ball State University. She has presented papers on Linnaeus' use of names from classical mythology for plant nomenclature and on honorific inscriptions dedicated to Romans in Greece. She is currently investigating appearances of the Gorgona as a theme in modern Greek literature and folklore.

Dora C. Pozzi is Associate Professor of Classics at the University of Houston. She is the author of a critical edition of Menander's *Dyskolos*, with Spanish introduction, translation, and commentary, and of articles on Pindar, Thucydides, and Greek drama. She is currently working on a monograph-length study of the Herakles plays by Euripides and on a project concerned with classical themes in the Latin American theater.

Robert A. Segal is Professor of Religious Studies at Louisiana State University. He is the author of *The Poimandres as Myth: Scholarly Theory and Gnostic Meaning; Joseph Campbell: An Introduction;* and *Religion and the Social Sciences: Essays on the Confrontation.* He has also written many articles on theories of religion and myth and is completing a book that surveys critically modern theories of myth.

Thomas J. Sienkewicz, Capron Professor of Classics at Monmouth College in Monmouth, Illinois, received a NEH Summer Fellowship in 1987 to visit Mali and to continue research for a book about the Sunjata epic. In 1989 he received an award for excellence in teaching from the American Philological Association. With V. Edwards of Birkbeck College, London, he is the coauthor of *Oral Cultures Past and Present: Rappin' and Homer,* which examines the oral literatures of a wide variety of cultures, both past and present, including those of Homer and the Afro-American rapper.

John M. Wickersham is Professor of Classical Studies at Ursinus College. He is the author of *Greek Historical Documents: The Fourth Century B.C.* (with G. P. Verbrugghe). He has published articles on Ptolemaic Egypt and on Greek myth and cult. His current projects include a translation of Manetho and an edition of Servetus' *Declaratio Jesu Christi.*

Index of Sources

Abydos Table, 61
Aelian: *De Natura Animalium*: *3.26*, 154
Aeschines, 23
Aeschylus, 52, 54, 55, 56, 57, 61, 62, 131;
  Bassarides, 39; *Eumenides*, 140; *735*, 140;
  Libation Bearers: *372–374*, 59; *Oresteia*,
  123; *Prometheus Bound*, 53, 61, 62;
  567–574, 681–682, 707–735, 53; *714–716,
  717–719*, 56; *723–728*, 57; *790–814*, 53;
  814–815, 54; *828–841*, 53; *839–841*, 57;
  846–847, 54; *848–851*, 53, 54; *853–856,
  855*, 53; *Seven against Thebes*, 97–98;
  642–648, 97; *662, 667, 670–671, 673, 681,
  718*, 98; *Suppliants*, 53, 63; *220, 234, 237,
  243*, 62; *254–259*, 61; *299–301*, 52;
  307–309, 392–395, 547–564, 53; *555, 558*,
  59; *746–747*, 63; *914*, 62
Alcman, 133; *Partheneia*, 129
Alexander Romance, 15, 164–181 passim;
  Letters of Wonders, 15, 166, 176
  Armenian version: *87*, 171; *90*, 169, 172;
    91, 172; *92*, 170, 172; *94*, 172
  Greek version: *I.1–14*, 168; *7.3, 17.4, 29.2,
    30.1–5*, 169; *30.6*, 170, 171; *31.1*, 170;
    32.1, 171; *32.2, 32.3*, 170; *32.4*, 167,
    171; *32.5–6, 32.6, 32.7, 33.1*, 171; *33.2*,
    170; *33.3, 33.4, 33.5, 33.6*, 171; *33.7*,
    172; *33.8, 33.9*, 173; *34*, 169; *34.7*, 173
  II.15.4–5, 21.2, 169; *37.5*, 165; *38.7–11*,
    165–176; *39.1–2, 39.11, 39.12*, 176;
    39.13, 40, 41.2–5, 177; *41.6*, 178;
    41.8–13, 165, 176

III.19.2–4, 169; *24.2*, 169, 172–173; *24.4,
  33, 34.1, 34.3*, 174; *34.4*, 174, 176; *34.5*,
  174, 175
Anaximander, 58
Antoninus Liberalis: *10*, 143
Apollodorus, 67, 79; *1.7.3*, 135; *1.116*, 67;
  2.2.2, 143; *2.6.4*, 27; *3.12.3*, 55; *3.14.4*,
  64; *3.15.1*, 135; *3.120*, 142; *3.182*, 67;
  3.183–185, 67
Apollonius of Rhodes: *Argonautica*, 37;
  1.494–515, 33; *1.499–500*, 33; *1.516–518*,
  37; *1.554*, 19; *1.1134–1138*, 37;
  2.684–693, 37; *2.927–929*, 37;
  4.303–1781, 55; scholia: *Argonautica
  1.554*, 19
Archilochus: *F 77 D.117 T*, 128
Aristeas of Proconnesus (*FGH* 35), 52
Aristophanes, 14, 147–149, 200
  Acharnians: *247–283*, 145
  Birds, 14, 144, 146, 149–161 passim, 162;
    5, 7, 149; *44*, 152; *82*, 151; *92, 110*, 152;
    121–122, 159–160, 160, 161, 151; *162,
    163*, 157; *180–184*, 152; *209*, 153;
    209–222, 152, 153, 157; *210*, 153–154;
    211, 213, 215–216, 216, 154; *227–262*,
    158; *255*, 160; *256, 313*, 157; *331*, 155;
    381, 434, 157; *451*, 158; *455, 460*, 157;
    462–463, 616, 637–638, 158; *642*, 151;
    643, 158; *654–655*, 152, 158; *663*, 159;
    676–684, 152, 154–155; *681*, 155;
    685–722, 155, 159; *723–751, 737*, 159;
    737–751, 152, 155–156; *746*, 156; *755*,

225

General Index

Achilles, 19, 27, 92–93, 100, 103 n 10, 107, 118; embassy to, 107–109
Adelphos, 93–95
Adonis, 64–85; gardens of, 64 n 1, 65, 70–71
Aegyptos, 53
Agōn, 40–42, 148
    antagonism in myth, 40, 44
    in drama, 126–127
    over dead warrior, 89–90
    over Patroklos' body, 107–108, 112
Aia and Aietes, 36
Aiakos, 18–19, 113, 115
Aidōs, 100, 110–120
Aition, 3, 24
Ajax, 17–21, 24, 26–31, 99–125; suicide of, 119–121
Alexander the Great, 2, 8, 164–181; and the Water of Life, 176–178
Alexandria, 170–173
Alkathoös, 24
Alterity, 36, 46, 49–51, 143; and wandering, 55–57, 61–63, 143
Amazons, 54–57
Ammon, 168–171, 176 n 44
Antigone, 86–98
Aphrodite, 64, 67, 71, 79, 83, 90; alterity of, 36
Apollo:
    and Dionysos, 40–42, 135, 137–138, 157 n 93
    in Euripides *Ion*, 135–140, 153–157
    and the Hyperboreans, 51, 59
    and Orpheus, 37–42
    Patroos, 135 n 31, 136

Archetype:
    "hero," 78–79
    mother, 73–80
    See also Great Mother; *Puer aeternus*
Aretē, 99, 124–125
Argives, 61
Argos (Io's watchman), 52
Argos (polis), 3, 52, 60
Arrhephoria, 136, 144
Athena, 24, 98, 114
Attendant squire. *See Therapōn*
Aulis, 8–9
Autochthony, 60, 136, 141–144

Barbarians. *See* Alterity; Hellenes and barbarians
Biē vs. *mētis*, 103–107, 109–111, 116
Body, symbolism of, 34
Burial. *See* Funeral practices

Canon:
    of *Iliad*, 17, 28–29
    of *Sunjata*, 188–202
    See also Myth: epichoric vs. canonical
"Carnival," 145
Catalogue of Ships, 28
Cattle, 54–55
Chadhir legends, 178
Chorus:
    authority of, 129–133
    choral performances, 126–129
Civilization vs. barbarism, 60. *See also* Alterity
Cocteau, Jean, *Orphée*, 46–47

Library of Congress Cataloging-in-Publication Data

Myth and the polis / edited by Dora C. Pozzi, John M. Wickersham.
    p.   cm. — (Myth and poetics)
  Includes bibliographical references and index.
  ISBN 0–8014–2473–9 (cloth: alkaline paper). — ISBN 0–8014–9734–5 (paper: alka-
line paper)
    1. Mythology, Greek.   2. Community.   I. Pozzi, Dora C. (Dora Carlisky), 1930–   .
II. Wickersham, John M. (John Moore), 1943–   .   III. Series.
BL785.M98   1991
292.1′3 — dc20   90–55716